EIL Education for the Expanding Circle

The teaching of English in the Expanding Circle, traditionally called EFL countries, has long been regarded as having no choice but to follow Inner Circle or Anglo-American norms, both in pedagogy and language models. This situation is in sharp contrast with that of the Outer Circle, or ESL countries, where the WE (World Englishes) paradigm, coupled with post-colonialism, has liberated the users of indigenous Englishes from the norms of Anglophone native speakers. Employing Japan as a primary sample, this book proposes a new paradigm of EIL (English as an International Language) education, by integrating relevant paradigms such as WE and ELF (English as a Lingua Franca), which enables users of English from the Expanding Circle to represent their own voices in international communication. Various examples of actual classroom practice in EIL are also presented, bridging the longstanding gap between theory and practice in this field.

Nobuyuki Hino (Ph.D.) is Professor at the Graduate School of Language and Culture, Osaka University, Japan. He currently serves on the editorial/advisory board of the journal *World Englishes* (Wiley) as well as of the book series *Intercultural Communication and Language Education* (Springer) and *Routledge Advances in Teaching English as an International Language* (Routledge).

Routledge Studies in World Englishes
Series Editor: Ee Ling Low
National Institute of Education, Nanyang Technological University,
Singapore and President of Singapore Association of Applied Linguistics

This **Singapore Association for Applied Linguistics** book series will provide a starting point for those who wish to know more about the aspects of the spread of English in the current globalized world. Each volume can cover the following aspects of the study of World Englishes: issues and theoretical paradigms, feature-based studies (i.e. phonetics and phonology, syntax, lexis) and language in use (e.g. education, media, the law and other related disciplines).

English Pronunciation Models in a Globalized World
Accent, acceptability and Hong Kong English
Andrew Sewell

Attitudes to World Englishes
Implications for teaching English in South Korea
Hyejeong Ahn

Teaching English as an International Language
Implementing, reviewing and re-envisioning World Englishes in
language education
Roby Marlina

Negotiating Englishes and English-speaking Identities
A study of youth learning English in Italy
Jacqueline Aiello

World Englishes
Rethinking paradigms
Edited by Ee Ling Low and Anne Pakir

EIL Education for the Expanding Circle
A Japanese model
Nobuyuki Hino

For a full list of titles in this series, visit www.routledge.com/Routledge-Studies-in-World-Englishes/book-series/RSWE

EIL Education for the Expanding Circle
A Japanese Model

Nobuyuki Hino

First published 2018
by Routledge
2 Park Square, Milton Park, Abingdon, Oxon OX14 4RN

and by Routledge
711 Third Avenue, New York, NY 10017

Routledge is an imprint of the Taylor & Francis Group, an informa business

© 2018 Nobuyuki Hino

The right of Nobuyuki Hino to be identified as author of this
work has been asserted by him in accordance with sections 77 and
78 of the Copyright, Designs and Patents Act 1988.

All rights reserved. No part of this book may be reprinted or
reproduced or utilized in any form or by any electronic,
mechanical, or other means, now known or hereafter invented,
including photocopying and recording, or in any information
storage or retrieval system, without permission in writing from the
publishers.

Trademark notice: Product or corporate names may be trademarks
or registered trademarks, and are used only for identification and
explanation without intent to infringe.

British Library Cataloguing-in-Publication Data
A catalogue record for this book is available from the British Library

Library of Congress Cataloging-in-Publication Data
Names: Hino, Nobuyuki, 1958– author.
Title: EIL education for the expanding circle : a Japanese model /
  by Nobuyuki Hino.
Description: London ; New York : Routledge, [2018] | Series:
  Routledge studies in world Englishes | Includes bibliographical
  references and index.
Identifiers: LCCN 2017057419 | ISBN 9781138630383 (hardcover) |
  ISBN 9781315209449 (ebook)
Subjects: LCSH: English language—Study and teaching—Japanese
  speakers. | Intercultural communication—Japan. | Language and
  education—Japan. | Bilingualism—Japan. | Applied linguistics—
  Japan.
Classification: LCC PE1130.J3 H56 2018 | DDC 428.0071/052—dc23
LC record available at https://lccn.loc.gov/2017057419

ISBN: 978-1-138-63038-3 (hbk)
ISBN: 978-1-315-20944-9 (ebk)

Typeset in Galliard
by Apex CoVantage, LLC

Contents

List of figures	vii
List of tables	viii
Preface	ix
Acknowledgements	xi
List of abbreviations	xiv

Introduction	1
1 Liberating the Expanding Circle through EIL	3

PART I
A paradigm of EIL education — 9

2 A holistic framework of EIL education — 11

3 Principles for EIL education — 49

PART II
Models, materials, and methodologies for EIL education — 55

4 Developing original production models — 57

5 Cultural content of teaching materials — 73

6 Locally-appropriate methodology — 82

PART III
Practices of EIL education — 89

7 Approaches and methods for teaching EIL — 91

vi *Contents*

8 A radio EIL education program   100

9 Integrated Practice in Teaching English as an International Language (IPTEIL)   113

10 Content and English as a Lingua Franca Integrated Learning (CELFIL)   128

Conclusion   137

11 Toward the ownership of English for the Expanding Circle   139

References   146
Index   164

Figures

2.1	Aims of EIL studies	14
2.2	Taxonomy of views on the forms of EIL	19

Tables

3.1	General principles for teaching EIL in the Expanding Circle	53
9.1	Results of a semester-end questionnaire on IPTEIL classes, July 2017	123

Preface

How can ELT (English language teaching) help fill this world with love and peace, instead of hate and conflict? The world today is plagued with intolerance, as terrorism and war are so often caused by the rejection of cultural, ethnic, and religious diversity. Under the circumstances, ELT has the important mission to provide a means of communication and cross-cultural understanding between those with a variety of linguistic and cultural backgrounds.

What is urgently required in this undertaking is a new model of ELT that will allow users of English to communicate their own values, not only to native but also to non-native speakers, rather than the conventional type of ELT which confines learners within the Anglo-American frame of reference. The present volume proposes one such model, based on my research and practice for nearly four decades, aiming to produce users of English who positively accept the linguistic and cultural diversity of "Englishes" including their own.

The past 40 years in ELT, in fact, have seen a gradual surge of interest in "post-Anglophone" (Kirkpatrick, 2010) approaches, which liberate learners of English from native-speaker norms, endowing non-native speakers with the "ownership of English" (Widdowson, 1994; Norton, 1997; A. Matsuda, 2003). Those innovative schools of thought include EIL (English as an International Language), WE (World Englishes), and ELF (English as a Lingua Franca), originating in Smith (1976), B. Kachru (1965), and Jenkins (2000), respectively. Though this book primarily employs the term "EIL" coined by Smith, the other two concepts, along with an indigenous Japanese philosophy known as "*kokusai-eigo*" (International English) (Kunihiro, 1970), are also incorporated where appropriate into my theoretical framework and pedagogical practices.

As the title suggests, this book puts a particular focus on the sociolinguistic and educational needs for the Expanding Circle (B. Kachru, 1985, 1988), or countries such as Japan where English has no official domestic functions. For the Outer Circle, or former territories of the U.K. and the U.S., the spirit of postcolonialism has often motivated the deliverance from the Anglo-American style of ELT imposed by their former colonizers, as evident in the support for the legitimacy of Outer Circle varieties such as Indian English. It is high time that the Expanding Circle, including large portions of Asia, Europe, the Middle East, Latin America, and Africa, should also stand up for the right to pursue

x *Preface*

an ELT of their own, rather than merely continuing to mimic Anglophone pedagogy that is not tailored to their needs (cf. Hino, 1992a; McKay, 2003). While discussions in the present book mainly draw on examples from Japan as shown in the subtitle "A Japanese model," many of them are expected to be applicable also to other Expanding Circle situations.

In essence, the teaching of EIL is an effort toward multicultural and symbiotic societies. It is hoped that EIL education, pictured in this volume, will ultimately contribute to the construction of a world that embraces diversity, where people with different values can live in peaceful harmony with one another.

Acknowledgements

Chapters 2, 4, 5, and 7 through 10 in the present volume are partly based, though with extensive revisions and updating, on the author's Ph.D. dissertation *Principles and practices for EIL education in Japan* (Osaka University, 2015), which in itself mainly consisted of revised versions of my previously published works. Although much revised and reorganized now, the below list shows the origins of parts of those chapters, along with those of Chapters 3, 6, and 11 that have also been extensively revised for this book.

Chapter 2:

Hino, N. (2001). Organizing EIL studies: Toward a paradigm. *Asian Englishes*, *4*(1), 34–65.

Chapter 3:

Hino, N. (2014). Teaching de-Anglo-Americanized English for international communication. *The Journal of English Language and Literature*, *60*(1), 91–106.

Chapter 4:

Hino, N. (2012). Endonormative models of EIL for the Expanding Circle. In A. Matsuda (Ed.) *Principles and practices of teaching English as an international language* (pp. 28–43). Bristol: Multilingual Matters.

Chapter 5:

Hino, N. (1988). Nationalism and English as an international language: The history of English textbooks in Japan. *World Englishes*, *7*(3), 309–314.

Chapter 6:

Hino, N. (2016). Negotiation between East Asian values and Anglophone culture in the teaching of English in Japan. In H.-H. Liao (Ed.) *Critical reflections on foreign language education: Globalization and local interventions* (pp. 29–45). Taipei: The Language Training & Testing Center.

xii *Acknowledgements*

Chapter 7:

Hino, N. (2010). EIL in teaching practice: A pedagogical analysis of EIL classrooms in action. In N. Hino (Ed.) *Gengobunka-kyoiku no aratanaru riron to jissen [New theories and practices in education in language and culture]* (pp. 1–10). Osaka: Graduate School of Language and Culture, Osaka University.

Chapter 8:

Hino, N. (1997). EIL in a radio English program in Japan. *Studies in Language and Culture*, *23*, 95–113.

Chapter 9:

Hino, N. (2012). Participating in the community of EIL users through real-time news: Integrated Practice in Teaching English as an International Language (IPTEIL). In A. Matsuda (Ed.) *Principles and practices of teaching English as an international language* (pp. 183–200). Bristol: Multilingual Matters.

Chapter 10:

Hino, N. (2014). The learning of EIL in EMI classes in higher education. In N. Hino (Ed.) *Eigokyoiku no konnichiteki kadai [Current issues in the teaching of English]* (pp. 1–10). Osaka: Graduate School of Language and Culture, Osaka University.

Chapter 11:

Hino, N. (2016). A socio-educational vision for the creation and diffusion of Japanese English: A prospect for the Expanding Circle. In N. Hino (Ed.) *Saishin no eigokyoiku-kenkyu [The latest research in English language teaching]* (pp. 1–13). Osaka: Graduate School of Language and Culture, Osaka University.

The content of this book partly reflects the results of research supported by JSPS KAKENHI, Grant Numbers JP03858090, JP17520375, JP20520548, JP24520700, and JP15K02678.

I am indebted to so many scholars for their help with my pursuit of EIL studies for almost four decades that it seems regrettably impossible to name each of them. Nonetheless, I would really like to express my special gratitude to my deceased mentors, the late Professor Larry E. Smith and the late Professor Masao Kunihiro, for inspiring me to the world of EIL and teaching me the importance of accepting diversity.

I am also extremely thankful to Professor Jack C. Richards, Professor Kaichi Ito, and Professor Stephen A. C. Boyd for their kind instruction, guidance, and advice as my mentors in ELT research since the beginning of my career.

Acknowledgements xiii

I would like to express my sincere appreciation as well to my respected colleagues at Osaka University, most notably to Professor Shigeo Kimura, Professor Tomoko Okita, and Professor Ichiro Koguchi, for their valuable comments on an earlier draft of this work. Last but not least, I am truly thankful to Mr. Simon Yu of Osaka University for helping me with proofreading.

Abbreviations

CALL	Computer-Assisted Language Learning
CELFIL	Content and English as a Lingua Franca Integrated Learning
EFL	English as a Foreign Language
EIL	English as an International Language
ELF	English as a Lingua Franca
ELT	English language teaching
EMI	English-Medium Instruction
ESL	English as a Second Language
ESP	English for Specific Purposes
IPTEIL	Integrated Practice in Teaching English as an International Language
NS	native speaker
NNS	non-native speaker
OSGD	Observed Small Group Discussion
TEFL	Teaching English as a Foreign Language
TEIL	Teaching English as an International Language
TESL	Teaching English as a Second Language
WE	World Englishes

Introduction

1 Liberating the Expanding Circle through EIL

Expressing original values in de-Anglo-Americanized Englishes

The purpose of this book is to present a new approach to English language teaching (ELT) that helps those who have traditionally been called "learners of English as a foreign language" (EFL) to function as "users of English as an international language" (EIL). The overall theme is to liberate non-native speakers of English from the conventional ELT aimed at the teaching of linguistic and cultural norms of Anglo-American native speakers. EIL is a means of communicating one's own thoughts, beyond the Anglophone frame of reference, to interlocutors including non-native speakers of English (Hino, 1988a; Smith, 1976, 1981b).

As implied by the use of the term EFL rather than ESL (English as a Second Language) in the above paragraph, a special emphasis is placed on the educational needs of the Expanding Circle (B. Kachru, 1985), where English is not normally employed between compatriots. Cases cited in the present volume are mainly from Japan, which makes the discussions particularly relevant to East Asian countries with their similar sociolinguistic environments, though many of the arguments are expected to be applicable also to other Expanding Circle regions.

It used to be, or still is to a great extent, taken for granted that learners of English should work toward a native-speaker target, or an Anglophone model. However, in light of the fact that Anglo-American English is a means of expressing Anglo-American values, such a model is inappropriate for representing the cultures of non-native speakers of English. For example, while it is normal to refer to one's sibling simply as "brother" or "sister" in American English, it does not make much sense unless specified in such a way as "older brother" or "younger sister" in East Asian culture, where seniority among siblings cannot be ignored.

Thus, in order to adequately express oneself in English, it is essential for those users of English to make necessary changes to Inner Circle or Anglo-American English, instead of merely copying it as it is, so that their English can better express their own values, culture, or thoughts. In fact, 90 years ago, even in the infancy of ELT in Japan, lexicographer Hidezaburo Saito pointed to the

4   *Introduction*

need for the indigenization of English to allow for the representation of Japanese culture, arguing that "the English of the Japanese must, in a certain sense, be Japanized" (Saito, 1928, preface). This call for an original model of English three generations ago should now be answered, at a time when many find it crucial to be able to communicate in English in the globalized world.

The English that one produces is required to be intelligible to the interlocutor or the reader, without imposing too much burden on the recipient. For example, while your accent may positively serve as an important identity marker, it also needs to be understood by your interlocutor. For this reason, it is often claimed from a conservative ELT position that the native-speaker model is the best orientation after all. However, contrary to general belief, studies in EIL and ELF (English as a Lingua Franca) have proven that native-speaker pronunciation is not the most intelligible in international communication involving non-native speakers (Smith & Rafiqzad, 1979; C. Nelson, 2011; Jenkins, 2000, 2002; Deterding & Kirkpatrick, 2006; Walker, 2010; Low, 2015). This is true with written English as well.

In addition to being representative of one's own values as well as being intelligible to both native and non-native users of English, we need to speak and write the kind of English respected by the listener or reader. This third condition is in line with Smith's classic tenet that EIL needs to be "appropriate for the situation" (Smith, 1976, p. 64) as to its sociolinguistic domains.

The Expanding Circle: left behind in World Englishes

In an effort to challenge the myth of the supremacy of native-speaker English, the World Englishes (WE) paradigm (B. Kachru, 1985, 1986, 1997) has been instrumental in raising awareness, among stakeholders of ELT, for the status of Englishes in the Outer Circle consisting of former colonies of the U.K. and the U.S. The theory claims the endonormativity of those varieties established through many years of their intra-national use. On the other hand, their counterparts from the Expanding Circle, without a history of domestic use, have not been regarded as legitimate Englishes (Hino, 1987b; Jenkins, 2006), viewed by WE scholars merely as exonormative varieties lacking in "range and depth." As a result, WE scholars have generally held that Inner Circle or Outer Circle Englishes, as established varieties of English, should be the models for learners in the Expanding Circle. In other words, the Expanding Circle has been left behind in the WE movement.

We must be aware that it is no less important for members of the Expanding Circle than it is for those from the Outer Circle to express their original values in English when the language is an indispensable means of global communication today. It is imperative to find a way to keep them from remaining mere parrots who can only convey someone else's ideas. The Expanding Circle should certainly be allowed, just like the Outer Circle, to represent their thoughts in their own Englishes. A new paradigm alternative to the conventional WE framework is urgently needed to achieve this goal through ELT.

Liberating the Expanding Circle 5

In fact, ELF researchers initially worked toward some model of English for international communication, particularly for the Expanding Circle, at the stage now called "ELF1" (Jenkins, 2015b) in the beginning of the third millennium. They made significant achievements in identifying the LFC (Lingua Franca Core) (Jenkins, 2000, 2002) which was expected to ensure mutual intelligibility despite the varieties of English as an international language.

Today, however, the need for a model has been de-emphasized since the ELF scholars' interest shifted to the "ELF2" stage, focusing on the fluid and dynamic nature of ELF communication that is collaboratively constructed through negotiation in each situational and interactive context. The concept of "variety" as a central notion of WE as well as of ELF1 is taken over by "variation" in ELF2. This stance largely remains the same at the latest "ELF3" or "English as a Multilingua Franca" (Jenkins, 2015b) stage, which views "translanguaging" such as codeswitching as a natural component of ELF interaction.

From the viewpoint of current ELF studies, any model could be viewed as too static to be applied to ELF communication. However, such a limitation is only inevitable with any model in human and social sciences if not in mathematics. All human behaviors and social practices are indeed fluid and dynamic, where no model works in its "default" form. Although any model of English surely has to be modified or accommodated *in situ*, we still need certain models that learners can turn to as a starting point. In this regard, it is recommendable to seek an indigenous model of English, such as the Model of Japanese English (MJE) proposed by Hino (2012a), which is intended to be expressive of Japanese values while being internationally communicative.

Along the lines of the Japanese philosophy of indigenized English rooted in the abovementioned Saito (1928), the present volume seeks to develop a new approach to ELT in order to relieve the Expanding Circle from native-speakerism, or belief in the supremacy of native speakers. For this scheme, I will employ Smith's EIL (1976) for a start, but will also adopt any useful theories as necessary, from a non-sectarian position, including those of WE and ELF.

It should be added here that the very concept of "the Expanding Circle" certainly has many limitations. One of them is that there is a diversity of sociolinguistic situations within the Expanding Circle. For example, while the domestic function of English in much of East Asia and Latin America is indeed as limited as is presupposed by the Kachruvian WE paradigm, some countries in Europe nowadays actually make extensive use of English intra-nationally. In fact, sociolinguistic studies such as Gerritsen, Van Meurs, Planken, and Korzilius (2016) on the Netherlands and Hilgendorf (2007) on Germany point to the difficulty of classifying European countries today into the conventional Outer and Expanding Circle categories. In this regard, it is safer to assume that discussions in the present volume, largely based on Japan, may apply to Expanding Circle countries only to a varying degree.

Before going further in our discussions, a note should be provided on the usage of the term "model." The word "model" is used in this book with a narrower or a wider meaning depending on the context. In the present chapter,

6 Introduction

for example, it is employed chiefly with the former definition, referring to a "language sample that learners can turn to." The latter is associated with cases such as the subtitle of this book, *The Japanese model*, as well as the use of the word in the Preface, where it points to a "paradigmatic sample that may be useful for those interested in pursuing similar undertakings." In the present discussion, the former is a central component of the latter.

Organization of the book

The aim of this book is two-fold. One is to investigate principles for the teaching of English as an International Language (EIL), and the other is to discuss their pedagogical application to the teaching of English in the Expanding Circle.

The concept of EIL entails a major paradigm shift in the teaching of English by arguing for the relativization of native-speaker norms, or the de-Anglo-Americanization of English. With rapid globalization evolving in many facets of our lives, where the traditional dichotomy between native and non-native speakers is now blurred, interest in the notion of EIL, or "global Englishes" (Jenkins, 2015a), has been growing in ELT across the world. However, as of today, a holistic approach to EIL education research, directed towards the development of pedagogical practice informed by sound theories, has been rather rare. The present volume is intended to address the gap between theory and practice in EIL education, citing Japan as a primary example, with respect to the global and social need for a new type of ELT in the Expanding Circle.

After this brief introduction (Chapter 1), a paradigm of EIL education research is proposed in Part I as an analytical framework for considering various problems in EIL education (Chapter 2), along with a summary of principles for EIL education (Chapter 3). The paradigm in Part I is applied to Part II with discussions of models (Chapter 4), materials (Chapter 5), and methodologies (Chapter 6) for the teaching of EIL in the Expanding Circle. Starting with an overall taxonomy of EIL pedagogy (Chapter 7), Part III reports on the author's own pedagogical efforts as examples of actual practices in teaching EIL in the Expanding Circle (Chapters 8, 9, and 10). Finally, the concluding discussion (Chapter 11) ventures to offer prospects for the development of original Englishes in the Expanding Circle as the ultimate road to the ownership of English, before summarizing the arguments put forward in this book.

This volume will hopefully make some contribution, however humble, to the identification of principles for EIL education as well as to the development of concrete methodologies for teaching EIL, with a special focus on the Expanding Circle including Japan that has so often been caught up with native-speakerism (cf. Houghton & Rivers, 2013).

Definitions

An attempt is made in this section to first define three key terms for global Englishes employed throughout the volume, namely, EIL, WE, ELF, as succinctly as possible to minimize confusion. They are divided into two kinds of usage, one as academic concepts and the other referring to academic schools of thought.

When employed as an academic concept in this book, EIL (English as an International Language) is defined as "English for international communication," while WE (World Englishes) means "varieties of English across the world." Likewise, summarizing the definitions given by various leading ELF scholars, ELF (English as a Lingua Franca) refers to "English used for communication among those with different first language backgrounds."

As a school of thought, EIL is regarded in the present volume as one initiated by Larry E. Smith. WE as used in this book points to Kachruvian WE, that is, a school of discipline founded by Braj B. Kachru. ELF is viewed primarily as one proposed by Jennifer Jenkins, though more broadly it refers to the school started by "the three mothers of ELF" (an expression attributed to Andy Kirkpatrick), namely, Jennifer Jenkins, Barbara Seidlhofer, and Anna Mauranen, with the support of Henry Widdowson.

Partly inspired by its use in Jenkins (2015a), the expression "global Englishes" is sometimes employed in this book as a cover term to represent any view of English oriented toward the deliverance from conventional Anglophone native-speaker norms. In this usage, "global Englishes" embraces various schools of thought including EIL, WE, and ELF.

Before closing this introductory chapter, explanation should be offered on another key concept mentioned above, that is, the three "Circles" of WE comprising the Inner Circle, the Outer Circle, and the Expanding Circle. Endeavors by WE scholars to define these three categories, ever since their origin in B. Kachru (1985), always seem to leave a certain ambiguity. In fact, despite its academic and practical significance, the three Circles of WE is a somewhat arbitrary construct for which a clear-cut definition may be impossible.

Nevertheless, in this book, the Inner Circle refers to Anglophone countries or regions traditionally viewed as native English-speaking countries or regions (though against the present realities), such as the U.K., the U.S., and Australia. The Outer Circle consists of former colonies of the U.K. or the U.S. where English is used intra-nationally as a second or an official language (though this is also an oversimplification), such as India, Singapore, and Nigeria. Last, the Expanding Circle includes all the rest, in other words, countries or regions where English is a foreign language and is employed primarily for international communication (though there are many exceptions today), such as Japan, Brazil, and Spain. While, as Saraceni (2015) observes, "the forms and functions of English as an international lingua franca in the Expanding Circle have traditionally featured comparatively rarely in World Englishes literature" (p. 80), the Expanding Circle is the main focus of the present volume.

Part I
A paradigm of EIL education

2 A holistic framework of EIL education

Introduction

The globalization of English has gradually attracted the attention of scholars of linguistic and cultural studies especially since the mid-1970s. Its significance for the promotion of international communication and cross-cultural understanding is becoming even clearer in the world today. A large inventory of works on global Englishes are available in international academic journals including *World Englishes*, a flagship periodical in WE studies, and more recently *Journal of English as a Lingua Franca*, a stronghold for ELF research, as well as in numerous books on the subject. Academic conventions, especially annual conferences held by the International Association for World Englishes along with its fast-growing ELF counterparts known as the International Conference on English as a Lingua Franca, constantly provide the newest research results in the field.

However, with the ever-increasing interest in global Englishes on one hand, we also seem to be somewhat lost in the abundance of research on the other hand. A large number of studies are being carried out daily, but it is by no means easy to identify what kind of contributions each specific research makes to the field of EIL. If one were to borrow a phrase from the American rock group Guns N' Roses, "Where do we go now?"

I suggest that it is time for reorientation. For this aim, the present chapter revisits Hino (2001), which proposed a tentative paradigm for grasping a holistic picture of EIL education with particular regard to the sociolinguistic and educational needs of the Expanding Circle. While the overall framework proposed in Hino (2001) still seems to serve the purpose, the discussions require drastic updating partly because the paper had been authored before Jenkins (2000) revitalized EIL studies with the concept of ELF.

A need of an analytical framework for EIL education

This chapter extensively revises and updates my discussions in Hino (2001), while retaining the basic framework, as a holistic approach toward an organization of major areas of EIL research. Its goal, however, is not to review existing research literature in EIL. Rather, I intend to present the whole EIL studies as

12   *A paradigm of EIL education*

an organic system to clarify the significance of each individual study, with the ultimate goal of constructing a paradigm of EIL studies that will help to give directions toward the solution of various problems in EIL.

It should be also noted here that my position is to consider the fundamental nature of the idea of EIL to be pedagogical, though the concept can be, and in fact has been, applied to many other aspects of language studies. Accordingly, the term EIL, as it is used in the present chapter, implies that it is essentially the basis of TEIL, or Teaching English as an International Language. This is akin to the use of the term and concept of ESL, or English as a Second Language, as it usually implies its connection with TESL, or Teaching English as a Second Language.

In this effort towards a paradigm of EIL, the distinctions between WE, ELF, and EIL need to be clarified first beyond the terminological definitions in Chapter 1, as discussed in the next section.

WE, ELF, and EIL

The concept of WE grew out of the observation of linguistic realities in postcolonial environments, chiefly in the British Commonwealth. In consequence, WE studies are primarily concerned with intra-national domains, and secondarily with international contexts. Likewise, WE research originally tends to be more interested in Outer Circle varieties such as Indian English and Singaporean English than Expanding Circle varieties such as Japanese English and Korean English.

On the other hand, the major social factor that prompted the birth of the concept of EIL (Smith, 1976) was the need for international communication. For this reason, EIL studies are primarily concerned with international settings and secondarily with intra-national contexts. It is also natural that EIL researchers generally view both Outer Circle and Expanding Circle varieties on an equal basis. Though with some subtle differences, many of the notable users of the concept of EIL also seem to employ the term with such connotations (e.g.,McKay, 2002; Sharifian, 2009; A. Matsuda & Friedrich, 2011).

Another important difference is that while the idea of EIL in its essence could also be applied to any language other than English, as discussed later in this chapter, the use of WE framework by its nature is restricted to languages that could be referred to as a world language. In other words, EIL considers English to be a language that merely happens to be the most frequently used for international communication, when WE regards English as a language with a specially unique sociolinguistic disposition.

This conceptual distinction between EIL and WE is not always clear cut, and it is often possible to work within the rough framework of EIL/WE (cf. Smith, 2004), but it is also useful to keep in mind that there are some essential differences in emphasis between EIL and WE. Though each concept has its own advantages and disadvantages, this book opts for EIL, rather than the higher-profile WE, as a basic foundation.

A holistic framework of EIL education 13

For the Expanding Circle, including Japan, the notion of EIL is often more relevant than WE, because the use of English for the Expanding Circle is more international than intra-national in nature. In fact, an indigenous school of thought in ELT in Japan known as *kokusai-eigo* ("international English," literally), which stemmed from the Expanding Circle environment of the country, presents a close resemblance to EIL. The popularity of Larry E. Smith's proposal on EIL among English language educators in Japan, especially from the late 1970s to the early 1980s, can also be explained in light of this background (Hino, 2017a).

There are also similarities and differences between EIL and ELF. Regarding the similarities, ELF indeed used to be referred to as EIL, most notably in Jenkins (2000). The close kinship between the two concepts is also evident in the fact that *Journal of English as a Lingua Franca* reprinted two of Smith's classic papers on EIL (1976, 1981b) in 2015 to recognize their pioneering contributions to ELF studies. As to the differences, ELF does not, theoretically at least, presuppose the nation-state framework, while EIL more or less draws on the conventional notion of nation-states, as implied by the word "Inter*national*" in its name. This difference has been further highlighted since the ELF studies reached the aforementioned "ELF2" stage, where ELF is viewed as a variation (Widdowson, 2015) rather than a variety or a collection of varieties (Jenkins, 2015b), when the EIL studies, under the influence of WE studies, still find the concept of varieties as an integral part of their paradigm.

This chapter employs EIL as the basic term to represent the position proposed in the present volume, attributing its origin to Smith's concept of EIL and the Japanese philosophy of *kokusai-eigo* (International English), while also incorporating various results of relevant ELF and WE research. In this respect, the stance of this book is in large agreement with Low (2015), who also synthesizes relevant paradigms such as WE and ELF in the name of EIL.

Organizing the field of EIL research

In attempting to organize the whole field of EIL, it is necessary, first, to clarify what EIL studies are aimed at. In Hino (2001), I argued that all the EIL research up to 1999 could be classified into six questions, also predicting that the same categorization would probably hold true for the future. Seeing that Hino (2001) seems to have proven to be on the right track in this regard, they are reproduced as (a) to (f):

(a) What is EIL?
(b) Why is EIL necessary?
(c) How is EIL possible?
(d) What does EIL look like?
(e) How is EIL used?
(f) How can EIL be taught?

14 *A paradigm of EIL education*

From the pedagogical orientation that the present volume draws upon, questions (a) to (e) are seen to constitute the foundations of TEIL, with question (a) referring to the definition of EIL, question (b) to the rationale for TEIL, and questions from (c) to (e) to the background of TEIL. Question (f) addresses the practice of TEIL. This holistic view of aims of EIL studies is visualized in Figure 2.1 (cf. Hino, 2003a).

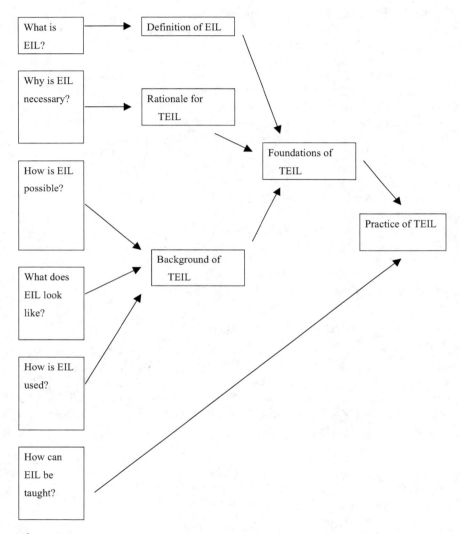

Figure 2.1 Aims of EIL studies

In the "background" section, question (c), which investigates the very entity of EIL, can be divided into two subsections. One is historical aspects, looking into the past to investigate the basic nature of EIL. The other is anthropological aspects, examining the theoretical feasibility of EIL from cultural viewpoints. Question (d) deals with linguistic and sociolinguistic aspects of EIL, in which features of WE are described and analyzed. Question (e) concerns communicative aspects of EIL, by covering human interactions through EIL.

The section on the practice of TEIL can be classified into five subcategories – curriculum, teaching materials, teaching methodologies, testing/evaluation, and teacher training.

In Hino (2001), based on the outlines described thus far, I proposed a holistic organization of EIL studies, which was slightly revised later in Hino (2003a) by adding a few details. While discussions under each section are extensively updated in this chapter to reflect recent developments such as those of ELF research, I have decided to retain the basic framework, though with several minor changes in wording, since it still seems to best serve the purpose of providing a bird's-eye view of EIL studies:

1 Foundations of TEIL
    1.1 Definition of EIL
        1.1.1 EIL, the term
        1.1.2 Concept of EIL
        1.1.3 Definition of an "international language"
        1.1.4 Forms of EIL
    1.2 Rationale for TEIL
        1.2.1 EIL for linguistic equality
        1.2.2 EIL for representing users' identities
        1.2.3 EIL for global awareness
    1.3 Background of TEIL
        1.3.1 Historical aspects of EIL
              1.3.1.1 International languages in world history
              1.3.1.2 Formation of EIL ideology and its development
        1.3.2 Anthropological aspects of EIL: the relationship between language and culture
              1.3.2.1 EIL and the Sapir–Whorf hypothesis
              1.3.2.2 Indigenization/nativization of language
              1.3.2.3 "Nation" as a unit of analysis
        1.3.3 Macro-sociolinguistic aspects of EIL
              1.3.3.1 Spread of English
              1.3.3.2 EIL in language policies
        1.3.4 Linguistic and micro-sociolinguistic aspects of EIL: features of World Englishes
              1.3.4.1 Description of syntax, phonology, lexicon, discourse rules, and sociolinguistic rules

16 *A paradigm of EIL education*

        1.3.4.2 Contributions from corpus linguistics
        1.3.4.3 Varieties of English in dictionaries
        1.3.4.4 Institutionalized varieties, performance varieties, and similects
        1.3.4.5 Contact linguistics/literature
            1.3.4.5.1 World Englishes and pidgin/creole
            1.3.4.5.2 Englishes in postcolonial literatures
  1.3.5 Communicative aspects of EIL
        1.3.5.1 Dilemma between identity and communication
        1.3.5.2 Intelligibility, comprehensibility, and interpretability
        1.3.5.3 Language attitudes toward varieties of English

2   Practice of TEIL
  2.1 Curriculum
    2.1.1 Administrative matters
    2.1.2 Syllabus
    2.1.3 Models in TEIL
    2.1.4 Four skills in TEIL
        2.1.4.1 Teaching of listening in EIL
        2.1.4.2 Teaching of speaking in EIL
        2.1.4.3 Teaching of reading in EIL
        2.1.4.4 Teaching of writing in EIL
    2.1.5 Cross-cultural/intercultural understanding in TEIL
    2.1.6 Analysis of courses of study
    2.1.7 EIL and ESP
  2.2 Teaching materials
  2.3 Teaching methodologies
  2.4 Evaluation/testing
  2.5 Teacher training/employment

Contents of each section: an overview of EIL studies

In the following, I will briefly describe what content each section of this framework entails, which will also serve as a concise overview of EIL studies.

1 Foundations of TEIL

As the first half of the paradigm, this part theoretically identifies EIL itself.

1.1 Definition of EIL

A clear definition of key concepts is a prerequisite for any academic discipline. However, in the study of global Englishes, the basic interpretation of fundamental concepts has often been blurred, resulting in unproductive circular arguments. Under the circumstances, it is especially important to start with the definition of EIL.

A holistic framework of EIL education   17

In this book, the concept of EIL refers to a paradigm constructed by the present author, developed on Smith's pioneering proposals on EIL (e.g., 1976, 1978, 1981b) as well as on the indigenous Japanese philosophy of *kokusai-eigo* (International English) (e.g., Kunihiro, 1970; T. Suzuki, 1975), while also incorporating many relevant elements from other useful theories of global Englishes including WE (e.g., B. Kachru, 1976, 1985, 1986, 1997) and ELF (e.g., Jenkins, 2000, 2015a; Seidlhofer, 2011).

Drawing partially on Smith (1976) and others, EIL is defined in the present volume as "English for international communication." This definition is meant to imply "English *when used* for international communication" as mentioned in 1.1.3.

1.1.1 EIL, THE TERM

There are various terms to express the concept of EIL or an idea overlapping with it, besides EIL (Smith, 1981b, 1983) itself. As those variations at times create confusion as to what they mean, the very examination of these terms should be an important subfield of EIL studies. They include, among others, English as an International Auxiliary Language (EIAL) (Smith, 1976), English as an International and Intranational Language (EIIL) (Smith, 1978), English for Cross-Cultural Communication (Smith, 1981a), English for International Communication (Brumfit, 1982), English as a World Language (Bailey & Görlach, 1982), New Englishes (Pride, 1982; Platt, Weber, & Ho, 1984), World Englishes (WE) (B. Kachru, 1985), International English (Trudgill & Hannah, 1982), English as a Global Language (Crystal, 1997), English as a Lingua Franca (ELF) (Jenkins, 2000), Lingua Franca English (LFE) (Canagarajah, 2007), and Global Englishes (Jenkins, 2015a).

In Japan, several thinkers have expressed their views on the implications of globalization of English for the learning of English, each creating his or her own term. Among them are *kokusai-eigo* (International English) (Kunihiro, 1970), *Englic* (T. Suzuki, 1971, 1975), and *Englanto* (Makoto Oda, 1970).

These terms have their own implications and semantic boundaries, as will be revealed in the due course in the present volume. Just for one example, although the concepts of New Englishes and WE both share their origin in the British (Commonwealth) linguists' study of postcolonial or Outer Circle Englishes, the latter includes all of the Inner, Outer, and Expanding Circle varieties whereas the former only refers to those of the Outer Circle.

1.1.2 CONCEPT OF EIL

What is the essence of the concept of EIL? Based on his observation of the global spread of English in the late 1960s, Japanese anthropologist Masao Kunihiro (1970) analyzed, in his original expression, that the "*datsu-eibei*" (de-Anglo-Americanization) of English was taking place. This position of Kunihiro could be seen as a forerunner of Smith (1976), who came up with the idea of

18 *A paradigm of EIL education*

EIL from his experiences in cross-cultural communication in English in Thailand and, subsequently, Honolulu. EIL may, indeed, be characterized as de-Anglo-Americanized English for international communication. In other words, EIL is the English language in situations where it is freed from the linguistic and cultural framework of Anglophone native speakers.

1.1.3 DEFINITION OF AN "INTERNATIONAL LANGUAGE"

While EIL stands for English as an International Language, definitions of an "international language" are a source of much confusion, as the term is subject to many different interpretations. Smith (1976) defines an international language as "one which is used by people of different nations to communicate with each other" (p. 38). While basically drawing on Smith's definition, it is my position to rephrase it as "a language when used for international communication," chiefly for two reasons. One is to emphasize the situational nature of an international language, and the other is to dilute the traditional nation-state framework by avoiding the word "nation" itself.

The former reason concerns an attempt to prevent EIL from falling into the pitfall of "linguistic imperialism," a problem pointed out in a number of influential works particularly in the 1990s, such as Phillipson (1992), Pennycook (1994), and Tsuda (1990). With my definition, any language can be an international language, depending on situational contexts. It is just that, by comparison, English is the most frequently used international language. In other words, it is entirely possible to conceptualize TIL (Turkish as an International Language), FIL (Finnish as an International Language), or MIL (Mongolian as an International Language) just as EIL, even though the actual use of these languages for international communication is relatively infrequent. EIL as a context-dependent notion does not endow the English language with any inherent privilege.

To follow up on this point, EIL is distinguished from English as a World Language, when the latter presupposes the global spread of English as its premise. Although it is certainly important for EIL studies to investigate the globalization of English in order to sociolinguistically grasp the way this language is used, the dominance of English itself is not a prerequisite for the concept of EIL.

Regarding the latter reason, a problem with Smith's definition of an international language is that it is inevitably accompanied with the notion of nationality, a legal concept to determine who belongs to what nation, which often fails to indicate one's linguacultural backgrounds especially in this age of mobility. In my definition, the word "international" is intended to mean "beyond nations," rather than "between nations" as used by Smith, thus comparatively de-emphasizing (though not discarding) the nation-state as a linguacultural unit.

1.1.4 FORMS OF EIL

What is the shape of EIL? In his lifetime, Smith constantly reiterated that "EIL is a function, NOT a form of the language" (Smith, 2014, p. 133. Emphasis

A holistic framework of EIL education 19

in the original), a position echoed by other EIL scholars including A. Matsuda and Friedrich (2011). While this characterization of the concept may have an advantage of ruling out the interpretation of EIL as a monolithic entity, one of the standpoints described later in this chapter, it does not preclude the need to identify what EIL looks like.

Though there are various views on the forms of EIL, they can be classified into two major dichotomous categories, namely, diverse EIL and monolithic EIL. Each is further broken down into two subcategories, with the former comprising "varieties of English" and "variations of English," while the latter consists of "neutral English" and "artificial English." This taxonomy of the viewpoints on the forms of EIL, representing the total of four different interpretations, is illustrated in Figure 2.2.

As a basis of EIL education toward a symbiotic and multicultural world, the concept of EIL as defined in the present volume primarily focuses on the diversity of English, the first of the two umbrellas in Figure 2.2. It also encompasses both the "varieties" and "variations" positions, neither of which can be disregarded in intercultural communication.

It is generally believed that the WE paradigm, as a study of varieties of English, is committed to diversity. This definitely is true with its treatment of Englishes in the Outer Circle, such as Indian English and Nigerian English, as it frees these varieties from Inner Circle norms. On the other hand, learners from the Expanding Circle, such as East Asia and Europe, have not been allowed to enjoy the same privilege when WE scholars hold that their models be established Englishes of the Inner Circle (Andreasson, 1994; Bamgbose, 1998) or of the Outer Circle. As long as the concept of exonormativity, instead of endonormativity, is associated with the Expanding Circle as such, the notion of diversity remains less than complete.

As for the ELF paradigm, it has been controversial whether ELF is oriented toward diverse or monolithic English. While representative ELF scholars

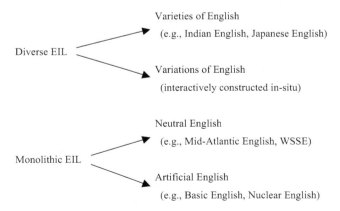

Figure 2.2 Taxonomy of views on the forms of EIL

20 A paradigm of EIL education

repeatedly emphasize that they are aiming for diversity (e.g., Jenkins, 2006, 2007, 2009; Seidlhofer, 2006, 2009), many actually regard ELF as monolithic, an interpretation that would fall into the second of the two umbrellas in Figure 2.2. For example, Rubdy and Saraceni (2006) consider the notion of ELF to be a "monomodel" (p. 11) in nature. Pennycook (2009) also interprets the concept on a similar note, writing of "an ELF approach with its supposedly centripetal focus" (p. 199). Most symbolic in this respect was a symposium at the 2007 conference of the International Association for World Englishes in Regensburg. Jenkins and Seidlhofer, both serving as panelists, received harsh criticisms from some participating WE scholars for allegedly belittling the diversity of English, despite their claim that it was by no means the case.

The impression of "monolithic ELF" largely comes from the Lingua Franca Core (LFC) proposed by Jenkins (2000), a common core, especially of phonology, which ensures intelligibility in the use of English for international communication. However, from my standpoint, LFC can actually promote diversity if "non-core" features are skillfully exploited as a free space where the speaker is allowed to express his or her own identity. For instance, it is my perception that English spoken with a syllable-timed rhythm (a non-core feature) better represents my Japanese identity, compared with an American-style stress-timed rhythm. This aspect is especially significant for the Expanding Circle, because such an approach is equally applicable both to the Outer and Expanding Circle, nullifying the discrimination produced by the WE paradigm.

Thus, from my point of view, in its early studies, or at a phase now called "ELF1" (Jenkins, 2015b), ELF research had unique potential for the diversity of English, opening ways for the chance of endonormative models for the Expanding Circle, concerning concepts such as Japanese English. However, the matter has been complicated since ELF studies moved on to "ELF2," focusing on the fluid and dynamic nature of ELF. It is still possible to regard ELF studies as subscribing to diversity, as evident in the plural form of the title of Jenkins (2015a), *Global Englishes*, yet the meaning of diversity has at least changed from "variety" to "variation" (Widdowson, 2015), in other words, to fluid and dynamic English interactively co-constructed *in situ*. It is diverse English, not as a collection of varieties but as situational variations. Jenkins (2015b) states that at the ELF2 phase "ELF, with its fluidity and 'online' negotiation of meaning among interlocutors with varied multilingual repertoires, could not be considered as consisting of bounded varieties" (p. 55). In other words, notions such as Japanese English are greatly de-emphasized here.

Jenkins (2015b) also discusses the "ELF3" phase, English as a Multilingua Franca, in which translanguaging is regarded as a natural process of ELF. However, as ELF3 can be regarded an extension of ELF2 rather than a fundamental paradigm shift, I will not go into the analysis of ELF3 in the present context.

ELF experts today hardly talk about the ELF1 stage any more, including Jenkins herself, who seems to have stopped mentioning LFC. ELF1 now tends to be treated as outdated. In my view, this is quite regrettable in terms of the potential of ELF1 mentioned earlier in this chapter.

A holistic framework of EIL education   21

In summarizing the author's interpretation of EIL, there is no one single form of EIL. Rather, EIL is represented by an enormous number of varieties, such as British English, American English, Indian English, Filipino English, Chinese English, and Japanese English, with their distinct cultural identities. On the other hand, those varieties are also accommodated and adjusted *in situ* through co-construction processes between interactants, resulting in countless situational variations. In other words, no variety of EIL is a static entity. To achieve international and intercultural communication, all varieties, be it Indian English or Japanese English, are required to change all the time, depending on various contextual factors often involving negotiations with one's interlocutor.

Although it is the author's position to pay special attention to the diversity of EIL with respect to the teaching of English for a symbiotic society, the second of the two umbrellas in Figure 2.2, that is, "monolithic EIL," is also a significant interpretation of EIL that deserves serious consideration.

The emergence of a unified, universal variety of English for international use has been observed for some time. Almost half a century ago, Kunihiro (1970) pointed out that, concurrently with the diversification of English, a neutral form of English appeared to be emerging. He named it "Mid-Atlantic English," as it looked half-British and half-American. A quarter of a century later, Modiano (1996) observed what he also called "Mid-Atlantic" among the unified European countries, endorsing Kunihiro's foresight as a result. Crystal (1997) argued as well that a new form of international English, which he named "World Standard Spoken English" (WSSE), would almost certainly arise. In other words, together with the diversification of English, the unification of English, which is a move in the opposite direction, has also been seen to occur. Along a similar line of thinking, Yano (2001), a frequently quoted paper by a Japanese scholar, also argues that English as a global language "should be as simple and regular as possible in its linguistic forms, in its rules of use, and socioculturally as neutral as possible" (p. 129), thus predicting a move toward neutrality.

"Artificial English," the second in the "monolithic EIL" category, also refers to unified forms of English, such as Basic English, proposed by Ogden and Richards (Ogden, 1930) and Nuclear English, proposed by Quirk (1981). Both Basic English and Nuclear English are aimed at simplifying English to facilitate learning as well as communication. Basic English is known to limit the basic vocabulary to 850 words. In Nuclear English, all instances of tag-questions, for example, are reduced to just one expression "Right?," sparing the speakers the burden of complex grammatical operations in coming up with appropriate forms such as "aren't they?," "do you?," or "shouldn't she?"

Basic English has come to be employed as a pedagogical tool for a method of ELT known as the Graded Direct Method (GDM), but has never been extensively used as a means of international communication. Nuclear English did not really go anywhere, as Quirk never described it in concrete detail. Although artificially devised English is not a focus of investigation in the present volume, they could have some potential as a means of international communication in terms of the functional effectiveness of restricted codes.

22 A paradigm of EIL education

1.2 Rationale for TEIL

Why is there a need to practice TEIL? What good does it do? Why are TEFL (Teaching English as a Foreign Language) and TESL (Teaching English as a Second Language) not sufficient? Three attributes of EIL, among others, serve as the rationale for TEIL – the promotion of linguistic equality, the representation of users' identities, and the raising of global awareness. Each of these points is briefly discussed in the following subsections.

1.2.1 EIL FOR LINGUISTIC EQUALITY

The concept of EIL promotes unbiased attitudes toward all varieties of English. In EIL, non-native varieties of English are deemed to be as valuable as native varieties. When the WE paradigm has some reservations on the equality between Englishes in the Outer Circle and those from the Expanding Circle, the EIL paradigm holds that Englishes from all three circles should be treated as equals. Another important aspect of the linguistic equality in EIL is that, unlike in ESL and EFL, native speakers as well as non-native speakers are equally responsible for making efforts to ensure successful international communication (Smith, 1981b).

On the other hand, the idea of realizing linguistic equality through EIL has at times been questioned from the viewpoint of "linguistic imperialism." As touched on in 1.1.3, some theorists pointed out, most notably in the 1990s, that EIL would actually result in enhancing the linguistic imperialism of the English language by promoting the preferred use of English for international communication over other languages (Phillipson, 1992; Tsuda, 1990, 2003; Oishi, 1993, among others). However, those criticisms are actually inapplicable to our discussions of EIL, since the concept of EIL as defined in the present volume by no means claims that English is the best language for international communication. The notion of EIL does not mean that more people should learn English, but that we should be aware of its linguistic and cultural diversity when learning English.

In this regard, to avoid confusing pedagogical issues of EIL with those of linguistic imperialism, it must be made clear that the concept of EIL is restricted within the domain of ELT. Succinctly put, one may support EIL and criticize the dominance of English at the same time with no contradictions.

It may be added, as briefly mentioned earlier in this chapter, that a large part of the EIL framework could be applied to any other language. For example, just as with EIL, it is also possible to propose JIL (Japanese as an International Language), no matter how limited such a situation may actually be. When Japanese is used for international communication, there is no reason for non-native-speakers of Japanese to be bound to its native-speaker norms. Native speakers of Japanese have no right to impose their own norms on non-native speakers. This is true with any language.

Last, Tupas (2006) points out, in response to Hino (2001), a limitation to the supposed equality in EIL. That is, such equality is ensured, after all, only for the rich and the elite who have access to quality education. Though this aspect is beyond the scope of the present volume, it is indeed a fundamental problem, also discussed in works such as Martin (2014) and Kubota (2015). The concept of "developmental World Englishes" proposed by Bolton, Graddol, and Meierkord (2011) shares the same ethos as well in dealing with the issue of inequality.

1.2.2 EIL FOR REPRESENTING USERS' IDENTITIES

Language varieties function as identity markers for the language users. Among many aspects of identity as a multi-faceted socio-psychological construct, national identity is the one most often discussed with regard to EIL, as EIL is expected to be capable of representing its users' identities beyond the Anglo-American frame of reference.

In world history, language has often served as a medium of nationalism, national unity, or national identity. The recognition of local varieties of English also arose in line with the call for independence in former colonies of Britain and, to a limited extent, America. For example, the notion of Indian English is symbolic of India's independence from the U.K. This idea of English for national unity is more closely related to WE rather than to EIL due to the emphasis on the domestic use of English in the former, but is still a factor also in EIL. For instance, the feasibility of using Japanese English as a means of expressing national identity in international settings has long been discussed in Japan (e.g., T. Watanabe, 1983; Hino, 1987b; Suenobu, 1990; Nakayama, 1990).

On the other hand, it should be also noted that the representation of national identity through EIL is not without danger in terms of attitudes toward cross-cultural communication. As discussed in Chapter 5, the Japanese Ministry of Education sought to de-Anglo-Americanize ELT textbooks in Japan during World War II, a policy that was driven not by the need for global communication but by the motive of promoting the ethnocentric belief in the superiority of Japanese culture. Nationalism is a double-edged sword for EIL (Hino, 1988a).

The conceptualization of identity in EIL and WE studies is at times also criticized by scholars such as Kubota (2012) for being too static or "essentialist". Indeed, identity is dynamically negotiated through interactions with various situational factors involving artifacts and interlocutors. In my position, however, such constructivist approaches should not go to extremes. It is true that identity is a fluid entity, but it must also have a certain core. In order to be true to oneself, it is worthwhile to try to retain and represent one's essential element no matter what language may be employed as a vehicle of the ideas. For the author, this is where "strategic essentialism" (Sewell, 2016, p. 64), a notion attributed to Gayatri Spivak, comes in. Though EIL concepts such as "Japanese English to express Japanese patterns of thought" would sound essentialist, those approaches are still useful efforts to oppose the imposition of Anglo-American values when the English language is going global.

24 *A paradigm of EIL education*

A concept known as "the third space" (Bhabha, 1994) is also suggestive in analyzing the role of identity in EIL. As shown in works such as Dunworth and Zhang (2014), this theory means, when applied to language learning, that second language learners neither fully accommodate themselves to the culture of the target language nor simply retain their original selves. Instead, they engage in negotiations to create their new identities in the third space. According to this notion, Japanese learners of English, for example, would neither give in to Anglo-American values nor cling to Japanese values, but would come up with a new identity through interactions between the two cultures. However, from an EIL perspective, while in reality such a mixing process must be inevitable to a certain extent, the intervention of English into learners' value systems is not considered to be desirable with respect to EIL ideals, which holds that one's thoughts should not be controlled by a language that he or she employs.

1.2.3 EIL FOR GLOBAL AWARENESS

EIL is a vital factor in integrating global awareness into ELT. Efforts have been made for years to incorporate global issues into foreign language teaching, as evident in the fact that many academic organizations involved in language education now have special interest groups (SIGs) in Global Education or in related areas. Kip Cates, a longtime key figure in "Global Issues in Language Education" SIG in the Japan Association for Language Teaching (JALT), defines the aim of Global Education as "to enable students to effectively acquire a foreign language while empowering them with the knowledge, skills, and commitment required by world citizens to solve global problems" (Cates, 2002, p. 41). He cites terrorism, ethnic conflict, social inequality, and environmental destruction as examples of global problems. In fact, also in my observation, peace, human rights, and the environment are the three central themes that have often been taken up in classrooms by ELT teachers interested in Global Education.

While the close kinship between "TEIL" and "Global Education in ELT" (henceforth, GEELT) has intuitive support, it seems that it has never really been explained how these two pedagogical concepts might relate to each other. The following lists are my attempts in this respect:

1   Both TEIL and GEELT are dedicated to the promotion of international understanding and cross-cultural awareness (cf. Obari, 1995).
2   The "English" in GEELT has to be EIL rather than American or British English, as the scope of global issues transcends the Anglo-American frame of reference.
3   Not being confined within the Inner Circle consisting of so-called developed countries, EIL reaches out to the Outer Circle and the Expanding Circle for communication, many members of which are developing countries often victimized by global problems such as war, human rights violations, and environmental destruction.

4 To support number 3 above pedagogically, the most common methodology for TEIL is the content-based approach, in which global issues may be naturally dealt with as the content.

Some of my pedagogical practices presented later in Part III exemplify these points. On a radio EIL program for which I served as the host, I discussed issues such as the exploitation of tropical rain forests in Malaysia, famines in Bangladesh, and interethnic problems in Sri Lanka with international guests from those respective countries (Chapter 8). In my university undergraduate EIL classes where Internet news media from across the world are explored real time, issues in war and peace, human rights, and the environment are naturally highlighted (Chapter 9).

1.3 Background of TEIL

The background of TEIL is explored from five angles, namely, historical, anthropological, macro-sociolinguistic, linguistic and micro-sociolinguistic, and communicative perspectives.

1.3.1 HISTORICAL ASPECTS OF EIL

The concept of EIL did not suddenly emerge from a vacuum. The analysis of its historical background provides important clues for identifying the essential nature of EIL.

1.3.1.1 International languages in world history English is probably the most conspicuous international language in history, but it is by no means the only one. In fact, there have been numerous languages that have played significant roles for international communication. They include Latin, Greek, Arabic, and Chinese, to name just a few.

Works on global Englishes have dealt with the historical international functions performed by these languages (e.g., Lowenberg, 1988; Mufwene, 2001; Trudgill, 2014; B. Kachru, 2017), but have not fully investigated specifically from EIL perspectives what problems they were faced with and how those problems were tackled. This kind of analysis should prove informative when we think about various issues surrounding EIL, as it would demonstrate what happens when a language frees itself from its original native speakers' linguistic and cultural framework.

For example, the New Testament, or a collection of various writings over time that came to be known by that name, was authored in what could be called GIL, or Greek as an International Language, which went beyond the border of native and non-native speakers. Some of its writers (such as Paul and Luke) were native speakers of the language with Hellenistic background, while others (such as the author of the Gospel According to Mark) were non-native

26   *A paradigm of EIL education*

speakers without Hellenistic values, both of whom were trying to communicate their messages to native and non-native speakers alike.

It is also quite significant from an EIL perspective that Bible scholars characterize the language used in much of the New Testament as "Palestinian Greek" (M. Silva, 1991) or "Jewish Greek" (Turner, 1991), an indigenized variety of Greek employed for international communication. When ELF, or English as a Lingua Franca, is sometimes assumed to take one single form, history testifies to the use of pluralistic "Greeks" as a lingua franca as far back as two thousand years ago. In other words, just as GIL or GLF was actually not monolithic despite the "contact-induced simplification" (Trudgill, 2014, p. 389) to function as a *koine*, but diverse enough to represent the local values of its users, ELF should also be viewed as pluralistic.

1.3.1.2   Formation of EIL ideology and its development   The history of EIL philosophy itself is an important component of EIL studies, since we need to look into the past if we wish to understand the present. In fact, the essential nature of the concept of EIL is grasped clearly only by reflecting on its roots.

The first explicit statement that ELT should be delivered from native-speaker norms is attributed to Halliday, McIntosh, and Strevens (1964), a book by leading British linguists. A criticism against their position by a noted American applied linguist Prator (1968) was in turn criticized by an Indian sociolinguist B. Kachru (1976) for exhibiting "linguistic chauvinism." This controversy from the 1960s to 1970s can be recognized as the beginning of WE studies, with B. Kachru's work on Indian English (e.g., B. Kachru, 1965) as one of its first products, while EIL studies, originally independent from WE thought, was initiated by Smith (1976).

B. Kachru and Smith soon came to work together, skillfully combining the concepts of WE and EIL, leading to the launch of the International Association for World Englishes (IAWE) in 1992. The term World Englishes itself was officially coined in an editorial of the journal *World Englishes,* jointly written by its co-editors B. Kachru and Smith (1985), which marked the remodeling of the periodical from its earlier version *World Language English.* However, the separate origins of WE and EIL have remained in the background. The concept of WE arose mainly from the observation of the development of domestic varieties of English in the former colonies of Britain. The idea of EIL, on the other hand, evolved from experiences in international communication through the medium of English involving both native and non-native speakers of the language.

The differences in the birth process between WE and EIL explain why the distinction between Outer Circle varieties and Expanding Circle varieties is always emphasized in WE, while EIL theorists are not so strongly concerned with this distinction. Although WE scholars by no means ignore Expanding Circle varieties, Outer Circle varieties are so frequently their primary concern because of the postcolonial emphasis of WE. While for WE theorists it is meaningless to discuss Indian English and Japanese English on the same platform, EIL theorists see no need to avoid treating these two as equals, because their international functions are the same regardless of the fundamental differences in their intra-national roles.

Another group of scholars, centered around Germany or Europe, has long been active in the study of varieties of English, with *English World-Wide* as their flagship journal. As evident in works such as Görlach (1991, 1995) as well as in papers published in the journal, approaches employed by this school of thought, tentatively called EWW here, are linguistic, theoretical, and academic by nature in contrast with the pedagogical orientations of EIL. In my observation, the EWW school had practically excluded Expanding Circle varieties from their major research themes until recently, due to their focus on describable varieties.

Although basically an independent school of thought, EWW is often categorized today under the WE umbrella. For example, a theory of postcolonial Englishes known as the Dynamic Model proposed by a representative EWW scholar Edgar W. Schneider (2003, 2007) is now regarded by WE researchers as a guiding principle for analyzing the development of Englishes in the Outer Circle.

In regard to ELF, a recent high-profile approach to global Englishes, its initial motives seemed to be multi-faceted. Generally perceived as a European school, ELF studies has been driven by the need for communication in the unified Europe, as evident in the works by two of "the three mothers of ELF" (an expression coined by Andy Kirkpatrick), Barbara Seidlhofer (e.g., 2011) from Austria, and Anna Mauranen (e.g., 2012) from Finland.

On the other hand, the seminal book by the other "mother of ELF," Jennifer Jenkins (2000), also had several other significant features. First, in my viewpoint from East Asia, the volume was another new wave from the U.K. along the line of Crystal (1997). For so long since Halliday et al. (1964), British and Commonwealth linguists had not cared very much about varieties of English outside of former British territories. In other words, they used to be concerned only with Englishes in the Inner and Outer Circle, while being indifferent to Expanding Circle varieties. Crystal (1997) brought about a change in this conventional attitude among British and Commonwealth scholars by analyzing English as a global language beyond the postcolonial framework, and Jenkins (2000) went even further by suggesting the chance of endonormative models of pronunciation for ELF, which would liberate not only the Outer Circle but also the Expanding Circle from native-speaker norms.

Second, Jenkins (2000) was a significant attempt to identity the core features enabling speakers of different varieties of English to understand each other. Some WE researchers had also been insightful enough to assume that there might be such cores (e.g., Hashiuchi, 1989), but had not ventured to find out exactly what they were.

Third, Jenkins (2000) also brought to attention the importance of "accommodation" in international communication, when WE studies had focused more

28 *A paradigm of EIL education*

on the freedom to speak one's own variety to project his or her distinct identity.

The first two of these three aspects of the initial ELF proposal by Jenkins were obscured as ELF studies proceeded to the next "ELF2" stage, while the third aspect, accommodation, came to be highlighted.

1.3.2 ANTHROPOLOGICAL ASPECTS OF EIL: THE RELATIONSHIP BETWEEN LANGUAGE AND CULTURE

"Language and culture may be inextricably tied together but no one language is inextricably tied to any one culture" (Smith, 1981b, p. 30. Also in Smith, 1983, p. 10). This is the view that the whole EIL theory is based upon concerning the relationship between language and culture. This position of EIL could be interpreted to counter a traditional belief on this issue, namely the Sapir–Whorf hypothesis.

1.3.2.1 EIL and the Sapir–Whorf hypothesis One of the most influential theories, or actually a hypothesis, in linguistic anthropology and sociolinguistics has been the Sapir–Whorf hypothesis, an original American version of the hypothesis suggested by German scholar K. W. Humboldt, which is interpreted to mean that language and culture are inseparable. A problem in EIL studies is that not much consideration has been given to the need for analyzing the implications of the Sapir–Whorf hypothesis for EIL, despite the fact that this view of the cultural aspects of language may be regarded as contradicting the premise of the theory of EIL. Among the papers published in the journal *World Englishes*, for example, Narasimhan (1997) critically analyzes Steven Pinker's idea of mentalese with an extensive reference to the Sapir–Whorf hypothesis, but what implications it would have for the EIL theory is yet to be discussed. In fact, it looks as if EIL researchers have largely been bypassing this issue. In view of the persisting influence that this hypothesis has in language study, it should be important for EIL researchers to be directly faced with the Sapir–Whorf hypothesis in order to provide the concept of EIL with a more solid theoretical foundation.

One major problem in dealing with this theme is the lack of clarity in the definition of the Sapir–Whorf hypothesis, which partly comes from the fact that this hypothesis is actually not a joint work between Edward Sapir and Benjamin Whorf but one that was formed in various manners by their successors in linguistic anthropology, who observed some common traits in the works by these two theorists.

For instance, this hypothesis is often referred to in two different forms, the strong version and the weak version. The use of terms such as "linguistic relativism" and "linguistic determinism," in addition to the Sapir–Whorf hypothesis, adds to this confusion, since some theorists consider these three terms to be interchangeable with each other, while others make a point of distinguishing them. Also, the relationship between "culture," "thought," and "world view"

A holistic framework of EIL education   29

is often in question in the analysis of the Sapir–Whorf hypothesis. Furthermore, the fact that this hypothesis is primarily meant for the first language, when EIL is a concept that covers both English as a native and non-native language, complicates the analysis.

The theory of EIL has its own answer to the relationship between language and culture. It is a concept known as "indigenization" or "nativization," discussed in 1.3.2.2. Its implications for the Sapir–Whorf hypothesis, however, have not been examined in any depth.

1.3.2.2 Indigenization/nativization of language   Indigenization (or nativization) refers to a sociolinguistic adaptation process in which a language undergoes changes in a new cultural environment. In the case of English, indigenization has usually been considered to occur in the former colonies of Britain or America. For example, in India, English has gone through this process as the language has been influenced by the Indian environment including Indian cultural values. In WE research, indigenization has been studied extensively in the form of case studies mainly concerning countries in the Outer Circle, such as India, Sri Lanka, Singapore, the Philippines, Kenya, and Nigeria.

When a language comes to be used by non-native speakers without the cultural values for which this language is originally supposed to express, either the language or the users, or both, must make adaptations to the other. From the viewpoint of EIL and WE, it is primarily the language that undergoes changes rather than the users (B. Kachru, 1986; Alatis & Straehle, 1997). This indigenization theory is placed at the core of WE studies, and is also an important basis of EIL studies.

A major research task is the analysis of indigenization at a fundamental level. What implications does the phenomenon of indigenization have for the Sapir–Whorf hypothesis? The indigenization theory may perhaps be viewed as an antithesis to the Sapir–Whorf hypothesis, but this issue requires greater investigation.

Another question that has not been sufficiently explored is whether indigenization occurs in countries in the Expanding Circle such as Japan and China. The concept of indigenized (or nativized) varieties of English has traditionally been used to refer to Outer Circle varieties like Indian English or Singaporean English (Richards, 1977; Pride, 1982; Platt et al., 1984), while linguistic adaptation in the Expanding Circle has largely been studied as a process of Englishization of the local language, for instance, how the Japanese language is influenced by English (e.g., Stanlaw, 2004; Takashi, 1990; Iwasaki, 1994, Fujiwara, 2014).

Along the lines of the WE paradigm that places emphasis on the indigenization of English in former colonies of Britain, WE scholars tend to be rather negative about the possibility of indigenization of English in the Expanding Circle. Schell (2009), for example, argues that no distinct Japanese English would be born unless oral communication in English becomes common among Japanese nationals. Schell's position can be seen as a direct application of the

30　*A paradigm of EIL education*

developmental process of postcolonial Englishes to the Expanding Circle, which should be more carefully discussed in view of the sociolinguistic and socio-educational differences between the Outer and the Expanding Circle.

This relates to the issue as to whether the Dynamic Model (Schneider, 2003, 2007) may be applicable to the Expanding Circle. The Dynamic Model is a theory on the developmental process of postcolonial Englishes, proposed by a leading scholar of what I call the EWW school, Edgar W. Schneider, which has come to be widely accepted not only by EWW but also by WE researchers. Although it provides a useful tool for analyzing how postcolonial Englishes such as Australian English (Inner Circle) and Indian English (Outer Circle) have been developed, a problem is that some WE scholars assume that the model can be applied to the Expanding Circle as well, an overgeneralization that Schneider himself has never intended.

The issue of indigenization will be taken up again in 1.3.4.4 in terms of the dichotomy between "institutionalized varieties" and "performance varieties."

1.3.2.3　"Nation" as a unit of analysis　A problem with EIL/WE studies so far is that the basic unit of analyzing EIL/WE has usually been the "nation."[1] Typically, varieties of English are classified in terms of nationalities, like American English, Indian English, or Japanese English. The nation has traditionally been considered the legitimate framework for analyzing language problems, but the validity of this practice, which relies on political rather than linguacultural categorization, is now questionable from sociolinguistic and anthropological perspectives. For example, the issue of "Ebonics" or African-American vernacular English as an ethnically oriented variety of English rather than a national variety cannot be adequately dealt with if we cling to the notion of "American" English.

At the moment, it is still not easy to find a clear-cut answer to this problem. For instance, merely replacing nationality with ethnicity is not a solution. It is true that ethnic groups often correspond to linguistic boundaries, but not always so. The relations between languages, nations, and ethnic groups are interwoven in a very complex manner. Furthermore, there are some advantages in using a nation or nationality as a basic unit of EIL analysis, as this approach can clearly point to the fact that there is often a homogeneous national variety of English regardless of the ethnicity of the speakers. For instance, while there are some differences in English used by Chinese, Malay, and Indian Singaporeans, there still exists a variety of English that can be defined as Singapore English or Singaporean English (Lim, 2004).

1.3.3　MACRO-SOCIOLINGUISTIC ASPECTS OF EIL

Who are the users of English in today's world? And, what policies does each country have for the use of English? These macro-sociolinguistic analyses are essential in order to understand the environment where this particular language is spoken and written.

A holistic framework of EIL education 31

1.3.3.1 Spread of English In order to identify the macro-sociolinguistic environment surrounding EIL, it is important to investigate the spread of English in the present world, as has been attempted by works such as Crystal (1997, 2003) and Graddol (1997, 2006). It is a reality, whether fortunate or unfortunate, that no language has been as widespread as today's English in human history.

An especially significant fact about the present use of English is that this language now has many more non-native speakers than native speakers as its active users (Honna, 1999; Jenkins, 2015a). In other words, it is nowadays a norm, rather than an exception, for users of English to communicate with non-native speakers. Pedagogically, this means that ELT today should be geared toward the need for communication with non-native speakers.

1.3.3.2 EIL in language policies Another important macro-sociolinguistic aspect of EIL is the analysis of language planning and language policies from EIL perspectives. For example, a comparison of language policies in Malaysia and Singapore highlights the fact that there are important differences in national attitudes toward English between these two countries in spite of their historical, cultural, and ethnic kinship. Since its independence from Britain, Singapore has basically been expanding the use of English for intra-national purposes as well as for international functions, while Malaysia has in a way been getting away from English as an intra-national language, limiting the use of the language to international situations.

As for language policies relevant to EIL in the Expanding Circle, there have recently been moves to employ English as a public language along with local languages in countries such as Japan and Korea, even with no history of Anglophone colonization. In Japan, for example, a government-sponsored committee by the name of *Nijuisseiki Nihon no Koso Kondankai* (The Prime Minister's Commission on Japan's Goals in the 21st Century) suggested the possibility of designating English as "an official second language" (Nijuisseiki Nihon no Koso Kondankai, 2000, p. 241) of Japan with the objective of "all citizens acquiring a working knowledge of English" (p. 241). It was speculated by many that the committee probably envisaged Singapore as a model, a fast-growing economy in contrast with waning Japan. Singapore's international competitiveness appeared, in the eyes of the Japanese, to be substantially due to its nationals' high proficiency in English, which had the status of an official language of the country.

Theoretically, the proposal by the prime minister's commission was tantamount to artificially making Japan go through the experiences of Outer Circle countries. It seems that its members were not really aware that it would be too unnatural to execute such a policy for Japan, a part of the Expanding Circle in Asia, with little authentic need for domestic communication in English. In fact, after causing sensation among the general public for some time, the proposal quickly fell into oblivion. The Japanese government never proceeded to take any concrete measures, either.

32 *A paradigm of EIL education*

1.3.4 LINGUISTIC AND MICRO-SOCIOLINGUISTIC ASPECTS OF EIL:
FEATURES OF WORLD ENGLISHES

What characteristics does each variety of English have? And also, what common traits do they share? These points have been studied extensively in EIL, and more so under the framework of WE. This subfield is one of the major areas in EIL and WE research.

1.3.4.1 Description of syntax, phonology, lexicon, discourse rules, and sociolinguistic rules The linguistic and micro-sociolinguistic analysis of WE encompasses such aspects as syntax, phonology, lexicon, discourse rules, and sociolinguistic rules. Concepts concerning register classifications, namely acrolect, mesolect, and basilect, provide a three-layered framework ranging from formal to informal domains. The study of features of Englishes identifies both differences and universals among varieties of English.

In EIL research from the 1980s, discursive and sociolinguistic rules have been considered a particularly important area of investigation, with awareness that how something is said is different from culture to culture, in other words, dependent upon each variety of English. This includes the way a specific speech act is performed, when and how silence is used, what topics are appropriate in what situations, etc. (e.g., Smith, 1987, 2001; K. Sridhar & S. Sridhar, 1986; Y. Kachru, 1992; Y. Kachru & Smith, 2008; C. Nelson, 1991; K. Sridhar, 1991; Barron, 2017). Rules for NNS/NNS interaction, or interaction between non-native speakers, are eminently characteristic of EIL, as they take place where native-speaker norms are irrelevant.

On the other hand, an aspect for which more thorough investigation may be anticipated in WE research is how the features of Englishes are accommodated in international communication. While the uniqueness of each variety of English is highly valued in WE philosophy, the need for accommodation has not been strongly emphasized, especially for established Outer Circle varieties. For example, what adaptations does a speaker of Indian English need to make to his or her own English in communicating with non-Indians?

Alsagoff (2007) is a study that suggests a prospect for this direction, proposing a new concept "International Singapore English" (ISE) (p. 35) for an international version of Singapore English to respond to global communicative needs. This stance can be seen as a further development on the notion of "English as a glocal language" (Pakir, 2000), which encompassed not only the local but also the global domains of Singapore English or Outer Circle Englishes in general. More recently, Low (2010, 2015) points out that two opposite forces are acting on Englishes in the Outer Circle, one towards globalized norms and the other towards localized norms.

Such dynamic aspects of global Englishes are an area where contributions from ELF studies, with its emphasis on the role of accommodation (Jenkins, 2000, 2015a), are greatly expected, although ELF research has thus far mainly focused on communication between Expanding Circle speakers.

1.3.4.2 Contributions from corpus linguistics Recent rapid developments in corpus linguistics, which constructs and analyzes computerized linguistic databases, are making an enormous contribution to the understanding of features of WE. The construction of corpora of non-native Englishes started with a historic proposal by British linguist Sydney Greenbaum (1988), which led to the compilation of the International Corpus of English (ICE) (Greenbaum, 1996; Greenbaum & G. Nelson, 1996). A problem, however, is that the Englishes involved in ICE have been restricted to Inner Circle and Outer Circle varieties such as New Zealander English and Sri Lankan English, respectively. The corpora of Expanding Circle varieties such as Japanese English and Chinese English have been compiled as a "learner corpus," in other words, as an "interlanguage corpus" for error analysis. A major example for this type of learner corpus is the International Corpus of Learner English (ICLE) (cf. Granger, 1996).

This hierarchy between the Outer Circle and the Expanding Circle is a reflection of the WE dichotomy between "institutionalized varieties" and "performance varieties," respectively.[2] In fact, while speakers of English in the former are usually called "users" of English, their counterparts in the latter tend to be referred to as "learners." Such discrimination is viewed as a problem from an EIL perspective. Building on Smith (1978), which defined even native speakers as learners of EIL, the present volume regards every speaker of English both as a learner and a user at the same time.

ELF studies, a newer school of thought, has produced a corpus that treats Englishes from the Expanding Circle as no less legitimate, known as the Vienna-Oxford International Corpus of English (VOICE), as a product of the project founded by Barbara Seidlhofer. In line with the region-free notion of ELF as a means of communication among speakers with different first languages, VOICE transcribes oral interactions between non-native speakers of English, mostly from the Expanding Circle (Seidlhofer, 2011, 2012). Focusing on interactions in academic situations, a team led by another leading ELF scholar, Anna Mauranen, has further produced the corpus of English as a Lingua Franca in Academic Settings (ELFA) (Mauranen, 2012).

While ELF studies initially centered around Europe not only in terms of the backgrounds of its researchers but also with respect to its scope of research, it is now expanding to other parts of the world. This is also true with ELF corpora, as seen in the Asian Corpus of English (ACE), constructed in a project headed by Andy Kirkpatrick as an Asian version of VOICE (Kirkpatrick, 2013), encompassing speakers both from the Outer Circle and the Expanding Circle with no discrimination between the two.

1.3.4.3 Varieties of English in dictionaries Partly due to the development of corpus such as ICE, some dictionaries today incorporate WE elements into their entries. The most notable is none other than the second edition of the *Oxford English Dictionary* (OED), which included in its 1989 edition a number of lexical entries from non-native varieties of English such as West African English

34 *A paradigm of EIL education*

and Indian English. *A dictionary of South African English on historical principles* (1996), edited by Penny Silva, was also a remarkable achievement in compiling a dictionary of a regional non-native variety of English. Another seminal work was the third edition of *The Macquarie dictionary* (1997), edited by A. Delbridge et al., which incorporated the lexicons of Southeast Asian Englishes into its entries (cf. Butler, 1997).

An interesting project that seemed to echo the ethos of Saito's pioneering work (1928) on the Japanization of English was *The new anchor Japanese-English dictionary* (1991). In the preface of this dictionary, the editor-in-chief, Katsuei Yamagishi, claims that he has tried to show how to express indigenous Japanese values in English. Considering the fact that it is often taken for granted in the WE framework that the speakers of "performance varieties" such as Japanese English should follow a native-speaker model, an effort like this is especially significant.

New dictionaries of regional varieties of English continue to be published. For example, Japanese researchers in Asian Englishes have compiled *Ajia-eigo jiten [Sanseido dictionary of Asian Englishes]* (i.e., Honna, Tajima, Enokizono, & Kawahara, 2002), focusing on the Englishes of India, Singapore, Malaysia, and the Philippines. Among more recent publications is *A dictionary of Hong Kong English* (i.e., Cummings & Wolf, 2011), one of the most comprehensive lexical descriptions of the variety to date (cf. Butler, 2012).

1.3.4.4 *Institutionalized varieties, performance varieties, and similects*

In WE studies, it has been assumed that Englishes in the Expanding Circle are essentially different from those in the Outer Circle, by calling the former "performance varieties" as opposed to "institutionalized varieties" attributed to the latter (B. Kachru, 1980). Performance varieties are also deemed as exonormative, or operating on external norms, while institutionalized varieties are regarded as endonormative, developing or possessing original norms (B. Kachru, 1986). Such a view of WE is understandable if we consider the postcolonial background as well as the sociolinguistic orientation of WE studies. However, in terms of EIL studies with its pedagogical objectives, this issue needs to be revisited.

The dichotomy of institutionalized and performance (also endonormative and exonormative) varieties very often leads to the argument that speakers of Expanding Circle varieties are simply supposed to follow native-speaker models, while the speakers of Outer Circle varieties are allowed to adopt their own regional models. This attitude, resulting in the imposition of native-speaker norms on some learners of English, could be construed as being against the basic egalitarian principle of EIL.

In fact, the lack of historical and sociolinguistic contexts for the use of English in the Expanding Circle should not be taken to mean that it is impossible to establish original educational models for Englishes in the Expanding Circle. This problem can be viewed from the two angles below.

First, though it is true that countries in the Expanding Circle, by definition, lack a history of intra-national use of English, it does not necessarily follow that their educational models are identical with native-speaker English. In fact, it is possible to argue that they have their own "institutionalized" varieties of English in education. For example, Shim (1999) analyzed that as a result of ELT in Korea, a "codified variety of Korean English," distinctly different from American English, had been developed. Matsui (1984) went so far as to suggest that "examination English" in Japan, developed over the years in a unique form that differed from native-speaker English, should be an appropriate tool for international communication because of its straightforwardness with the lack of native-like elements such as ambiguous rhetoric and confusing idiomatic expressions.

Second, even if the distinction between institutionalized and performance varieties is accepted as the sociolinguistic description of historic and present realities, it is still possible to have indigenous models for ELT in the Expanding Circle as individual samples. As a matter of fact, local teachers' English should serve as models for students in the Expanding Circle. This issue will be discussed once again in 2.1.3.

With the increasing presence of European and Asian users of English, including those of mainland China studied by Bolton (2003) and others, Englishes in the Expanding Circle, sometimes neglected before, have come to attract many researchers' attention. In light of the new research interest, the distinction between institutionalized and performance varieties, which the present author has questioned for long (e.g., Hino, 1987a), is now controversial at least. For example, Davydova (2012) discovered significant resemblances between the linguistic features of Indian English and Russian English beyond the conventional dichotomy of institutionalized and performance varieties. Low (2010) compared the rhythmic properties of Englishes of Chinese-dominant Singapore and mainland China, in addition to that of Britain, yielding somewhat mixed results. While mainland China English indeed exhibited phonological exonormativity vis-à-vis British English, its rhythmic pattern also showed considerable similarities with that of Singapore English.

A relevant concept that has come to be frequently cited in ELF studies is "similect," proposed by a representative ELF scholar Anna Mauranen (2012), referring to a lect that is based on the common first language background. According to this notion, speakers of English whose first language is Japanese speak similar English due to the common transfer. Similect could be a useful concept for reexamining the WE concept "performance variety."

1.3.4.5 Contact linguistics/literatures When two or more languages are in contact with each other, there emerge new unique linguistic entities. This phenomenon leads EIL researchers to the study of pidgins and creoles in terms of contact linguistics, and also to the study of postcolonial English literatures as contact literatures.

1.3.4.5.1 World Englishes and pidgin/creole   One of the sociolinguistic issues in EIL studies is to investigate the relationship between pidgins/creoles

36 *A paradigm of EIL education*

and WE, which has been both a complicated and controversial problem. When pidgins/creoles were regarded as mere degenerate, substandard languages with limited functions and repertoire, it was in a way easy to claim that EIL/WE were completely different from them. However, now that pidgins/creoles are often viewed by linguists as full-fledged languages, the matter is not so straightforward.

Are WE and pidgins/creoles placed in the same continuum? Or, do they essentially differ from each other? (cf. Siegel, 1997). A difficulty in answering this question seems to be demonstrated in Mufwene's recent notation that English creoles can be regarded as "the nonstandard varieties of the acrolectal Englishes spoken in the same territories" (Mufwene, 2015, p. 11), reminding us that being "non-standard" and "acrolectal" may indeed go together.

1.3.4.5.2 Englishes in postcolonial literatures   An analysis of postcolonial English literatures, which explores what B. Kachru (1986, 1987) calls "bilinguals' creativity," is an integral part of WE studies. The importance of this literary study is somewhat self-evident, in view of the fact that the philosophy of WE originally stemmed from a postcolonial background.

The analysis of postcolonial English literature, or literatures chiefly in the Outer Circle, such as those by Raja Rao from India and Wole Soyinka from Nigeria, is particularly significant in that it shows the extent to which local non-Anglophone values can be expressed through the means of English (Kimura, 2004). It thus provides an empirical ground on which the concept of EIL may be built. This aspect should be encouraging and empowering also for learners of English in the Expanding Circle, even with its sociolinguistic differences from the Outer Circle.

1.3.5   COMMUNICATIVE ASPECTS OF EIL

Since the primary aim of EIL is to ensure communication between people with different national and cultural backgrounds, communicative aspects of EIL is an area that is of the most immediate concern to EIL studies.

1.3.5.1 *Dilemma between identity and communication*   The basic philosophy of EIL entails the use of English as an expression of the speaker's own identity. However, this is often in conflict with understanding (Anderson, 1996), which in the theory of EIL is divided into intelligibility, comprehensibility, and interpretability, as discussed in 1.3.5.2.

A typical example cited in Hino (1997), discussed also in Chapter 8 of the present volume, was a Bangladeshi believer of Islamic faith, who made a point of using expressions such as "maybe" or "I don't know, but I will try" even when he willingly agreed to perform some task that was requested of him. For him, making a promise constitutes blasphemy against Allah, as the future is beyond human control. This way he expresses in English his own identity as a

A holistic framework of EIL education 37

Muslim, but at the same time runs the risk of being misinterpreted by those who do not share the same world views. Another Bangladeshi man who is also a believer of Islam told the author that although he understands he should not make a promise, he nonetheless makes a compromise and uses expressions such as "sure" or "certainly" in order to avoid misunderstanding.

This dilemma between identity and communication is a basic problem in EIL, and therefore one of the most fundamentally important research areas in the field. From the EIL viewpoint, which honors the diversity of culture, it is clear that one should not give up expressing his or her own values. A key concept here is the "negotiation of meaning," which enables the interactants to achieve mutual understanding through means such as clarification, even if it can be a time-consuming and laborious process.

1.3.5.2 Intelligibility, comprehensibility, and interpretability In order to analyze the issue of communication in EIL in detail, the concept of "understanding" is broken down into three levels – intelligibility, comprehensibility, and interpretability (Smith & C. Nelson, 1985; Smith, 1988, 1992, 2001; C. Nelson, 2011). Intelligibility refers to the degree of phonological recognition of an utterance. Comprehensibility means the extent of understanding the locutionary meaning, or the literal meaning of what is directly said, while interpretability concerns illocutionary meaning, that is, what is meant by the speaker or the writer in an indirect manner. The example of English spoken by the Islamic Bangladeshi in the previous subsection is a matter of interpretability, as he performed the speech act of agreeing to a request in a manner very different from mainstream native-speaker English.

Even after the epoch-making study known as Smith and Rafiqzad (1979), which showed that non-native varieties of English were no less intelligible than native-speaker English, Smith actually held that the problem of intelligibility itself should be relatively easy to solve, as difficulties in listening to unfamiliar styles of pronunciation tend to diminish after some exposure (e.g., Smith & Bisazza, 1982). He paid more attention to the issue of interpretability, as evident in Smith (1987), since this problem is not easy to detect, and therefore can often be a cause of serious misunderstanding. In this regard, Jenkins (2000) was one that drew attention once again to the issue of phonological intelligibility among varieties of English, though the concept of "varieties" was later de-emphasized in ELF studies.

Cecil L. Nelson, a pioneer who worked with Smith on this theme, succinctly summarizes one of the crucial aspects of intelligibility (also applicable to comprehensibility and interpretability) in EIL as "[n]ot accommodating one another for improved intelligibility will be personal (or group) failures, not deficiencies in our Englishes as such" (C. Nelson, 2011, p. 111). This view echoes Smith's position that in EIL even native speakers need to learn to speak intelligibly (Smith, 1978) and is also in agreement with Jenkins's argument on the significance of accommodation (Jenkins, 2000, 2007).

38 *A paradigm of EIL education*

1.3.5.3 Language attitudes toward varieties of English The issue of language attitudes has been a matter of major concern for EIL researchers, as a positive and unprejudiced attitude toward varieties of English, including their own, is a prerequisite for successful communication in EIL. This is also one of the areas in which EIL studies closely overlaps with sociolinguistics. A large number of empirical research projects have been conducted to measure language attitudes toward varieties of English, many of which reveal persistent preference among the learners of English for native-speaker English (e.g., Matsuura, Chiba, & A. Yamamoto; 1994; Chiba, Matsuura, & A. Yamamoto, 1995; A. Matsuda, 2003). It has also been pointed out that teacher training is a key for promoting fair attitudes toward the diversity of English (e.g., K. Brown, 1993; Honna & Takeshita, 1998; Bayyurt & Sifakis, 2017; Hino, 2017a; A. Matsuda, 2017b).

2 *Practice of TEIL*

Based on the theoretical foundations of EIL, what does research in the actual practice of the teaching of EIL entail? This matter will be discussed with an emphasis on its differences from the traditional teaching of ESL/EFL. If we employ the recent term "post-native-speakerism" (Houghton & Hashimoto, 2018), or its adjectival form "post-native-speakerist," TEIL is essentially a practice in pedagogy for the post-native-speakerist teacher of English (Hino, 2018).

Research in the practice of TEIL was relatively scarce until recently, compared with the rich accumulation of research relevant to many of the previous sections on the foundations of EIL. A dramatic change came around 2010, with a number of books on EIL education appearing from major international publishers. Particularly symbolic was the nearly simultaneous publication of two edited volumes, A. Matsuda (2012a) and Alsagoff, McKay, Hu, and Renandya (2012), with almost identical titles by chance, *Principles and practices of teaching English as an international language* and *Principles and practices for teaching English as an international language*, respectively. This new trend is surely a reflection of the global social need for learning English for international communication. With such a rapid shift in research interest, pedagogy has now become one of the most popular fields of EIL studies.

2.1 *Curriculum*

The word "curriculum" is used here in a rather wide sense that encompasses broad organizational factors beyond the management of one class, while the term "syllabus" refers to the content arrangement of a specific course.

2.1.1 ADMINISTRATIVE MATTERS

Whether the concept of EIL has any implication for language education policies at a macro level is a very subtle question.

It is the author's position that EIL studies basically have no say about issues such as how much time and money should be spent on the teaching of English in a certain country. EIL is often interpreted as an idea to promote ELT, but in my conception of EIL, this is not the case. EIL is a concept within the framework of English language education, and should not be regarded as being directed towards matters outside of its realm, for example, the selection of languages to be taught in schools. The schema put forth with the concept of EIL is "teaching EIL vs. teaching EFL/ESL" (when it is the case that English is indeed taught), and not "teaching EIL vs. teaching French (Korean, Tamil, or any other language)." Likewise, the concept of EIL has absolutely no claim against the efforts to create and spread a language of international communication such as Esperanto. Failure to recognize this basic position could mislead EIL supporters to much-criticized English language imperialism.

EIL could have some implications on administrative aspects within the framework of ELT; for instance, at what age students should start learning English. This has indeed been a hotly debated issue in countries such as Japan where the start of ELT has been lowered to the 5th grade (10 or 11 years old) in 2011 and is planned to be extended to the 3rd grade (8 or 9 years old) in 2020, though these changes are rather slow compared with many other Asian countries.

Studies in second language acquisition (SLA) on the controversial notion of critical period largely indicate that a second language learner who started late would probably fail to gain native-like pronunciation, but may not necessarily lose out in other areas of language learning. With the findings in EIL studies that non-native English pronunciation is by no means inferior to native-like English pronunciation in international communication (e.g., Smith & Rafiqzad, 1979; Deterding & Kirkpatrick, 2006; Kirkpatrick, 2010), there seems to be no strong reason to lower the starting age for learning English, as far as the acquisition of phonology is concerned. In fact, with respect to the need for learning local and national language(s) in Asia, Kirkpatrick (2012) argues that "English should be delayed until children have literacy and fluency in local languages" (p. 30).

On the other hand, there is a chance that an early start could enhance intercultural understanding, which can be an advantage for young students as future EIL users. Otsubo (1999a, b), in discussing the possibility of applying Larry E. Smith's EIL theories to the learning of English in Japan (cf. Otsubo, 2017), also suggests that ELT in elementary school taught by Japanese teachers may promote the growth of communicative Japanese English as EIL or WE. It is an interesting idea, although in reality many of the English classes in Japanese elementary schools are presently dependent on native English-speaking ALTs (Assistant Language Teachers) with a very limited contribution from Japanese teachers.

2.1.2 SYLLABUS

What types of ELT syllabus are appropriate for TEIL? Since the primary purpose of EIL education is the nurturing of communicative skills, instead of traditional mental training through the application of grammatical rules, a

40   *A paradigm of EIL education*

"communicative" syllabus has been identified with the EIL syllabus. As EIL greatly concerns language functions or speech acts (Smith, 1987; Y. Kachru & Smith, 2008), it is understandable that the notional-functional syllabus originally developed by Wilkins (1976), which is the most basic form of communicative syllabus as opposed to the structural/grammatical syllabus, has often been associated with TEIL.

In applying the notional-functional syllabus to TEIL, a crucial point from EIL perspectives is the fact that the way a certain speech act is performed differs from culture to culture, which makes it necessary to diversify the content of the notional-functional syllabus, typically in regard to NNS/NNS interaction where native-speaker norms are irrelevant. On the other hand, partly due to various limitations of the notional-functional syllabus, including the considerable difficulty in trying to combine it with the prevalent "structural syllabus" such as the grammatical syllabus employed for public school ELT in Japan, it seems that the actual implementation of TEIL with the notional-functional syllabus has never come true in a substantial manner.

With the waning interest in the notional-functional syllabus coupled with the emphasis on task authenticity in ELT today, among the more promising syllabus types for TEIL now are the task-based syllabus and the content-based syllabus. A necessary condition for the former is to concretely identify EIL tasks, pioneering attempts for which can be found in ELT textbooks developed by Larry E. Smith with his colleagues Via and Smith (1983) for speaking as well as Weiner and Smith (1983) for writing. In light of the fact that, though TEIL practice on the whole is still rather limited in quantity and frequency, the content-based approach is a popular, and perhaps the most realistic, pedagogy for TEIL (Hino & S. Oda, 2015), the content-based syllabus will naturally be a major type of TEIL syllabus along with the task-based syllabus.

2.1.3   MODELS IN TEIL

As mentioned earlier in this chapter, it has been a prevalent stance among WE theorists that learners of English in the Outer Circle may adopt their own regional varieties of English as their educational models, but that their counterparts in the Expanding Circle are supposed to follow a native-speaker model. Established varieties from the Outer Circle are sometimes recommended by WE scholars as alternative models for the Expanding Circle, but such advice could even strengthen the impression that Englishes in the Outer Circle are superior to those from the Expanding Circle.

This position in the WE paradigm stems from the view that Englishes in the Outer Circle are established "institutionalized varieties" and that those in the Expanding Circle are mere idiosyncratic "performance varieties," as briefly discussed in 1.3.4.4. If we go along this line of thinking, it will end up with the idea that speakers of English from the Expanding Circle will have to go through the same process, before they are entitled to their own models, as the one that those in the Outer Circle have experienced. This means many years of domestic

A holistic framework of EIL education 41

use of English among fellow nationals (cf. Schell, 2009), when those in the Expanding Circle usually find such intra-national use of English sociolinguistically unnecessary.

Redefining "performance varieties" as "similect" (Mauranen, 2012), mentioned in 1.3.4.4, helps eliminate the hierarchical perception between the two circles (though it may not be what Mauranen aims for). For example, many who listen to Japanese speakers of English feel that they speak more or less similar English. Those commonalities can be partly utilized as a basis on which a model of Japanese English may be developed.

Chapter 4 will discuss how endonormative models of English can be set up for ELT in the Expanding Circle in order to allow the users of English from the Expanding Circle to express their own voices in international communication. However, those models are not exactly the same as the English currently spoken or written by Expanding Circle users of English, which is a product of ELT with native-speaker models, but are more creative ones tailored both to the learners' linguacultural backgrounds and global needs.

An original EIL position on this issue, which is not the same as the WE perspective, is found in Smith (1978), who claimed that models in EFL countries (or the Expanding Circle in WE terminology today) can be "any educated English speaker (native speaker, local, or regional)" (p. 6. The notation in the parenthesis in the original). This is a remarkable foresight, which implies that the model does not necessarily have to be based on an established variety, and that individual models would serve the purpose.

2.1.4 FOUR SKILLS IN TEIL

What impact does the concept of EIL have on the teaching of four language skills – listening, speaking, reading, and writing? In the early days of EIL, or the 1970s, when traditional ELT especially in countries such as Japan still put emphasis on the written language, the concept of EIL was one that highlighted the importance of oral skills. However, now that the integration of the four skills is taken for granted in ELT today, equal attention should basically be given to each skill.

2.1.4.1 Teaching of listening in EIL In the teaching of listening in EIL, unlike in the traditional teaching of Anglo-American English, it is important to enable the students to understand varieties of English, including non-native Englishes. For this objective, in all the three phases of intelligibility, comprehensibility, and interpretability, exposure to varieties of English is one of the most basic activities to be incorporated into the teaching of listening in EIL education. It is desirable that students are given opportunities to listen at least to the varieties that they are likely to encounter in their future use of English (cf. Smith, 2001).

Hino (1989–1990), discussed in Chapter 8, was an early attempt to expose Japanese learners to varieties of WE through a radio English program. Also in

42 *A paradigm of EIL education*

Japan, Nishinoh, T. Yamamoto, and Taguchi (1994) was a pioneer university ELT textbook in this regard, which introduced, with an audio tape, Outer Circle Englishes from Ghana and Singapore in addition to less-represented Inner Circle varieties from New Zealand and Ireland.

A considerable number of audio WE materials have recently been published. Most notable among them is an audio CD that accompanies Kirkpatrick (2007), containing several regional varieties from Asia and Africa, along with various ELF interactions. Tsuruta and Shibata (2008) also comes with a CD that presents the recording of speeches at the World Economic Forum, given by delegates from 20 countries. Focusing on one non-Anglophone variety, Enokizono (2012) offers a detailed explanation of linguacultural features of Indian English for Japanese learners of English, with a CD recording of role-play skits in various situations for listening practice. Nowadays, the Internet also allows us to listen to varieties of English across the world, including videos on YouTube, ranging from acrolectal to basilectal levels.

Cultural understanding plays a major role in listening comprehension, especially in terms of "interpretability" (Smith & C. Nelson, 1985; C. Nelson, 2011). Most significantly, the way a certain speech act is performed is often culture specific (Smith, 1987; Y. Kachru & Smith, 2008). For instance, a speaker of EIL may not necessarily make a request or complaint in a manner commonly accepted in the U.S. In TEFL/TESL, the understanding of native English-speaking cultures is considered sufficient in this respect, but it does not hold true in TEIL. For example, knowledge of Islamic values, which are different from Judeo-Christian values traditionally associated with English, is sometimes a key factor in correctly interpreting the intention of interlocutors from the Islamic world.

Most of the basic techniques used in the teaching of listening in modern-day communicative TEFL/TESL (i.e., not the old practice that often puts an undue emphasis on the decoding of sounds per se rather than comprehension or interpretation of the message) are applicable to EIL. In fact, the notion of "interactive listening" advocated by Baxter (1980) for TEIL can be seen as one of the pioneering works also in TESL/TEFL with its foresight on the importance of viewing listening as a dynamic process. Today, the interactional perspective further leads to the discussions on the significance of negotiation of meaning, such as clarification requests, in oral communication in EIL (Berns, 2008; Seidlhofer, 2009; Hilgendorf, 2015). Though negotiation of meaning is an integral aspect of communication even within the Inner Circle, it is a particularly important skill in EIL with respect to the cross-cultural complexity and intercultural unpredictability of EIL interaction.

2.1.4.2 Teaching of speaking in EIL The teaching of speaking in EIL presents a considerably different picture from its counterpart in conventional TEFL/TESL.

In the teaching of pronunciation in EIL, native-speaker phonology is not the absolute standard any more. In international situations where interactions often

A holistic framework of EIL education   43

take place between non-native speakers, non-native phonology has proven no less intelligible than that of native speakers (Smith & Rafiqzad, 1979; Kirkpatrick, 2010; C. Nelson, 2011).

It is already established in WE studies that the indigenous pronunciation of each variety of English can serve as educational models in the Outer Circle. For the Expanding Circle, native-speaker models have generally been assumed to be the norm by WE theorists (e.g., Andreasson, 1994; Bamgbose, 1998), but the feasibility of "glocal" models may be explored also in these countries as in Chapter 4, though understandably controversial.

Another aspect of the teaching of speaking in EIL is the fact that, as was briefly mentioned in 1.3.4.1 and 1.3.5.1, it is not always easy to determine what norms of conversational discourse, including sociolinguistic rules, should be followed in what situations. Unlike in TESL/TEFL, where it has been taken for granted that native-speaker norms are the ones to be adhered to, each speaker of EIL is basically allowed to express his or her own values with their indigenous discursive and sociolinguistic rules. This issue has been studied extensively since Smith (1987), but still remains one of the most complex points of teaching in EIL. At this point, recent ELF studies emphasize the fluidity and dynamism of intercultural interaction in EIL (Baker, 2015).

As to practical techniques for teaching speaking in EIL, one classic example is "Talk-and-Listen" (Via, 1981; Via & Smith, 1983; Smith & Via, 1983), which is an easily accessible type of role-play with an emphasis on expressing one's own self. The EIL education program launched by Smith in 2007, now known as GCEP (Global Cultural Exchange Program), provides students with opportunities for interactive speaking in authentic EIL environments in Hawaii (Smith, 2014; Hino, 2015a).

2.1.4.3 Teaching of reading in EIL   As long as we have communicative language teaching (CLT) in mind, that is, unless we try to use more classical methods such as the Grammar-Translation Method or the Audio-Lingual Method, methodology of reading instructions in EIL itself is not radically different from that of EFL/ESL. For example, the balance between top-down and bottom-up approaches, a major principle for reading in TEFL/TESL, is equally important in TEIL. Likewise, reading techniques employed for TEFL/TESL, such as skimming, scanning, and reading for specific information, are applicable to TEIL as well. However, a subtle but important difference lies in the fact that, unlike in ESL/EFL, reading materials in EIL do not necessarily reflect Anglo-American styles of text organization, as mentioned again in 2.1.4.4. Readers of EIL cannot expect, for instance, that a topic sentence is likely to occur at the beginning of a paragraph.

2.1.4.4 Teaching of writing in EIL   Although "deviations" from native-speaker norms generally have a better chance of being accepted in speaking compared with writing (A. Matsuda & P. Matsuda, 2010), the teaching of writing in EIL can be significantly different from that of ESL/EFL, especially

44 A paradigm of EIL education

with respect to text organization. For example, in the teaching of argumentative writing in ESL/EFL, the prevalent approach is to lead the students to put the thematic sentence or the conclusion itself at the head of the paragraph, which is to be elaborated on in the following sentences. As M. Watanabe (2007) has found in her exploration into the historical background of this practice, this is an educational model more or less based on pedagogical and sociolinguistic values in the U.S., though how much it actually reflects American discourse rules for written texts is another question. A problem is that in some non-Anglo-American cultures, other types of text organization could be more natural, such as the one that starts a paragraph with details, also with non-linear progression.

For instance, a traditional construction of argumentative writing in Japanese is composed of four parts known as *ki-sho-ten-ketsu* (introduction-development-turn-conclusion), which is usable in any language, including English. In light of the philosophy of EIL, which honors indigenous cultural values, local text organization should be respected even in the writing of English, as a reflection of original thought patterns. This position may appear as a naive application of the classic observation by Kaplan (1966) along with the successive "constrastive rhetoric" studies, which are now often criticized for being "essentialistic," but there actually is no intention of stereotyping or labeling in my argument. This is an attempt to present alternative approaches in order to put the philosophy of "post-native-speakerism" (Houghton & Hashimoto, 2018) into practice.

Weiner and Smith (1983) is an early attempt to incorporate the concept of EIL into a classroom ELT textbook for writing.

2.1.5 CROSS-CULTURAL/INTERCULTURAL UNDERSTANDING IN TEIL

TEIL puts a great emphasis on cross-cultural understanding, or intercultural understanding, as one of the important keys to successful international communication, or to the acquisition of ICC (Intercultural Communicative Competence) (Byram, 1997).

One way to go about this objective is to use teaching materials with content that directly reflects cross-cultural values. Such an approach goes well with Content-Based Instruction (CBI) (cf. Widdowson, 1978; Mohan, 1986), as well as with Content and Language Integrated Learning (CLIL) (e.g., Coyle, Hood, & Marsh, 2010), and also has an advantage of incorporating global issues into ELT (e.g., Cates, 2002).

In recent ELF studies, the term "intercultural" is usually preferred over the more conventional "cross-cultural," as the latter could connote a static view of culture while the former implies a dynamic and interactional construct of culture (e.g., Baker, 2015).

2.1.6 ANALYSIS OF COURSES OF STUDY

Many countries, such as Japan and Korea, have official courses of study for English as a school subject issued by their governments, which define the content of English language education. It is an important area of research in English teaching curricula to analyze those courses of study from the viewpoint of EIL. For example, the analysis of the courses of study for junior high schools in Japan reveals the fact that there was a shift in the national policy regarding the cultural content of English teaching materials from an Anglo-American focus to a wider coverage of varieties of culture, as discussed in Chapter 5.

2.1.7 EIL AND ESP

The relationship between EIL and ESP (English for Specific Purposes) can be controversial. Bhatia (1997) suggested that genre analysis, as a basis of ESP, should take the reality of WE into account, but how ESP essentially relates to WE was still not made clear. Widdowson (1997) argued, after his years of involvement in EIL/WE studies, that EIL was indeed ESP itself, but this interpretation of EIL seems a little too narrow, and is dependent on the definitions of EIL and ESP after all.

One aspect that the concept of ESP clearly has in common with EIL is that the native/non-native distinction is not an issue, as the model of ESP is the language used by experts in the field or in each specific discourse community. This perspective has lately been pursued especially in ELF studies. For example, in regard to academic English as ESP, Kuteeva (2015) reports that internationally active Swedish scholars perceive English as an academic lingua franca to be "nobody's land," where non-native speakers are not really disadvantaged.

2.2 Teaching materials

Developing teaching materials in TEIL is an area that presents a sharp contrast with TEFL/TESL. Whereas the content of materials in traditional TEFL/TESL is one that reflects Anglo-American culture, TEIL materials could deal with any cultural value, whether it is native English-speaking or non-native English-speaking culture. They may also be based on a Judeo-Christian, Islamic, Hindu, Buddhist, or agnostic world view. An emphasis may be put on the students' own cultural values, or if appropriate, some specific cultures that students are likely to encounter in their future use of English.

As for research in this issue of materials in TEIL, cultural components in the existing ELT textbooks have been analyzed rather extensively (e.g., Fujita, 1987; Hino, 1988a; A. Matsuda, 2002; Erikawa, 2008; Nakagawa, 2011), but it is hoped that there will be more discussions on the actual practice of using materials that represent non-native English-speaking values.

2.3 Teaching methodologies

While traditional foreign language teaching placed an emphasis on grammar and translation, modern TEFL/TESL focuses on communicative skills. In this respect, it used to be assumed that there are no distinctive differences in

46 *A paradigm of EIL education*

teaching methodologies between TEFL/TESL and TEIL. According to this stance, any communicative language teaching methodology proposed in TEFL/ TESL can also be basically applicable to TEIL situations, except that the language model is relativized in TEIL (cf. Smith, 1984).

However, there is a growing awareness among researchers today on the importance of locally-appropriate pedagogy for EIL. Though this issue is not necessarily specific to TEIL, we should indeed be aware that it becomes even more important in TEIL to investigate what methodologies may be suited for the learners' indigenous values, including sociolinguistic or educational traditions (e.g., Hino, 1988b, 1992a; Holliday, 1994; McKay, 1992, 2002, 2003; Kern, 2000; A. Matsuda, 2012b; McKay & J. Brown, 2016). Just as local cultural values are respected in the development of TEIL materials, locally-appropriate methodologies should be sought for the benefit of the students.

2.4 *Evaluation/testing*

Evaluation/testing is a key issue in TEIL. We are so familiar with traditional examinations that are far from the idea of EIL. A typical example in Japan is pronunciation questions in conservative university entrance examinations. Certain parts of given English words are underlined, and the examinee is required to choose which of those are pronounced alike or differently. The answer often depends on which variety of English the examinee has in mind, but the examiner allows only one answer, that is, the one based on General American or Received Pronunciation, in other words, so-called standard American or British English.

As a pioneer work in testing from EIL perspectives, Lowenberg (1993) observed that in major standardized examinations, little consideration was given to non-native varieties of English because the examiners had a tendency to regard American or British norms as the sole standard. Multiple-choice questions, for example, could have more than one "correct" answer, depending on what variety of English each examinee has learned. Cultural content of examination questions also presents a problem, as it is often biased toward Anglo-American values. An important task for EIL researchers is to set up certain criteria that will satisfy EIL needs for testing and evaluation.

More recently, Hu (2012), for example, lists five principles for the test of EIL, such as "Determine linguistic norms for a test according to its intended use" (p. 134) and "Broaden the construct of EIL tests to incorporate intercultural strategic competence" (p. 137). Newbold (2015) reports on a project that produced an entrance test based on the notion of ELF for use at European universities, in which test-takers were required to "react to spoken and written texts produced by NNS" (p. 207). With the fluidity of ELF in mind, the task-based approach was employed for this test, presenting ELF tasks in the context of higher education such as "Listening to lectures giving information about courses." Indeed, a major homework for EIL test developers is to identify authentic EIL tasks that can be assigned to examinees in exam situations.

A *holistic framework of EIL education* 47

Among major standardized tests, for instance, TOEIC (Test of English for International Communication) has diversified its spoken English, but is still limited to Inner Circle varieties. The American bias of TOEFL (Test of English as a Foreign Language) used to be largely free of criticism by EIL researchers since it was, after all, an exam for those who wished to enroll in American universities. However, in view of the fact that many American universities nowadays claim themselves to be international institutions, even TOEFL is not immune from the need for EIL any longer, because EIL (or ELF) is the kind of English to be used at international universities (Jenkins, 2014, 2016).

2.5   Teacher training/employment

Teacher training in TEIL is another area that will be significantly different from TESL/TEFL, as was predicted by Smith (1976).

In Richards and Hino (1983), a survey on teacher training needs conducted 35 years ago by Jack C. Richards and the present author, "varieties of English" was found to be really underrepresented in graduate ELT teacher training curricula in the U.S. and U.K. Later, K. Brown (1993) also showed that ESOL teacher training programs tended to lack WE perspectives.

However, it is changing now. Pedagogical implications of global Englishes are the theme of the opening chapter of Richards (2015), a recent high-profile reference book for language teachers. Also, the latest development in this field is the publication of A. Matsuda (2017a), an edited collection that compiles a number of reports on actual practices in EIL teacher training across the world, along with the discussion of theoretical backgrounds. We have come a long way in EIL teacher training.

As to issues of qualifications of EIL teachers, reexamination of the concept of "native speaker" has been underway, represented by works such as Davies (2003) and Holliday (2006), further questioning the conventional dichotomy between native and non-native speakers.

The participant population of the JET (Japan Exchange and Teaching) program, a governmental project to invite young people from foreign countries to schools in Japan mostly as ALTs (Assistant Language Teachers), used to typically exhibit the lack of EIL perspectives in teacher training and employment. Even after opening ALT opportunities to non-native speakers in the mid-1990s, the overwhelming majority of those hired as ALTs long remained to be from the Inner Circle countries such as the U.S., Britain, Canada, Australia, and New Zealand (e.g., Ministry of Education, Culture, Sports, Science and Technology, 2001), reflecting the beliefs held by the Japanese administration that native speakers are the ones who speak "real" English.

However, there has been a tangible change, if not an extremely significant shift, in the employment policy of the JET program in the direction of EIL. In 2016, for example, among the total of 4,536 ALTs, 105 are from Jamaica, followed by 46 from Singapore and 37 from the Philippines.[3] It is also

48   *A paradigm of EIL education*

becoming increasingly common to encounter non-native English-speaking ALTs, such as from India and Russia, among those hired at the local level.

On the whole, if quoted from E. Llurda's views on non-native language teachers, research in EIL teacher training/employment is expected to "identify NNS teachers' qualities, improve teacher training programs, and guide administrators in their selection of the best possible teachers for a given setting" (Llurda, 2005, p. 8).

Last, it should be added that in analyzing native-speakerism present in university policies for teachers, Rivers (2013) draws our attention to an important perspective that is often overlooked. That is, not only non-native speakers but also native speakers can be victims of native-speakerism. Indeed, when a decision on teacher employment depends upon whether the applicant is a native speaker, the hired teacher is expected to behave as a "native speaker." Vital aspects such as his or her true ability and commitment as a teacher are downplayed.

Conclusion

It is not always easy to determine what goes into the realm of EIL research and what does not. Topics included in this chapter are largely restricted to problems specific to EIL. In other words, issues that are equally relevant to EFL/ESL and to EIL are generally excluded from this plan. It is hoped that this attempt to systematically organize the whole field of EIL will serve as a meaningful step toward the ultimate goal of constructing an EIL research paradigm.

Notes

1 Here I will not go into the complicated distinctions between "nation," "state," and "nation-state," though in a more thorough discussion these concepts would have to be clearly defined.
2 An early exception to such a tendency in corpus studies was the corpus of Thai English in the ASIACORP developed by scholars at Macquarie University. For a discussion of the ASIACORP, see Butler (1997).
3 JET Program. http://jetprogramme.org/ja/countries/ (Accessed on May 25, 2017).

3   Principles for EIL education

Introduction

This chapter succinctly presents general principles for EIL education as basic guidelines for administrators and teachers trying to introduce the concept of EIL into their educational programs and pedagogical practice in the Expanding Circle, with regard to materials, methodologies, testing, teachers, learners, and models. A brief summary of those principles, partly incorporating the discussions in Chapter 2, are also provided in a table.

Materials

In the teaching of EIL, materials for receptive skills (listening and reading) need to provide varieties of English with their linguistic and cultural diversity, and materials for productive skills (speaking and writing) should present an English that is capable of expressing the user's own values as well as being internationally communicative. Combining both receptive and productive skills, materials for interactive skills should prepare students for intercultural interaction by helping them use various communication strategies such as accommodation and negotiation of meaning.

In Japan, for example, there have been significant changes over time in the direction of widening the cultural scopes – in other words, more toward EIL – in junior high school English textbooks approved by the Ministry of Education. Below is an excerpt from a popular junior high school English textbook in use from the late 1960s to early 1970s, in which an American junior high school student, a leading character of this text, travels to Britain:

UNCLE: It's half past two now. Where shall we go next?
ROY: I want to see the British Museum.
UNCLE: All right. I often go there to read.
ROY: Is it a library?
UNCLE: Yes, it is. It's a museum, too. You'll find a great many books there.

(*New prince readers 2*, 1968, p. 41)

50   *A paradigm of EIL education*

Representing the traditional educational philosophy that associates the teaching of English with Anglo-American cultures, this textbook revolves around American life. Even in a situation where the main character went abroad, Britain was chosen by the authors apparently to ensure that the story would take place in an Anglo-American setting. On the other hand, the following example from a current junior high school English textbook typically shows a major shift in cultural orientations:

NANA: It smells really good!
SONIA: Have you ever eaten Indian food?
NANA: Yes, I have. I like curry.
SONIA: When we eat, we only use our right hand. And we don't use spoons or forks. It's a custom here.

(Total English 3, 2016, p. 40)

In English textbooks for junior high schools in Japan today, leading characters are normally Japanese junior high school students, rather than American students, just like the users of the texts themselves. Those textbooks center around the daily life of Japanese students, and it is common for the main characters to travel to places other than Britain or America. In the above excerpt, a Japanese girl traveling in India learns how to eat Indian food from a local lady. In fact, varieties of culture, including those of the Outer and the Expanding Circle, are described in recent textbooks. In this respect, the cultural content of public school textbooks in Japan is already in accord with the idea of EIL to a considerable extent.

On the other hand, those textbooks still adhere to "the Inner Circle" or native-speaker English, as far as linguistic aspects are concerned. For instance, the above excerpt shows no sign of Indian English or Japanese English, but abides by the linguistic rules of American English regarded as the norm for ELT in Japan. Another fact that should be noted is that most CDs accompanying junior high school English textbooks in Japan are entirely recorded by native speakers of English.

Methodologies

In the teaching of EIL, just as indigenous varieties of English have been treated with respect, the significance of locally-appropriate methodologies is now accepted as well (e.g., McKay, 2002, 2003; McKay & Bokhorst-Heng, 2008; A. Matsuda, 2012b). For the teaching of English in Japan, for example, the use of translation and oral reading may be two possible candidates suitable for its sociocultural environment.

Japan has a long tradition of reading, learning, and teaching a foreign language via word-by-word translation (Hino, 1992a). It dates back to over a thousand years ago when the Japanese managed to read Chinese by reordering Chinese words in accordance with Japanese syntax. This approach was gradually established as a systematic method of reading Chinese by using some special symbols to facilitate the reordering. This method, known as *kundoku* or *yakudoku* in Japanese, possibly learned originally from Korea in ancient times, was applied to the teaching of Dutch in the 19th century, and subsequently to the teaching of English. Considering that *yakudoku* is deeply embedded in the sociolinguistic and educational traditions of Japan, it could be more productive to make some effective use of translation than to attempt to eliminate it altogether. Support for an appropriate employment of translation in ELT has recently been proclaimed and fairly well accepted also in Western pedagogies (Cook, 2010), but it has a special cultural meaning in Japan.

In the same manner, the practice of repeated reading aloud, conventionally coupled with *yakudoku* in Japan, should deserve some place in terms of its compatibility with local sociolinguistic and educational values, despite the fact that this activity has been generally neglected in Anglo-American methodologies.

Models

The issue of production models, or models for speaking and writing, has been a point of controversy. In the influential "Kachruvian" WE paradigm, indigenous models have been considered to be of crucial importance for varieties in the Outer Circle, or postcolonial Englishes such as Indian English and Singaporean English, but have been regarded as infeasible for those in the Expanding Circle. However, I have been seeking a possibility of original models for Englishes from the Expanding Circle such as Japanese English and Korean English for international communication.

As mentioned earlier, Anglo-American English is by no means the most intelligible or comprehensible variety of English for global communication. Another fundamental problem with the conventional native-speaker model is that the variety that has developed in the Anglo-American context is not suited for expressing non-native English-speaking cultures. I have been attempting to develop a pedagogical model of Japanese English, capable of expressing Japanese values as well as being internationally communicative, which may be given to Japanese learners of English as an alternative option to the American English model. This issue will be discussed in more detail in Chapter 4.

Testing

The testing of receptive skills (listening and reading) in EIL measures abilities to understand varieties of English. In the testing of productive skills (speaking and writing) in EIL, abilities to express one's own thoughts in internationally communicative English are evaluated. In other words, approximation to Anglo-American English is not the criteria for EIL tests. For example, pronunciation with limited elision and linking, characteristic of non-native Englishes, can be positively accepted, because it tends to be more intelligible than native-speaker

52   *A paradigm of EIL education*

phonology in communicating with non-native speakers (Jenkins, 2000; Deterding & Kirkpatrick, 2006; Kirkpatrick, 2007, 2010).

Integrating the receptive and productive skills, tests for interactive skills need to measure abilities to interact interculturally, with the use of various communication strategies.

Teachers

For the teaching of Anglo-American English, native speakers have usually been preferred as teachers. On the other hand, it is desirable for local teachers to play central roles in the teaching of EIL. Also, in the employment of teachers from abroad, there is no reason to make a distinction between native and non-native speakers.

Positive changes are in sight in Japan. For example, a shift from native-speakerism is taking place, though slowly, in the hiring policy at Japanese universities. Tamagawa University, a private university in Tokyo that established the Center for English as a Lingua Franca in 2014, now employs ELT faculty from an ELF perspective, with no discrimination between native and non-native speakers (Masaki Oda, 2017). Similarly, a major national university in western Japan, which used to specify "a native speaker" as a qualification for international ELT faculty positions until several years ago, now has one from Singapore (the Outer Circle) and another from Russia (the Expanding Circle) among six full-time international ELT faculty members.

Interaction with non-native English-speaking ALTs at public schools in Japan is a valuable authentic experience in EIL for students. When I invited an ALT (then known as AET) from the Philippines working at a junior high school in Chiba Prefecture to my radio program in January 1990, she was probably the only non-native English-speaking ALT in Japan. In fact, even in 1995, among the 4,230 assistant English teachers in the JET program, 2,248 teachers were from the U.S., 790 from Britain, 692 from Canada, 243 from Australia, 194 from New Zealand, and 63 from Ireland (*STEP News*, May 1, 1996, p. 4). In other words, everyone was from the Inner Circle in 1995, although the door was gradually opened to non-native speakers in the late 1990s. However, these days we quite frequently encounter non-native English-speaking ALTs, especially among those employed at the local level outside the national JET program, which is a welcome trend in terms of EIL.

For example, when I observed a class with a Russian ALT in elementary school English classes in Kyoto Prefecture in July 2009, I was able to see that she was really instrumental in helping her students in EIL communication. Outside her classes taught in cooperation with Japanese homeroom teachers, many students gathered around the Russian ALT during the recess, talking in English, as if she was their favorite elder sister. It was evident that they had successfully established a rapport between them. My brief interviews with her Japanese colleagues including the principal also verified a high level of trust placed in her. The fact that she was a non-native speaker of English was in no way felt to be a problem by her fellow teachers.

With regard to teacher training, based on their experiences in Turkey and Greece as the Expanding Circle, Bayyurt and Sifakis (2017) propose three phases of "EIL-aware teacher education," consisting of exposure, awareness, and action plan. In my EIL teacher education class in Japan reported in Hino (2017a), this "exposure" phase is practiced as authentic EIL interactions among local and international students.

Learners

While learners in the teaching of English as a second or foreign language are, by definition, non-native speakers of the language, learners of EIL include both native and non-native speakers (Smith, 1978). This is one of the salient features of EIL education, based on the idea that it is imperative for native speakers to learn how to communicate with non-native speakers. Not only non-native speakers but also native speakers are responsible for making efforts to achieve successful communication in EIL.

For example, native English-speaking students are not exempted from my undergraduate English classes at Osaka University (described later in Chapter 9), but are required to learn EIL with Japanese classmates. A student from New Zealand expressed to me that it was an interesting cross-cultural experience for him, as he was exposed to varieties of English with a diversity of values, including English spoken by the Japanese.

Conclusion

This chapter has briefly summarized the main features of educational practice in EIL. Synthesizing the discussions provided in Chapter 2 and the present chapter, general principles for materials, methodologies, models, testing, teachers, and learners are outlined in Table 3.1.

Table 3.1 General principles for teaching EIL in the Expanding Circle

	Teaching of Anglo-American English	*Teaching of EIL*
Materials for receptive skills	Anglo-American English	Varieties of English, with possible emphasis on specific varieties
Materials for productive skills	Expression of Anglo-American values	Expression of the students' own values
Materials for interactive skills	Based on Anglo-American norms of interaction	Intercultural interaction with the use of communication strategies
Methodologies	Communicative language teaching	Communicative language teaching, with the consideration of locally-appropriate methodologies

(*Continued*)

Table 3.1 (Continued)

	Teaching of Anglo-American English	*Teaching of EIL*
Models	Codified Anglo-American English	Individual models, along with models under development
Testing for receptive skills	Ability to understand Anglo-American English	Ability to understand varieties of English, with possible emphasis on specific varieties
Testing for productive skills	Ability to produce Anglo-American English	Ability to express oneself in internationally communicative English
Testing for interactive skills	Ability to interact in accordance with Anglo-American norms	Ability to interact interculturally, with the use of communication strategies
Teachers	Native speakers of English preferred	Central roles played by local teachers, with no distinction between native and non-native speakers made for foreign teachers
Learners	Non-native speakers	Both native and non-native speakers

Part II

Models, materials, and methodologies for EIL education

4 Developing original production models

Introduction

In this chapter, chiefly building on my arguments in Hino (2012a), the feasibility of endonormative production models for learners of English in the Expanding Circle is discussed. It will be shown that it is possible for users of English in the Expanding Circle, just like their counterparts in the Outer Circle, to enjoy non-Anglo-American models of their own.

The WE paradigm may be correct in describing the present status of Expanding Circle Englishes as "norm-dependent" (B. Kachru, 1985, p. 17) or exonormative. However, I have been trying to help change such a state of affairs by applying what may be called "Japanese English" to university EFL classes as an optional model or a sample for the students, in the hope of enabling them to express their original values in international communication. The model of Japanese English (henceforth MJE) that I employ is different from American or British English in some subtle but important ways with respect to various aspects such as phonological, grammatical, lexical, discursive, and sociolinguistic features. Using the MJE as an example, the current chapter explores the possibility of indigenous models for the Expanding Circle.

Thus far, even among teachers supportive of the notion of EIL, the prevalent stance has been to give the students American or British English as a model and tell them at the same time that they do not have to worry about it too much. Such an attitude is confusing and demotivating for the learners. We teachers are responsible for providing the students with a model or models that they can seriously work toward.

The Model of Japanese English (MJE): a case in the Expanding Circle

First, it should be made clear that the MJE is not an attempt to create a national variety of English. Rather, it is a pedagogical alternative to conventional Anglo-American English in educational contexts, as a possible option for those who seek a means of expressing themselves in international settings.

58 *Models, materials, methodologies*

Though Hino (2012a) has often been misquoted on this point, the MJE is also not intended to be a description of English presently spoken or written by the Japanese, because the present reality of Japanese English, a large part of which is the degenerate product of copying native-speaker English, may not be the appropriate target. Instead, the MJE is a reflection of its proponents' grasp of the kind of English that is capable of expressing Japanese values as well as being internationally intelligible, comprehensible, and interpretable. In other words, the MJE is a sample model that exemplifies the range of possibilities for Japanese users of English to communicate effectively in international situations while maintaining their Japanese voice.

The concrete features of the MJE have been developed via the following process. In the first stage, hypotheses are made on what kind of English may be capable of representing Japanese values as well as being internationally communicative, gaining clues through multiple channels. One of them is research results in the studies of EIL and ELF, particularly on the issues of intelligibility, comprehensibility, and interpretability. Another source is my observation of the use of non-Anglo-American English by Japanese users of English. While trying to use American or British English, they sometimes produce innovative usages by accident under the influence of Japanese linguaculture. This is what may be called "Japanese English by serendipity." Still another source is my own experiences in EIL, frequently seeking original English expressions when using English.

In the next stage, the hypotheses have been field-tested in my use of those items in authentic EIL communication, and some of them have been finally incorporated into the model when judged appropriate.

Although the content of the MJE may be considered subjective at this point, such an effort is necessary for moving the teaching of English in the Expanding Circle away from the restrictions of native-speaker norms. It is also my hope that other teachers and users of EIL will join me in this creative process, sharing observations and experiences, to develop concrete models of Japanese English, East Asian Englishes, or Expanding Circle Englishes.

Historically speaking, the MJE is an effort toward the realization of the long-cherished dream of having an original model for Japanese users of English, dating back 90 years to the vision expressed by noted lexicographer Hidezaburo Saito in the preface of his Japanese–English dictionary:

> The mastery of a language has for its final object the expression of the exact light and shade of meaning conceived by the speaker. In a word, the Japanese speaker of English should be original. . . . In short, the English of the Japanese must, in a certain sense, be Japanized.
>
> (Saito, 1928, preface)

In this quote, H. Saito points out the need for the indigenization of English for fully representing Japanese culture in English. Similar views have been expressed by various works by later Japanese scholars, such as T. Suzuki (1975) and Yamagishi (1991).

Last, in this section, it is presumed that the process for developing the MJE could be applied to any other country in the Expanding Circle. With the MJE approach, we can set up original educational models of EIL that suit the needs of local students, irrespective of the fact that such English may not exist as a national variety. The example of the MJE will help pave the way for the autonomy of ELT in the Expanding Circle, a privilege that has been allowed in the WE paradigm only for the Outer Circle equipped with national varieties of English.

The paradigm of EIL

The conceptual framework that the MJE relies upon is a version of EIL originally proposed by Larry E. Smith (e.g., Smith, 1976, 1978, 1981b) and later developed by the present writer (e.g., Hino, 2001, 2009). A significant element that distinguishes EIL from WE is its equal treatment of Englishes in the Outer Circle and the Expanding Circle. In his classic proposal, Smith (1978, p. 10. Reprinted in Smith, 1983, p. 18) stated that "any educated English speaker is acceptable" as a model of English for international communication, implicitly suggesting the possibility of original models not only for the Outer but also for the Expanding Circle.

EIL is also clearly different from WE as to its position on the intra-national or domestic use of English. Since B. Kachru (1976), the general lack of intra-national use of English in the Expanding Circle has often been cited in WE studies as a factor against the chance for their indigenous models (e.g., Schell, 2009). However, from the viewpoint of EIL as English for international communication, the paucity of the use of English among compatriots is irrelevant.

With its equal treatment of the Outer Circle and the Expanding Circle, ELF had been a strong support, at least until recently, for the egalitarian position of EIL as to the issue of endonormative models. Jenkins (2006, p. 38) defined ELF as "an attempt to extend to Expanding Circle members the rights that have always been enjoyed in the Inner Circle and to an increasing extent in the Outer." As another leading scholar of ELF, Seidlhofer (2006) held that "non-core" features identified by Jenkins's research on LFC were not "pronunciation errors but manifestations of (L2) regional variation, which allows the speakers' identities to 'shine through' while still ensuring mutual intelligibility" (p. 43). Such views help enable any user of English, not only from the Outer but also from the Expanding Circle, to have their own models. Lately, however, with the de-emphasis on the concept of "variety" in ELF studies in favor of situational and dynamic "variation" (Seidlhofer, 2011; Widdowson, 2015), interest in the issues of "model," regarded as static in nature, seems to have waned in ELF research.

The author's position of EIL is placed between constructivism and essentialism in this respect. That is, while it is true that EIL is fluid, dynamic, and collaboratively constructed *in situ*, there still are certain core elements. It is useful to have some models of EIL for pedagogical purposes, even though they certainly have to be constantly modified in their actual use in authentic situations.

60 *Models, materials, methodologies*

Foundations for the MJE

Definition of "Japanese English"

In this chapter, "Japanese English," a highly controversial concept even among Japanese scholars (cf. Toh, 2015), is defined as "English for expressing Japanese values in international communication." Unlike some common usages such as in Stanlaw (2004), in the present discussion this term is not intended to mean English incorporated into the Japanese language. Also, it does not merely refer to "English used by Japanese for international communication," which is just a description of current use of English by the Japanese.

In the meantime, we must be reminded once again that such a notion as Japanese English has the risk of leading to insular nationalism, if handled inappropriately, as it presupposes the existence of shared values among the Japanese. As I illustrated in Hino (1988a), nationalism is a double-edged sword for the promotion of EIL philosophy. Caution must be taken so that the concept of Japanese English will not inadvertently help promote parochial nationalism.

It should also be kept in mind, in light of the plurality of one's identities, that there is the danger of overestimating the significance of national varieties (Hino, 2001). Attention should be drawn to the fact that "Japanese English," specifically associated with the concept of national identity, is just one of the many ways to characterize one's English.

As many leading ELF scholars argue (e.g., Seidlhofer, 2011; Jenkins, 2015b), ELF goes beyond national boundaries, which is also true with EIL. However, it is the author's position that EIL users should be also allowed to represent their "roots" if they wish to.

Rationale for the MJE

From the EIL perspective, the need for endonormative pedagogical models of English for the Expanding Circle seems rather obvious. Without indigenous models, it is often difficult to enable students to express their own values. Just for one example, forcing East Asian students to put their given names in front of their family names, a common educational practice with the conventional Anglo-American model, deprives them of the expression of their cultural identities. In this case, an autonomous model that allows the learners to order their names in accordance with their cultural values should also be provided as an alternative option.

It is quite another matter that the learning of Anglo-American English expands the learners' horizons. Although exposure to the British and American values inherent in the traditional English language could certainly benefit the students by widening their cultural viewpoints, imposition of those patterns of thought is detrimental. "If you want to speak real English, you have to think like Americans," a catchphrase commonly found in advertisements for materials and language schools for learners of English in Japan, typically illustrates the problematic attitudes that should be overcome with the use of the MJE.

The MJE as pedagogical creation

In WE studies, models of English are usually interpreted as a description of already existent varieties. It is partly because of this lack of "codification" that the possibility of original models for the Expanding Circle has often been neglected in the WE studies. It is true that a systematic description of Japanese English as it is used today is not available at the moment, but it is not necessarily indispensable to the MJE, which is not intended to be a simple reproduction of the current usage of English by the Japanese. Education is an act toward the creation of a desirable future, whose purpose is not merely to adapt our students to the present realities. The MJE is a representation of what kind of English I would recommend my students to learn, if they find it useful, for their speaking and writing.

In terms of the recent ELF concept "similect" (Mauranen, 2012), the MJE is not a description of Japanese similect of English either, but is a reference sample for Japanese learners of English.

At least two issues need to be discussed with regard to the MJE approach. One is that the MJE may be viewed as an imposition of the teacher's values on the students. However, ELT in Japan has often been monopolized by Anglo-American values, so to speak, and it would make sense to liberalize it by providing the students with an alternative that may better reflect Japanese values. Most importantly, the MJE is not to be forced on the students, but to be merely suggested to them when appropriate as one possible option.

Another question comes from a comparison with the experiences in the Outer Circle, where education has not really played such a crucial role in the development of nativized varieties of English. Those Englishes in the postcolonial environment are basically not the products of pedagogical planning, but are ones that have more or less "emerged" through local uses. From this history, efforts to set up the MJE in educational contexts may appear incompatible with the "ecology of language evolution" (Mufwene, 2001, 2008). However, the MJE itself is not an attempt to give birth to a national variety of English called "Japanese English," but is a pedagogical model to help the students learn to express their Japanese values in English. Whether this educational effort will eventually contribute to the development of a national variety is not the issue for pedagogical discussions in the present chapter. Such a socio-educational possibility, extended beyond classrooms, will actually be analyzed in Chapter 11.

Unlike the Outer Circle, education is a key factor for English in the Expanding Circle, because this is where students have the most regular and intensive contact with the language. In fact, the English spoken and written by the Japanese today is in large part a direct reflection of what they were taught in EFL classes in school. In this respect, the well-known Dynamic Model by Schneider (2003, 2007), a highly useful sociolinguistic theory that explains the developmental process of postcolonial Englishes in the Outer Circle and the Inner Circle, is not directly relevant to our present concern for ELT in the Expanding Circle (Schneider, 2014).

62 *Models, materials, methodologies*

Criteria for the MJE

What is "good Japanese English" (Hino, 1989b, p. 43), or "educated Japanese English" (D'Angelo, 2005, p. 331), which could be used as a target model for ELT in Japan? Such English is required to meet at least two criteria – (1) capability of expressing Japanese values and (2) international communicability. Social appropriateness (Smith, 1976, 1981b) may be added as the third criterion, but the present discussion mainly focuses on these two essential factors, partly because (1) and (2) could be interpreted to include social appropriateness as a component.

If we draw on the framework proposed by Smith and C. Nelson (1985), which should not be confused with another influential paradigm by Munro and Derwing (1995), communicability in (2) may be broken down into intelligibility, comprehensibility, and interpretability, but "communicability" here is intended to cover all aspects concerning the understanding of spoken and written language, including illocutionary forces.

A basic difficulty with these criteria is the conflict between identity and understanding (cf. Anderson, 1996, p. 17). In fact, expression of unique indigenous values and international communicability may even be inversely proportional with each other. Therefore, the need for expressing Japanese values is accommodated and compromised for the MJE, though pushed to the limit where communication is still possible through a tolerable degree of negotiation of meaning. There can be no model of Japanese English, or any English whatsoever, usable in all situations without accommodation. Communicability is dynamically negotiated and constructed *in situ* by way of collaborative efforts. In this sense, the MJE only provides some ideas with a limited generalizability.

As to (1) as a necessary condition for the MJE, "what are Japanese values?" is also a question, which tends to be either subjective or stereotypical and may even run the risk of leading to some exclusive categorization. Indeed, it is quite possible to criticize this sort of presupposition of national characters (e.g., Kubota, 1999, 2012). However, given how it has been taken for granted that users of English must accept Anglo-American values, it is still quite useful to put forth the concept such as "Japanese values" as a countermeasure, no matter how obscure it may be, in order to free the learners from the conventional Anglo-American framework of ELT.

As for (2), a lingering question is "intelligible/comprehensible/interpretable to whom?," as communicability involves not only the speaker/writer but also the listener/reader. Though it is often a difficult pedagogical task to decide on the international communicability of each specific linguistic feature, the author has been trying to look into a more or less universal tendency.

Description of the MJE

As Smith (1978, p. 10. Reprinted in Smith, 1983, p. 15) put it, the model of EIL can be "any educated English speaker." In this regard, the MJE presented in this chapter is no more than one of the many possible models.

Developing original production models 63

Generalized description of a model of EIL is not an absolute necessity in view of the fact that the most common method of teaching EIL is a holistic approach such as Content-Based Instruction and participation in a community of practice (Hino, 2010). In other words, the MJE may be shown to the learners in an inductive manner.

On the other hand, it is also clear that efforts in describing a model would facilitate the teaching process as well as the sharing of the knowledge with other teachers. In the following, a few examples of the features of the MJE will be provided, which has been developed through day-to-day decisions by the present writer for his university EFL/EIL classes. It should be made clear here, to avoid misunderstanding, that the lists in the following sections are not a description of English presently used by the Japanese but a proposal for pedagogical models.

Phonological models

For suprasegmental domains, learners of English have traditionally been required to learn to speak with native-like phonology that comes with frequent elision, linking, reduction, or assimilation, which are also the features contributing to the formation of stress-timed rhythm. However, it is evident from empirical studies (e.g., Jenkins, 2000; Deterding & Kirkpatrick, 2006) that these features of connected speech can even reduce intelligibility in interactions between non-native speakers. Such research results are also in agreement with daily experiences of non-native speakers, many of whom find their fellow non-native speakers' lack of elision, linking, reduction, and assimilation to be helpful to their listening comprehension. Therefore, with the MJE, it is recommended to speak English with relatively limited elision, linking, reduction, and assimilation (Hino, 1989c).

For segmental features, although actual intelligibility may not always be determined at the phonemic level but could sometimes be related to the phonetic level, the MJE is generally based on phonemic considerations. This is partly because it has been the author's experiences and observations that learning pronunciation at the phonemic level, without going into allophonic differences, seldom causes misunderstanding, and also because this approach to pronunciation has long been accepted by Japanese learners of English with relative ease.

Jenkins (2000) includes some phonetic or allophonic aspects in her LFC core, which are subject to some criticisms. For example, a presentation by a Japanese group of researchers at IAWE2006, which was based on Jenkins (2000), that defines the aspiration for the word-initial voiceless plosives as a core feature (e.g., [pʰ] in "pet"), was questioned by several international participants. Most notably, Paroo Nihalani, an influential scholar of phonology, pointed out that the word-initial voiceless plosives are normally not aspirated in Asian Englishes without causing any communication problem. This position of his was later reiterated in Nihalani (2010).

The issue here is if a lack of aspiration with the word-initial plosives would lead to confusion between voiceless and voiced plosives, such as "pet" and

64 *Models, materials, methodologies*

"bet." In the author's experiences, though my unaspirated voiceless word-initial plosives seem to have been mistaken by native speakers as its voiced counterparts once or twice, it has hardly been a problem for non-native listeners. On the whole, in addition to the fact that aspiration on word-initial plosives could sound rather unnatural for the Japanese (i.e., an extreme mimicking of native pronunciation), it seldom appears to create communication problems. For these reasons, the MJE allows the learners of English to pronounce the word-initial plosives without aspiration.

Grammatical models

Rules of grammar are a difficult issue for any attempt to set up an endonormative model. In Smith's classic notion of EIL, the grammar of educated English was regarded as basically the same as that of native speakers (Smith, 1976, 1978), which is a position generally shared also in later WE research at least for the acrolectal level.

However, some researchers have recently been exploring the possibility of unique non-native usage of the definite article ("the"), once held in ELT as a sacred place for which only native speakers have any authority. Concerning the definite article employed when the speaker/writer assumes that his or her listener/reader is familiar with what he or she is referring to, Komiya (2007) points out the Japanese tendency to use "the" where it is null for native speakers may be a reflection of the Japanese belief in high-context culture. In Komiya (2016), she further suggests that the frequent use of "the" might be a politeness strategy for Japanese users of English, by which they respectfully recognize their interlocutors' knowledge of the subject. In the MJE, such a use of the definite article can be acceptable even though it may sound like an overuse to native speakers.

Dewey (2009) also observes that the definite article is often utilized by ELF speakers for emphasis, which actually makes better sense than the rather idiomatic exploitation of the word by native speakers. Indeed, a lot of the Inner Circle usages of the definite article (or lack of it) appear nonsensical to non-native speakers. In the MJE, the usage of the definite article corresponds to that of Anglo-American English only so far as it is within the realm of the basic function of the word "the" (i.e., referring to something specific), which does bear some meaning for the Japanese.

Another example of grammar is the distinction between "will" and "be going to." For instance, it looks perfectly all right to the majority of Japanese speakers of English to say, "I will play tennis" when asked, "What are your plans for the weekend?," though many native speakers find this use of "will" a little strange because they are supposed to be talking about an event already in progress.

In the MJE, "will" and "be going to" are basically regarded as synonymous for two reasons. First, the lack of this distinction, common even among highly competent Japanese users of English, seldom seems to cause any misunderstanding in international communication involving both native and non-native speakers. Second, the Japanese do not appear to be interested in clearly distinguishing those two kinds of future in the first place.

The latter point needs some elaboration. American anthropologist Margaret Mead pointed out in her classic work (1942) that the belief that one's future primarily depends on his or her efforts, though with help from God, is at the heart of traditional American values founded on Puritan ethics. On the other hand, we are aware that the lives of the Japanese have historically been radically and abruptly changed over and over again by major natural disasters including fatal earthquakes.

I myself barely survived the Great Hanshin Earthquake in 1995 when a more devastating tsunami disaster was yet to occur in Japan in 2011. It is not surprising if the Japanese experience over the centuries, where future is felt to be predominantly determined by the overwhelming power of nature beyond human control, have shaped a perception of future that does not match Anglo-American future expressions such as "will" and "be going to."

Partly out of such concern, the MJE allows the students to use "will" and "be going to" interchangeably. It would be unfair if a certain world views different from the learners' own were forcibly imposed upon them.

However, the MJE does not necessarily accept all usages of English prevalent among the Japanese. For example, the traditional Japanese usage of the expression "You had better ~" is labeled an error in this model. A lot of Japanese speakers of English, particularly those who were educated before the 1980s, employ this phrase in making a polite suggestion, as if it were synonymous with "It would be better for you to ~." They assume that the English expression "You had better ~" is much more courteous than "You should ~." This is clearly different from the native-speaker usage in which "You had better~" is often a strong command that can even be uttered as a threat. The traditional Japanese interpretation comes from a literal translation of the word "better."

In the MJE, using "You had better~" for courteous advice is treated as an error, though longstanding in ELT in Japan until quite recently. Saying "You had better~" as a polite suggestion does not add anything to the representation of Japanese values. It is in no way useful in expressing Japanese ways of thinking.

Moreover, while it is interesting to see that this usage creates no problem with speakers of some non-native varieties of English who tend to use "You had better~" in the same way as Japanese do (e.g., a lot of Chinese), the author has observed that Japanese users of English often cause serious misunderstanding with this usage of "You had better~" in their communication with native speakers of English. This includes a mishap 40 years ago for which I myself was responsible, when I inadvertently frightened two elderly Canadian ladies traveling in Japan who asked me on a station platform which train they should take. When I confidently answered, "You had better take the next train," they looked confused, but I did not know why. "You had better~" as a polite suggestion is excluded from the MJE, since EIL needs to be understood both by native and non-native speakers.

66 *Models, materials, methodologies*

Lexical models

When I showed a newspaper headline "the first anniversary of Michael Jackson's death" to my college EFL/EIL class, most of the Japanese students said it sounded really weird, which is a feeling I also share in spite of my knowledge that it is perfectly normal in the native-speaker usage. The majority of Japanese feel that "anniversary" should be used only for a happy event that is to be celebrated. There is a notable cultural difference here – in the Christian tradition, while death is a sad thing, it is also considered to be worthy of celebration. In fact, some Japanese go through a cultural shock when they experience the unexpectedly positive atmosphere in attending a funeral at a Christian church.

There is no reason that Japanese users of English should suppress their hesitation about using the same word both for happy and tragic occasions. For those who feel uncomfortable with this native-speaker usage, the MJE proposes the use of the word "commemoration" for sad events, while reserving the word "anniversary" for celebration. This original usage has won support among my students and has also proven comprehensible in my actual use in several instances of international communication.

From a Japanese point of view, "the first commemoration of Michael Jackson's death" is an expression that displays proper respect for the deceased. Also, no Japanese should be forced to use expressions such as "the fifth anniversary of the Great East Japan Earthquake," which could sound extremely discourteous.

Using the expressions "the third year" and "the fourth year" to refer to undergraduate statuses usually called "junior" and "senior" respectively in American English is another example of lexical choice in the MJE. For instance, in Hino (1989b), an essay-style EFL/EIL textbook authored as an attempt to demonstrate a sample of Japanese English for international communication, I wrote, "I was in my third year of college." One of the two American editors claimed that it should be revised as "I was in my junior year of college." The other American editor disagreed with his fellow countryman, pointing out that the author wrote this in EIL instead of American English. The latter interpretation was exactly the author's own intention. Defining the third year as "junior" does not mean anything to Japanese, as it is an idiomatic usage in the U.S. Besides, while the use of "junior" in this context is commonly understood by American readers, it may not be always communicative to non-Americans. Here, "the third year" is the expression that ensures international comprehensibility.

Idiomatic expressions rooted in Anglo-American values are not included in the repertoire of the MJE. For example, there is no need to say "That's not cricket," which is based on a British sport largely unknown to the Japanese. Not only is this phrase of little use for expressing Japanese values, but it also has relatively low comprehensibility outside of the British Commonwealth.

On the other hand, expressing Japanese metaphors in English can be useful as a representation of Japanese culture. Some metaphors can be easily understood in international communication due to cultural universality, while other

Developing original production models 67

metaphors require a certain negotiation of meaning because of cultural differences (cf. Honna, 2008, 2013). Japanese metaphorical expressions that I have been trying to use in English in the hope of conveying Japanese values to international interlocutors include "rice cake in a picture" and "sesame grinding," which are the equivalents of "pie in the sky" and "apple polishing" in American English, respectively. The former is understood fairly easily, while the latter needs some explanation.

In ELF studies, Pitzl (2009, 2016) works on the theorization of non-English metaphors such as "We should not wake up any dogs." Such research can also be seen as a significant effort to apply cognitive linguistics to the analysis of EIL.

Discourse models

Starting first with a minor aspect, one example of discourse features of the MJE is relatively frequent back-channeling in conversation. Japanese learners of English find it necessary to lessen their back-channels (e.g., nodding, saying "yes," etc.) if they are to adhere to the native-speaker model. However, frequent back-channeling, sending the sign that they are listening attentively, is an important part of Japanese culture as a courtesy to the interlocutor. It is psychologically painful for the Japanese if they have to withhold this custom in their discourse just because it is not normal in interactions between native speakers. Besides, in my observation, frequent back-channels by Japanese speakers of English seem to be usually warmly received in international interactions as a sign of respect for others. In the MJE, frequent back-channeling is regarded as positive transfer, rather than interference, from the native language.

More importantly, argumentative writing is another area where the issue of models plays a significant role at the discourse level. In teaching both undergraduate and graduate courses, I find it worrisome that the great majority of Japanese students construct their argumentative essays in one and the same manner. They start with the conclusion, state some reasons in support of the argument, and end their writing by restating and reinforcing the conclusion. The students also follow this pattern when a speech task is given.

Below is an example that I made up to illustrate their typical style of writing (Hino, 2011, p. 258). Here, I call it Pattern A. The topic for the essay is "Should Japan change the war-renouncing Constitution?"

Pattern A

We should change the Article 9 of the Constitution which prohibits Japan from possessing a military. Firstly, the Constitution was imposed upon Japan by the United States. Secondly, the Article 9 is overly idealistic. Thirdly, any country has a right to have its own military force. For these reasons, I am convinced that the Article 9 of the Japanese Constitution should be revised.

68   *Models, materials, methodologies*

This organization certainly has an advantage of presenting a clear conclusion, but ends up with a one-sided argument. The students seem to be obsessed with this manner of argument that Japan has learned largely from the U.S. (M. Watanabe, 2007).

The fact that such a construction is dominantly taught in ELT in Japan is evident, for example, in a popular reference book for takers of the speaking test in the STEP 1st grade exam, a standardized English examination in Japan often deemed even as the goal for Japanese learners of English. As a strategy for the 2-minute argumentative speech task, the book recommends the examinees to construct a one-sided argument – "It is advisable to clearly side with one standpoint so that your argument will be consistent . . . It is better not to touch on opposite viewpoints" (Obunsha, 2016, p. 300. In Japanese. Translation mine). However, what about the Oriental "middle-of-the-road" philosophy, which values moderation and balance rather than a dichotomous conflict (cf. Y. Kachru, 1997)?

Actually, Japan has an indigenous style of argument traditionally employed in Japanese, which is a unique adaptation from the organization of classical Chinese poetry known as *ki-sho-ten-ketsu* in Japanese. This construction consists of four parts, namely, introduction, development, reflection on the other side, and conclusion. The third section *ten* is the salient feature of this text organization, where alternative viewpoints are reviewed to ensure a balanced argument. When this approach is applied to English, a passage such as the following example, Pattern B, is produced (Hino, 2011, p. 258):

Pattern B

There is a growing demand among Japanese people for changing the Article 9 of their Constitution. This movement is based on the idea that this Constitution was imposed upon them by the United States. Many also argue that its Article 9 is overly idealistic and that any country has a right to have its own military force. However, when we turn our eyes to the roles that the Constitution of Japan has played all these years after the war, the matter may not be that simple. It is a solid fact that Japan has not entered into a single warfare under the present Constitution. Although I understand the need for reexamining the value of the Constitution drafted over 60 years ago, I suggest that we should carefully discuss if it is really necessary to revise its unique Article 9 right now.

It is deplorable that the Pattern B argument has now been almost totally discarded, when the Pattern A argument has been firmly established, in ELT in Japan. As I reported in Hino (2016b), for example, after comparing the two passages above in June 2014, one of my Japanese graduate students stated, "My ELT teachers through my senior high school and university years taught me to write with Pattern A. . . . (Pattern A was) imprinted on me" (In Japanese. Translation mine). Another Japanese graduate student also wrote, "When I drew up my draft for a speech contest in junior high school, I first wrote it with Pattern B. But then our ALT (native English-speaking Assistant Language Teacher) changed it to Pattern A completely" (In Japanese. Translation mine).

Both of these two students were also in agreement that Pattern B can better express their real thought. In other words, in learning to write in English, they had been forbidden to express their own ideas. Their stories are very similar to the cases of other Japanese students that I discussed in Hino (2012a). Teachers should be aware that such educational practice could result in forcing Western dichotomy on Japanese learners of English at the sacrifice of the East Asian "middle-of-the-road" tradition.

The above proposal may remind some readers of the classic and controversial notion of "contrastive rhetoric," which was initiated by Kaplan (1966) and later developed by Hinds (1990) and others, as well as its critical follow-ups such as "intercultural rhetoric" (Connor, 2004) and "critical contrastive rhetoric" (Kubota & Lehner, 2004). However, the present discussion does not go into those concepts, since they are not directly relevant to our current efforts to devise new pedagogical models, while they certainly provide useful insights for analyzing existing texts.

Sociolinguistic models

In many EFL-speaking classes in Japan, it is often taken for granted that students should call each other by their given names instead of their family names, in accordance with the American norms for friendly conversations. In those classes, even the elderly are called by younger students simply by their given names, despite the fact that such practice is against East Asian culture rooted in the Confucian tradition. In fact, a senior citizen enrolled in such a class in Tokyo complained about having to put up with being called "Kazuo!" by his Japanese classmates who were as young as his own son. In the MJE, first-name calling as a term of address is not imposed on the learners.

The Japanese belief in seniority should be able find its expression in Japanese English also in describing relationships with one's siblings. In fact, just an ordinary English sentence such as "He is my brother," common in any beginning EFL textbook, is a major culture shock for Japanese learners of English in their first encounter. It does not make sense to the Japanese unless specified in terms of seniority such as "He is my older brother (*ani*)" or "He is my younger brother (*ototo*)." *Ani* and *ototo* are completely different entities from each other in the Japanese conceptual framework, as are *ane* (older sister) and *imoto* (younger sister). With the MJE, it is considered simply natural to constantly indicate the seniority of siblings by always qualifying them with the words "older" or "younger," no matter how clumsy it may sound in American English.

In Japan, it is a good manner to say "*itadakimasu*" before each meal as an expression of gratitude to everyone (or even every being) involved. However, Japanese learners of English, who are supposed to always imitate American behaviors, have generally been taught to say nothing before meals, with the

70   *Models, materials, methodologies*

exception of grace for Christians. From the viewpoint of the MJE, there is no reason to suppress such a beautiful indigenous custom, whether in a domestic or an international setting. Adapted from a suggestion in Lummis (1982), the MJE recommends the use of "I will take this food with thanks."

Likewise, again partly based on Lummis (1982), the MJE has "With your kind influence . . ." in order to express a common Japanese phrase "*okagesa-made*" in English. An example is "With your kind influence, I am safely back." The interlocutor actually did not do anything. The feeling here is "Things went well, because your existence always has a good influence on me." This expression represents a virtuous aspect of Japanese culture, which should not be easily discarded.

Implementation of the MJE

The MJE for feedback to the students

Presented in the previous section are some examples from the inventory of the MJE, utilized for giving feedback to the students' speaking and writing in my EFL/EIL classes. However, the MJE is never imposed on the students but are only used for suggestions when deemed helpful. Any variety of English is accepted in my class, including in exam situations, as long as it meets the student's own communicative needs. It certainly presents no problem if a Japanese student wishes to follow an American, Indian, or any other model of English rather than the MJE.

Demonstrating the MJE in class

I also demonstrate my own English in class as a sample representation of the MJE. It has always been my policy as an EFL/EIL teacher to present my own English as a primary sample of production for the students, as mentioned in Chapter 9, rather than relying on English produced by native speakers.

This also includes a weekly radio ELT program discussed in Chapter 8, which was broadcast nationwide in Japan and for which I served as the lecturer. In a series aired from July 1989 to March 1990 (Hino, 1989–1990), against the unquestioned convention that guests for ELT programs should be native speakers, almost every week I invited non-native English-speaking guests from countries such as Malaysia, Hong Kong, Bangladesh, Sri Lanka, the Philippines, and France, giving the radio audience chances to be exposed to EIL interactions between Japanese English and varieties of non-native English. Some audience members wrote to me that they were pleased to find that Japanese English does communicate effectively in international settings.

For a radio series from April to October 1992 (Hino, 1992b), a native-speaker partner was assigned to me by the radio sponsor, but from EIL perspectives I at least played the role of a Japanese man myself for skits that were also written by myself. This practice is in contrast with CDs accompanying the official school

Developing original production models 71

textbooks in Japan in which the roles of Japanese are still played by native speakers in the conservative belief that native English should be the sole model.

Dörnyei (2009), in discussing the construction of the "Ideal L2 Self," points out "the impact of the role models that the students have seen in films, on TV or in real life" (p. 33), arguing that igniting the students' vision of the Ideal L2 Self involves "presenting powerful role models" (p. 33). It is an important job of local teachers to serve as role models for their students as speakers of EIL. It is hoped that the MJE will provide the teachers with useful guidelines for this purpose.

Learners' reactions to the MJE

In Hino (2012a), I presented the results of the questionnaire administered after three and a half months in my IPTEIL classes (Chapter 8) in the spring semester of 2010. In those classes, I demonstrated my English based on the MJE, along with other varieties of English available on the Internet and satellite television.

The anonymous questionnaire (N=182) found that many of the students supported the positive view of Japanese English. In response to the question "Do you agree with the educational concept that 'good Japanese English' is a valuable means of international communication?," 75 students (41.2 percent) strongly agreed, 67 (36.8 percent) moderately agreed, 29 (15.9 percent) were neutral, 10 (5.4 percent) moderately disagreed, and 1 student (0.5 percent) strongly disagreed.

As shown later in Table 9.1 in Chapter 9 with regard to the latest anonymous survey in 2017, students continue to be dominantly supportive of the idea of "good Japanese English" capable of representing Japanese values as well as being internationally intelligible. Below are some of the open-ended comments on my notion of Japanese English in the recent questionnaire (July 2017. Translation mine):

> "Before taking this class, I thought that Japanese English was something undesirable. Professor Hino's concept was new and interesting to me, in that Japanese English is easily comprehensible."
>
> "In this class, I learned about Japanese English for the first time. Japanese English is much more suitable for me than those spoken in native English speaking countries."
>
> "It seems really appropriate for us to claim ourselves to be users of Japanese English, since we are trying to learn the kind of English that can truly communicate to the world."
>
> "I have been strongly motivated to participate in this class, partly because I agree to the idea of 'good Japanese English.'"

There was no negative opinion given on Japanese English in the open-ended section of the questionnaire. These comments suggest that the students, just like their predecessors, learned to appreciate "good Japanese English," for which the MJE is intended.

72 *Models, materials, methodologies*

Conclusion

While the WE paradigm may be descriptively correct in calling Expanding Circle Englishes exonormative, we should be aware that they are not doomed to be reliant on external norms. As presented in this chapter with the example of Japanese English, it is actually possible to create endonormative pedagogical models for the Expanding Circle by drawing on several resources such as relevant research results and actual experiences in international communication. Each of us in ELT can start designing such models at any time, no matter how vague and incomprehensive they may initially be. Once we begin, we can refine the models through educational efforts. This approach will enable us to stop forcing native-speaker norms on our students, and will empower the future generations with vital tools to effectively express themselves in intercultural communication.

5 Cultural content of teaching materials

Introduction

In conventional ELT, it used to be taken for granted that the cultural content of teaching materials should cover Anglo-American values, or those of the Inner Circle. A classic ELT methodology textbook in Japan exemplifies such a traditional position by stating:

> Each English word and each English phrase bears the weight of its history. Therefore, we believe that it is best to learn English in such contexts as it is spoken and written in Britain and America.
> (Ando, Kuroda, Narita, & Osawa, 1978, p. 60. Translation mine)

Although the cultural content of ELT textbooks in Japan was, as discussed later in the present chapter, actually going through changes already at the time this textbook was published, the above citation represents the typical attitudes of teachers who were primarily trained in English literature and linguistics before the 1970s.

On the other hand, the WE paradigm leads to the idea that it can be more appropriate for ELT materials to focus on local cultures when aimed at the teaching of English as an intra-national language in the Outer Circle. For the teaching of EIL in the Expanding Circle, as discussed in Chapter 3, it is desirable for teaching materials to represent varieties of culture, including indigenous values.

Revising and updating my study in Hino (1988a), the present chapter examines the cultural components of English textbooks in Japan during the past 150 years, divided into five periods, as a case study of ELT materials in the Expanding Circle. This research reveals that the cultural content of English texts clearly reflects the socio-political environment of each period. When Anglo-American culture was uncritically admired in Japan, English textbooks exclusively dealt with British and American values. When Japanese culture was unconditionally worshiped, the content of English texts extensively reflected traditional Japanese values.

Another salient point that emerges from these findings is the role of nationalism in the teaching of English for cross-cultural communication. While it has long

74 *Models, materials, methodologies*

been claimed that chauvinism of native speakers is a negative factor in promoting the idea of EIL and WE (e.g., Smith, 1981b; B. Kachru, 1976; Lummis, 1976), this chapter exemplifies the impact of nationalism of non-native speakers upon the teaching of EIL.

As is also true with the development of postcolonial English literatures, the movement toward the recognition of non-native varieties of English rose with the belief in self-determination among former colonies of Britain and America. In this sense, non-native speakers' nationalism was undoubtedly a driving force for WE or EIL. But, can we assume that it is always a positive factor for EIL? This question will be discussed in the following sections.

The history of English textbooks in Japan

In this chapter, the history of Japan for the past 150 years is divided into five periods. For each period, the socio-political environment and its influence on the cultural content of English textbooks are presented.

First period

After over 200 years of international isolation during the *Edo* period with the *Tokugawa* shogunate, Japan resumed diplomatic relations with other countries in 1853, under pressure from Western powers including the U.S. As Japan opened up to the world, the study of English became popular among the elite. The Japanese in those days strove to learn all kinds of things from the U.K. and the U.S., because these two countries were both technologically and academically advanced. It was essential for Japan to imitate Anglo-American cultures to achieve rapid modernization. This situation continued for about 60 years.

Among the materials used for teaching English in high schools during this period were literary works by Carlyle, Emerson, Lamb, Hawthorne, Irving, Dickens, and Shakespeare. Books such as *Political economy* by J. S. Mill, *Study of sociology* by H. Spencer, and *Character* by Samuel Smiles were also in use (Ikeda, 1968).

It is natural that those English texts dealt mainly with British and American values. The contents of *New crown readers V* (1916) illustrate this fact:

> "Franklin's First Entry into Philadelphia" by Benjamin Franklin
> "David Copperfield and the Waiter" by Charles Dickens
> "An English Sunday" by Arthur Cliff
> "Rural Life in England" by Washington Irving
> (Reprinted in Shimaoka, 1968, pp. 311–312)

By following Britain and America as ideal models of advanced countries, the Japanese came to adore and admire those cultures. This attitude is reflected even in grammar texts. Below is an example passage found in *New epoch English grammar* (1922):

Cultural content of teaching materials 75

The island of Great Britain is only a small spot on the globe, but it is one of the greatest countries in the world. It had many colonies which are found all over the world. "The sun never sets on the British Empire."

(Reprinted in Shimaoka, 1968, p. 316)

Second period

The next period is characterized by the rise of nationalism in Japan. Although Japan enjoyed some liberalism from the 1910s to the 1920s, known in Japan as "*Taisho* Democracy," it turned out to be very brief, drawing parallels with the short-lived democracy of the Weimar Republic.

In the 1930s, militarism gained enormous power in Japan, and, with its strong military force, Japan tried to expand its territories. Following the invasion of northeast China in 1931, it founded the Manchuria government there in 1932. Japan entered a full-scale war with China in 1937. America and Britain supported China, and Japan's relations with both countries sharply worsened.

The content of English texts in Japan was strongly influenced by this tide of nationalism. Japanese culture gradually began to be represented in English textbooks, such as English translations of the oldest anthology in Japan and of poems written by the Emperor of Japan (Ikenaga, 1969).

Third period

Japan joined World War II in 1941 as a member of the Axis against the Allies, including the U.S. and the U.K. During this war, the Japanese called these two countries "demons and beasts." They also believed in the absolute supremacy of Japanese culture. With strong censorship by the Ministry of Education, textbook writers in this period were forced to exclude much of Anglo-American cultures, and to put a focus on indigenous Japanese values. The following are some of the guidelines given by the Education Ministry to the writers of English texts:

1   Develop materials that will promote patriotism.
2   The Christian era must not be used. Use the Imperial era.
3   Pro-British or pro-American materials are prohibited.
4   Materials that imply the superiority of the British and Americans or the inferiority of the Japanese are not permitted.
5   Use materials about Japanese territories rather than about Europe and America.
6   Topics about academic disciplines, arts, biographies should be taken from Japan.

(Hoshiyama, 1980, p. 60. Translation mine)

In accordance with these criteria, Admiral Nelson, for example, was replaced by Admiral Yamamoto, the commander-in-chief of the Japanese navy. The

76   Models, materials, methodologies

British national anthem and a chapter on Christianity were deleted (Hoshiyama, 1980). Anglo-American names such as Tom, Harry, John, and Mary were substituted with Japanese names such as Taro, Masao, Hanako, and Yukiko. Illustrations were added that presented Japanese people in their national clothes (*The Asahi Shimbun*, December, 1, 1943. Reprinted in Kawasumi, 1978).

Below is an excerpt from a junior high school text published in the middle of the war. This passage reflects the nationalistic values held by the Japanese in those days:

> When we get up, it is still dark. We stand in a line, turn towards the Imperial Palace and bow. We thank our soldiers and sailors for their brave deeds. We pray for our success in war.
>
> (*Eigo*, 1944. Reprinted in Kawasumi, 1978, p. 773)

The following is a view expressed by an influential scholar Ryuzaburo Shikiba in 1942. His comment represents the philosophy of the teaching of English in Japan during the war:

> English has already become an international language. It is by no means owned solely by America and Britain. When we fight against Anglo-Americans, we should make use of the language in order to let them know Japan's strength. . . . It should be regarded as a good strategy to use English as a weapon in beating the Anglo-Americans. . . . We ought to make a point of giving up the admiration for Britain and America or the idea of treating them like advanced countries. In short, we should change our attitude toward the learning of English.
>
> (Reprinted in Kawasumi, 1978, p. 571. Translation mine)

Shikiba's argument appears to bear, on the surface, some resemblance to the concept of EIL declared today (cf. Nakayama, 1980). However, the question is whether this is really compatible with the basic philosophy of EIL.

Fourth period

In 1945, the U.S. and Britain along with their allies defeated Japan. The Japanese were obliged to radically change their values. They had believed in the absolute supremacy of Japanese culture, but now they regarded American and British cultures as undoubtedly superior, just as in the first period described earlier.

The first English textbook written after the war in Japan was *Let's learn English* (1947) for junior high schools. Cultural components found in this text are exclusively Anglo-American, as illustrated below with its chapter titles:

> All Fools Day, Pippa Passes by R. Browning, May in England, London Season, Independence Day, Bed in Summer by R. L. Stevenson, Thanksgiving Day,

Cultural content of teaching materials 77

Christmas, Queen Victoria, Home Sweet Home by J. H. Paine, Lincoln's Birthday, British Parliament.

(Reprinted in Ikenaga, 1969, p. 353)

The Course of Study issued by the Ministry of Education after the war, which established guidelines for writing textbooks, specified the goal of studying English in high school to be "Understanding the daily lives, viewpoints, and customs of native English speaking countries" (cf. Takanashi, 1975). In accordance with this provision, textbooks placed a heavy emphasis on native English-speaking cultures.

In post-war Japan, American influence was particularly strong in many phases of Japanese life, including the teaching of English. *New approach to English* (1960) for junior high schools is one example that embodied this trend. This textbook focused on American values, as seen in some of the titles of its lessons:

A Farmhouse in Colorado, The First Thanksgiving Day, The United States, Abraham Lincoln, American Games, American Sayings, The Arrow and the Song by H. W. Longfellow

The following excerpt exemplifies the main type of cultural content of this text:

The United States produces many things. Fruits and vegetables are grown in many parts of the country. A lot of wheat and corn are grown in the northern states. Cows are raised for milk in the northern states, and for meat in the southern states. Here the cowboys ride their horses to bring the animals together. These horses are rather small, fast, and strong. The cowboy's horse is his friend.

(*New approach to English* 2, 1960, pp. 83–84)

Indeed, even outside of English textbooks, the early 1960s were the days when Japanese television was occupied by American Western dramas, such as *Bonanza, Rawhide, The Rifleman*, and *Wanted dead or alive*.

Fifth period

The 1964 Olympiad was held in Tokyo, Japan, with participants from 94 countries. This international event greatly widened the cultural perspectives of the Japanese. So did Expo 1970, a world exposition in Osaka with participants from 77 countries. Though the American influence was still strong, the Japanese began to realize that the world consisted of varieties of culture.

With regard to the goal of cultural learning in ELT stated in the Course of Study for senior high schools, as Takanashi (1975) points out, the wording "native English speaking countries" up to the 1960 version was replaced by "foreign countries" in successive versions, as seen in the phrase "Understanding

78 Models, materials, methodologies

through English the ways of living and the viewpoints of people in foreign countries" (Translation mine).

This tangible shift in cultural emphasis, from native English-speaking cultures to foreign cultures in general, also held true with junior high school textbooks analyzed in the present chapter. The Education Ministry's directive in the Course of Study for junior high schools until 1958, "Getting the students to acquire, through the learning of a foreign language, the basic understanding of the daily lives, ways of living, and viewpoints of people who daily use the foreign language" (Translation mine), was changed to "Getting the students to acquire, though the learning of a foreign language, the basic understanding of the lives and viewpoints of people in foreign countries" (Translation mine), implying that cultures treated in ELT do not have to be restricted to those of native speakers of English.

Those shifts and changes in the social mood as well as in the governmental policies were gradually realized in English textbooks. The following is an excerpt from the *New prince readers* (1968) with a description of German values, that is, a non-native English-speaking culture. Though its overall content was still predominantly American, this textbook is an example of the transitional period, when a limited amount of non-native English-speaking cultures began to be introduced:

> I live in a town in Germany. Our town on the Rhine is famous for its wine. My father knows how to make good wine. It is autumn now, and the time for making wine.
>
> (*New prince readers* 2, 1968, p. 53)

In the textbooks used in the 1980s, cultural content was not restricted to the values of native English-speaking countries anymore, but varieties of culture were included. The following are some examples:

> Singapore became an independent country in 1965. It is a young country, and is really a "clean and green" country. You should not drop litter in the street. If you do, you have to pay five hundred dollars. Malaysia is famous for its rubber trees. Malaysia has been an independent country for about thirty years. It became independent in 1957. There are many different races in both Malaysia and Singapore – Chinese, Malayans, Indians, and others – and there have been some language wars among them.
>
> (*The new crown English series* 3, 1984, pp. 23–24)

> What do you know about Africa? Probably you know something about the pyramids or the great deserts. For a long time, people called Africa the "Dark Continent," because they knew little about it. But Africa has changed a lot since the end of World War II. It is rich in natural resources, and

Cultural content of teaching materials   79

African people are learning to use them. We should study more about Africa and its people.

(*New horizon English course 3*, 1986, p. 45)

Such extensive coverage of Southeast Asian and African cultures would have been hardly imaginable before.

With the remarkable economic growth of Japan after the war, the Japanese gradually regained confidence in their indigenous values. In consequence, Japanese culture came to be frequently mentioned in English textbooks. Examples from the mid-1980s are cited below:

There are three ways. They are *kanji*, *hiragana*, and *katakana*. We have 46 *hiragana* letters and 46 *katakana* letters. We must learn these 92 letters at primary school. . . . You have only 26 letters. We also must learn more than one thousand *kanji*. *Kanji* came to Japan from China. . . . You know something about the *Manyoshu*, don't you? The writers wrote the poems in *kanji* only. Our ancestors made *hiragana* and *katakana* from kanji. *Hiragana* and *katakana* are very simple ways of writing.

(*The new crown English series 2*, 1984, pp. 44–46)

They admired the Great Buddha in the Todaiji. "This beautiful Buddha has been here for over a thousand years," said the guide. In Nara Park they played with the deer. "Have these deer lived here for a long time?" Sadao asked. "Yes, they have," said the guide. This shrine has kept deer for over 300 years."

(*Total English 3*, 1984, p. 9)

Erikawa (2008) discusses the increasing presence of Japanese characters as one of the significant changes in junior high school textbooks. In his statistics, in the 1993 versions, Japanese people appeared in 74 percent of all chapters, while American people were seen in 53 percent of them. This is a major boost in the representation of Japanese characters compared with the 1981 versions, which gave 62 percent to Japanese and 63 percent to Americans. From our EIL perspectives, this shift can be regarded as showing the increasing sense of "the ownership of English" (Widdowson, 1994; A. Matsuda, 2003) in ELT in Japan.

One of the highlights of today's textbooks is the description of Japanese contribution to the international community. Contribution to the global society is also what is expected of EIL users. As the last example in this chapter, below is an excerpt from the latest 2016 version of a junior high school textbook:

In 1964, Nishioka went to Bhutan. He learned the language spoken there. He wanted to teach the Bhutanese a new way to grow rice. But most of them were not interested. So he decided to grow vegetables first.

(*Total English* 3, 2016, p. 60)

80 *Models, materials, methodologies*

Just in case one feels that the word "teach" in the second line may sound a bit imposing, it probably cannot be helped due to the restriction in vocabulary and sentence structures at this level. Active participants in the global community, like Mr. Nishioka above, are role models for EIL learners. This example is particularly interesting in that "the language" in the quote is not English but Bhutanese known as Dzongkha. This can be a response, though humble, to the popular criticism that ELT tends to promote English language imperialism as well as to the call for the acknowledgment of multilingualism in recent ELF studies.

In summing up the fifth period, junior high school English textbooks in Japan since the 1980s, ones officially approved by the Ministry of Education, present fairly balanced cultural content. They cover Anglo-American, European, Asian, and African cultures, with a particular emphasis on Japanese values (cf. Fujita, 1987). American junior high school students as the leading characters of the textbooks, with "Jack and Betty" being the most famous in history, have been replaced by their Japanese counterparts like the users of the books themselves. These features are in agreement with the concept of EIL. In other words, at least as far as the cultural content is concerned (though the linguistic norms have remained those of American English), school English textbooks in Japan have been EIL materials for three decades already.

Conclusion

In 1982, when alleged involvement of the Japanese Ministry of Education in the description of Japan's war-time actions in senior high school history textbooks made newspaper headlines, an education ministry official said to me and several other ELT researchers in an informal conversation, "There is no politics in English textbooks," suggesting that we did not need to care about such issues at least with regard to the subject of English. Indeed, in those days many ELT professionals naively believed that English textbooks were free from political concerns. However, the present chapter reveals that the reality is otherwise. Historically, English textbooks have constantly reflected socio-political transitions.

During the period when the Japanese tried to achieve rapid modernization, they uncritically venerated Anglo-American culture. Before and during World War II, they were converted to an extreme appreciation of Japanese culture. After the war, the Japanese drastically changed their attitude, and once again, they worshiped Anglo-American values. The cultural content of English textbooks was directly impacted by those attitudinal changes. This cycle draws a parallel with the swing of a pendulum, pointed out by Otani (1985, 2007), between Anglophelia and Anglophobia in Japan.

While sheer admiration of Anglo-American culture without critical literacy interferes with the idea of EIL, absolute belief in indigenous values also poses a serious problem. It is true that nationalism may function as a support for the concept of EIL in terms of the fact that nationalism on the part of the

Cultural content of teaching materials 81

non-native speaker shifts the cultural orientation away from the Anglo-American framework. However, when nationalism goes to extremes, it is quite doubtful that it really facilitates international communication. The radical nationalism in Japan during the war resulted in the exclusion of foreign cultures and strong emphasis on indigenous values. This attitude contradicts the basis of EIL, because EIL entails an enlargement of cultural scope where varieties of culture receive fair treatment without prejudice.

Just as the chauvinism of native speakers of English stands against EIL, and just as uncritical appreciation of native English-speaking cultures by non-native speakers works as a negative factor for EIL, radical and narrow nationalism of non-native speakers is incompatible with EIL. Here we are reminded that materials for the teaching of EIL need to be developed on the foundation of cross-cultural and intercultural awareness.

6 Locally-appropriate methodology

Introduction

Just as the English language itself, ELT pedagogy developed in Britain and the U.S. has been imported to the rest of the world usually without scrutiny. Some researchers questioned such practice early, pointing out that appropriate ELT methodology depends on local contexts (e.g., Hino, 1988b, 1992a; Henrichsen, 1989; Holliday, 1994; McKay, 1992; Kern, 2000). For example, I argued in Hino (1988b) that "in developing or selecting teaching methodology suitable for an EFL country, it is essential to investigate its indigenous sociolinguistic tradition" (p. 52), while Henrichsen (1989) also claimed that "[u]nderstanding antecedents is a crucial part of the process of analyzing or planning any effort to diffuse and/or implement an educational innovation" (p. 101).

However, this issue was long discussed separately from EIL research, as it was generally assumed that methodology for teaching, unlike other aspects such as models and materials, was largely unaffected by the notion of EIL. In fact, when I proposed a tentative framework of EIL studies in Hino (2001), I added the following notation:

> one of the popular areas in the study of foreign language education these days is an investigation of methodologies which are appropriate to indigenous values (e.g., Holliday, 1994; McKay, 1992; Hino, 1992a), but this topic is not included in this paper. Though the issue of locally-appropriate methodologies definitely has implications for TEIL, it is also equally relevant to TEFL/TESL. However, in an attempt to ultimately construct a comprehensive EIL research paradigm, inclusion of such subjects might also be taken into consideration.
>
> (Hino, 2001, p. 59)

It was McKay (2003), an article that followed her 2002 book, which first explicitly included locally-appropriate pedagogy on the agenda of EIL research, by stating that "just as the content of EIL materials must be separated from native-speaker models, so too must EIL methodology, by allowing locally appropriate pedagogy to be implemented" (p. 140). The issue of locally-appropriate

Locally-appropriate methodology 83

methodology is now becoming one of the major themes of EIL studies, including successive works by McKay herself (e.g., McKay & Bokhorst-Heng, 2008; McKay & J. Brown, 2016).

The impact of a traditional Japanese approach to Chinese on ELT in Japan

In the case of Japan, the conventional Japanese attitudes toward foreign languages are evidently displayed in the way the Chinese language has been learned in Japan over the centuries (Kawasumi, 1976, 1978). For more than a millennium, the Japanese have been studying classical Chinese as an integral part of their education. In fact, it is still taught in most senior high schools in Japan today as a mandatory subject in accordance with the Course of Study set by the Japanese government. Classical Chinese literature taught in Japanese high schools includes many cultural heritages of China such as works by Mencius, Sima Qian, Du Fu, and Li Bai, to name just a few.

Below is an example from a high school textbook of classical Chinese designated by the Japanese Ministry of Education, presenting a poem by Song dynasty poet Su Shi. In those textbooks, classical Chinese is written vertically as in the original, but is horizontally arranged in the present chapter for the sake of simplicity:

花　有　清　香　月　有　陰

(_Kotogakko koten kanbun-hen_, 2010, p. 21)

As seen in this example, symbols such as 一, 二, and レ are put beside the Chinese words as an aid for the reader. These symbols, used in Japan for centuries, are called _kunten_, which literally means "symbols for reading by translating." The function of _kunten_ is to facilitate word-by-word (also word-for-word) translation by directing how the Chinese words should be reordered to match Japanese syntax.

This method of reading classical Chinese, known as _kundoku_ (literally "reading by translating"), is highly significant in that it underlies both first language literacy and foreign language literacy in Japan (Hino, 1992a). While the Japanese writing system was historically built on _kundoku_, the same method has also been applied to the reading and learning of modern Western languages including English.

How does _kundoku_ operate with the use of _kunten_? レ is put between two characters to indicate that they should be reversed. 二 is a sign modeled after the Chinese numeral for "two," which commands the reader to bypass the character on the left, to go forward to the right as far as 一 ("one"), and to come back to the character that was skipped at first. The Chinese sentence is reordered in

84 Models, materials, methodologies

this way for the purpose of word-by-word translation into Japanese. If the reordering is shown by numbers, it appears like the following:

花　有　清　香　月　有　陰
1　4　2　3　5　7　6

Below, I also supply literal translation of this sentence in English. As in this example, it usually does not require much reordering to translate classical Chinese into English word-by-word because of the coincidental syntactical similarities between the two languages including the SVO word order, while it calls for very complicated operations to do the same into Japanese, an agglutinative language with an SOV construction:

花　有　清　香　月　有　陰
Flowers have clean fragrance The moon has shade

Going back to the *kundoku* method, the Japanese *katakana* letters (historically developed by simplifying some Chinese characters) 二 (*ni*) and リ (*ri*) put beside the Chinese characters are there to supplement grammatical elements required in the Japanese language. 二 is a postpositional particle, and リ is an inflectional suffix.

In reading this sentence, 花 (flower), 有 (have), 月 (moon), and 陰 (shade) are translated into indigenous Japanese words, as *hana*, *ari* (verb stem "*a*" plus inflectional suffix "*ri*"), *tsuki*, and *kage*, respectively. Original Chinese pronunciation is retained for 清香 (clean fragrance), which is treated as a borrowing from Chinese, while phonologically Japanized as *sei ko*. Thus, the whole sentence is read in Japan as "*Hana ni seiko ari, tsuki ni kage ari,*" where only *seiko* has any trace of the original Chinese pronunciation.

Likewise, when written out in Japanese, this sentence appears as "花二清香有リ 月二陰有リ." This is the same as the way Japanese is written even today, except that the *katakana* letters are usually replaced by soft-looking *hiragana* equivalents. In fact, as alluded to earlier, *kundoku* historically served as a basis for the formation of the writing system of Japanese. This fact shows how deeply *kundoku* is ingrained in the linguaculture of Japan, playing a key role not only for foreign language literacy but also for first language literacy.

It may be added here that it is theoretically possible to read the entire classical Chinese sentence with a Japanized pronunciation of ancient Chinese, that is, without translating any of them into indigenous Japanese words. In this case, this sentence would sound like "*Ka* (花) *yu* (有) *sei* (清) *ko* (香), *getsu* (月) *yu* (有) *in* (陰)," but it is not very common to read classical Chinese in such a manner with the exception of the reading of Buddhist scriptures.[1]

Kundoku is essentially an attempt to read a foreign language as if it were Japanese. Indeed, an important fact is that classical Chinese, taught with *kundoku*,

Locally-appropriate methodology 85

constitutes a part of the National Language (i.e., Japanese as the first language) curriculum in senior high schools. In other words, through the *kundoku* technique, classical Chinese is taught not as Chinese, but as Japanese.

Kundoku as a method of reading, learning, and teaching Chinese in Japan was passed on to the study of Dutch, and subsequently to that of English when Japan opened its diplomatic channels at the end of the *Shogunate* period in response to external pressure after over two hundred years of international isolation. The following are excerpts from a textbook in 1859 entitled *Eibei Taiwa Shokei* (*A shortcut to English conversation*):

	言		早
おまえ	ことなり	はなはだ	はや
	二		一
ユー	スパーカ	ツー	ハースタ
You	speak	too	fast.

(Reprinted in Inui, 2010, p. 55)

The second line of this example consists of Japanese translations for each English word, some of which are also partly transcribed in Chinese characters in the first line. The fourth line provides Japanese transcriptions of English pronunciation. The most interesting part is the third line, where 一 and 二, the symbols for reading Chinese, are employed. In other examples found in this textbook, the symbol レ is also in extensive use. Those signs direct the readers to translate the English sentence word-by-word just as they do for classical Chinese.

In the history of ELT in Japan, the reordering symbols later came to be replaced, for the sake of simplification, by numbers put for each English word, but the principle of the *kundoku* process remained exactly the same. The long history of *kundoku*, or *yakudoku* (Hino, 1988b) as it is usually referred to when used for reading modern foreign languages, at least partly explains why Japanese teachers of English tend to take it for granted that translating English word-by-word into Japanese should be a basic activity in English classes.

All through my own school years in the 1970s, I wondered why my teachers seemed to have no doubt that rendering each and every English word into Japanese is a must while ignoring the chance of understanding English directly in the original. It looked as if the teachers were controlled by some invisible force. When I learned that their approach to the teaching of English is a descendent of *kundoku* of classical Chinese, it really made sense. That is, word-by-word translation of foreign languages is a cultural practice for the Japanese, firmly established upon centuries of tradition.

Another sociolinguistic tradition in Japan is the emphasis on written language, an attitude also evident in the *kundoku/yakudoku* approach that concentrates on reading at the sacrifice of listening and speaking. Acceptance of Chinese characters in Japan with their logographic nature seems to have led the Japanese to regard written language as the primary aspect of language in sharp contrast with the Western tenet of linguistics, or the Saussurean paradigm, that language is primarily speech (T. Suzuki, 1975; Hino, 1991).

86 *Models, materials, methodologies*

Such linguistic attitude is especially evident among older generations. In fact, that is why the present author was given a name at birth that is extremely cumbersome to pronounce. As the family name precedes the given name in Japan like most other parts of East Asia, my name is Hino Nobuyuki (日野信行). A problem for me in living with this name is that I tend to stammer every time I try to utter my own name, because the last syllable of my family name "*no*" is immediately followed by the same sound at the head of the given name. Why did my father give such a tongue-twister to his son?

What happened is that my father did not care about how the name sounded. All he was concerned with was how the name appeared in Chinese characters, and 日野信行 looked good. As for semantic aspects, 信 means to "believe," and 行 is to "act," which was what the father wished his new-born son to do throughout his life – "Act with belief." No matter how awkward it may sound when pronounced, this name is perfect when written in Chinese characters.[2] My name is an example to show how much written language is valued in Japanese culture.

Appropriate methodology for local contexts

My earlier works on the impact of *yakudoku* tradition on ELT in Japan have been followed up by some noted scholars. For example, Kern summarizes Hino (1992a) as, "Instructional change, then, is dynamically negotiated at the juncture of professional discourse and larger sociohistorical forces" (Kern, 2000, p. 123). A. Matsuda also comments on the significance of such works as Hino (1988b) from EIL perspectives:

> Each culture has a way of teaching and learning that is historically situated in the local context. Although there is nothing wrong with introducing a new pedagogical approach, it cannot be expected to work well without any adjustments in a new context and should not be assumed to be more effective or better than the local practices.
>
> (A. Matsuda, 2012b, p. 178)

One of the important implications of the *kundoku* tradition for ELT pedagogy in Japan is that it is merely counterproductive to try to eliminate translation in this local context (Hino, 1992a). Given such a deeply rooted sociolinguistic convention, it is indeed more realistic to attempt to make effective use of translation in order to ensure compatibility with indigenous educational values. While it is certainly important for teachers to guide their students not to form the habit of always translating English into Japanese, translation may be strategically utilized in the learning process.

In addition, the Japanese inclination toward written language should also be taken into consideration as another local sociolinguistic factor in developing appropriate ELT pedagogy. In this regard, it was a proper decision, made by the Japanese Ministry of Education, to introduce reading and writing into ELT

Locally-appropriate methodology   87

for 5th and 6th graders in 2018, bringing a change to their previous policy to concentrate on the oral aspects of English in elementary school education.

The Grammar-Translation Method has been, though with a few exceptions such as Cook (2010), negatively viewed in the mainstream ELT dominated by Anglophone schools of thought. This stance is evidently displayed in a representative resource book for teachers. Richards and Rodgers (2014), the latest edition of "the" standard methodology book, still maintains that "though it may be true to say that the Grammar-Translation Method is still widely practiced, it has no advocates. It is a method for which there is no theory" (p. 7). In terms of the fact that there was no real scientific background for the way the Grammar-Translation Method arose in Europe from the teaching of Latin (Kelly, 1969), such critical account of this classical approach to language teaching surely holds true. On the other hand, it should be worth reexamining whether the Western perspectives are precisely applicable, for instance, to East Asian situations.

It was Koike (1983) and Koike (1985), two seminal nationwide surveys administered in the early 1980s, which substantiated the dominance of *yakudoku* approach in ELT classrooms in Japan. Three decades later, the results of my mini-survey in 2013 (Hino, 2016a) suggest that teachers' attitudes toward translation seem to have changed only slightly. It is quite understandable from the sociolinguistic perspective discussed in this chapter. Although the Japanese Ministry of Education now stresses that ELT classes should be taught basically in English, the success of such a reform will depend on negotiations with the indigenous sociocultural values as to the use of the native language.

With regard to the importance of locally-appropriate methodology, or "methods suited for the Japanese" (Ito, 1978, p. 204) in the case of Japan, we can learn from the experiences of H. E. Palmer, one of the most influential scholars in the history of ELT (Kelly, 1969; Howatt with Widdowson, 2004), who taught in Japan from 1922 to 1936. Along the lines of modern Western approaches to language teaching initiated by Sweet (1899) and Jespersen (1904), Palmer at first tried to introduce the original version of his pedagogy, known as the Oral Method (Palmer, 1921), to ELT in Japan. That is, he heavily emphasized spoken language, especially at the beginning level, while minimizing, if not eliminating, translation. However, as he became familiar with the reality of ELT in Japan, he gradually modified his methodology (Ozasa, 1995; Imura, 1997; Ando et al., 1978). He came to pay more attention to the teaching of reading and writing, and to make effective use of translation. While much has been told about the greatness of Palmer, we may also call him a pioneer of EIL pedagogy in this respect.

Conclusion

We have become so accustomed, especially in Asia, to identifying globalization with Westernization that its consequences seem to be seldom questioned. Unfortunately, language education has been no exception to this dominant tendency.

88 *Models, materials, methodologies*

Teachers of English in this region should stop suppressing Asian values, and instead try reconciling them with Anglophone culture in their educational practice. That is the spirit of EIL. We must now consider the positive role that indigenous values could play in helping the learners become owners, rather than renters, of English for global communication.

Notes

1 For example, the opening line of the Buddhist scripture adopted by most Japanese Buddhist denominations, 無上甚深微妙法 百千万劫難遭遇 ("It is difficult to meet with the supreme and deep truth of the teachings of Buddha, no matter how long we may try") is usually read aloud as "*Mu jo jin jin mi myo ho, Hyaku sen man go nan so gu.*" Here, the entire sentence is pronounced in Japanized phonology of ancient Chinese rather than in *kundoku* reading. This method of reading Buddhist scriptures, though commonly practiced by many Japanese priests, is an exception to the *kundoku* tradition.

2 Nobuyuki (信行) is a *kundoku* name itself, as both 信 (*nobu*) and 行 (*yuki*) are read with their indigenous Japanese equivalents. It would have been theoretically possible for my father to assign the other pronunciation system (the one based on ancient Chinese) to these characters, which are "*shin*" and "*gyo*" respectively, but it would be rather uncommon for this particular name.

Part III
Practices of EIL education

7 Approaches and methods for teaching EIL

Introduction

As seen in previous chapters, the theories of EIL (or WE, ELF, etc. depending on your preferred school of thought) have been extensively studied for years now. Educational principles based on those positions have also been discussed since their inception, as evident in Smith (1976), B. Kachru (1976), and Jenkins (2000), though to a much lesser degree compared with linguistic and sociolinguistic analyses.

Lately, EIL studies has seen a number of publications dedicated to its pedagogical aspects, including A. Matsuda (2012a), Alsagoff et al. (2012), Marlina and Giri (2014), and Bayyurt and Akcan (2015), which have proven to be valuable contributions to the field. On the other hand, even in those recent works on EIL education, a major focus often seems to be placed more on the raising of students' awareness in EIL, or providing learners with the knowledge on the sociolinguistic reality of global Englishes, rather than the teaching of actual EIL skills. In other words, while we have now become relatively familiar with how to "teach *about* EIL," there still remains a strong need to keep exploring how to "teach EIL," that is, concrete methods of teaching linguistic and pragmatic skills in EIL.

For the purpose of identifying some pedagogical features of classroom practice in EIL, this chapter will classify and analyze some examples of ELT classes, though still limited in number, where attempts are made to teach EIL. The findings reveal, among others, a tendency toward the content-based approach, teachers' belief in demonstrating their own non-native varieties of English, and the teachers' awareness of the value of engaging their students in real EIL interactions in person.

Teaching *about* EIL

In categorizing examples of actual classroom practices, four ways of teaching EIL are identified, in addition to "teaching about EIL" mentioned in the previous section. This section first describes the "teaching about EIL" approach briefly, as it is the one most commonly practiced when attempts are made to

92   Practices of EIL education

incorporate the idea of EIL into classrooms, before going on to the next section to discuss the four methods of teaching actual skills in EIL.

In teaching "about" EIL, the emphasis is put on raising the students' awareness in the significance of English for international communication, including its wide range of diversity. An example of this is seen in Honna, Kirkpatrick, and Gilbert (2001), a textbook for university ELT classes in Japan, as is evident in its chapter titles such as "Whose English?," "English Literature or Literature in English," and "Attitudes of Japanese to Varieties of English." For instance, Chapter 1 "Whose English?" starts with "English is unique. It is the only language in the world that has more non-native speakers than native speakers."[1]

This approach was also employed in a trial EIL class for senior high school students taught by two graduate students from the Graduate School of World Englishes, Chukyo University, from 2007 to 2008 (N. Murata & Sugimoto, 2009). The student teachers introduced the high school students to the notion of WE, including the Kachruvian concept of Three Circles of English (B. Kachru, 1985), asking them questions such as "How many countries use English?"[2]

In the European Expanding Circle context, Bayyurt and Altinmakas (2012) reports on a communication skills course for first- and second-year students at a Turkish University, which is based on the concept of WE. Classroom debate topics, intended for nurturing the awareness of EIL/WE, include, "What is 'standard' English? Can one talk about the existence of a 'Turkish English variety'?" and, "How should the curriculum of English language and literature departments be revised to reflect the current status of English as a world language?"

As for the Asian Expanding Circle other than Japan, Baker (2012, 2015) analyzes, from ELF perspectives, an e-learning course in Thailand which explicitly deals with the issues of intercultural communication and global Englishes as course content.

It is interesting that even in A. Matsuda and Duran (2012), a seminal compilation of actual classroom practices in EIL, many of the topics dealt with in the classes concern EIL itself (e.g., Tanner, 2012; O'Dwyer, 2012), such as the ones mentioned thus far. Although those practices are surely significant and worthwhile, the following section explores further pedagogical possibilities for teaching EIL.

Teaching EIL: four types of classroom practice

Four classroom methods for teaching EIL skills (Hino, 2010, 2013) are discussed in the following subsections, consisting of "exposure to varieties of English," "role-plays as cross-cultural training," "content-based approach to EIL," and "participation in a community of practice in EIL."

Exposure to varieties of English

The first type of EIL methodology is one that exposes the students to varieties of English, spoken and/or written, for the purpose of helping the learners

Approaches and methods for teaching EIL 93

become familiar with the linguistic and cultural diversity of EIL. As was shown by Smith and Bisazza (1982), exposure to varieties of EIL is one of the keys to successful international communication.

My own approach for first-year and second-year EFL classes at Osaka University (Hino, 2012b), namely IPTEIL discussed in Chapter 9, is one such example. With this method, the students watch real-time news on Internet websites such as those of *Channel NewsAsia* (Singapore), *NDTV* (India), *ABS-CBN* (the Philippines), *KTV* (Kenya), and *Al Jazeera* (Qatar), through which they can listen to and read varieties of English, including non-native Englishes, which are both linguistically and culturally diverse. Lessons presented in Bayyurt and Altinmakas (2012) also include one that introduces the students to the diversity of Englishes via the Internet.

Another example of my own is a nationwide radio ELT program *English for Millions*, discussed in Chapter 8, for which I was a lecturer from 1989 to 1992. In a series aired once a week from 1989 to 1990, I invited non-native English speakers from various countries, such as Malaysia, Hong Kong, Bangladesh, Sri Lanka, the Philippines, and France, in order to provide the Japanese audience with opportunities to experience the diversity of EIL (Hino, 1989–1990). Responses sent from the listeners all over Japan showed that many of them found this radio program to be a valuable chance to be exposed to varieties of English.

An early example of college EFL textbooks intended to familiarize the students with varieties of English is Nishinoh et al. (1994). This coursebook consists of four essays on the language and culture of Ghana, Singapore, New Zealand, and Ireland, written by scholars from each country, with recordings by those authors themselves.

Nowadays, textbooks as well as self-study materials with audios of varieties of English are fairly abundant. An internationally known example is Kirkpatrick (2007), a book on WE that comes with a CD of native and non-native varieties of English, such as those of Australia, Sri Lanka, Hong Kong, and Nigeria.

Quite a few domestic publications on this theme are also available in Japan today, including Tsuruta and Shibata (2008), with a CD that collects Englishes spoken by delegates from 20 countries at the World Economic Forum, encompassing all of the Inner, Outer, and Expanding Circles. Focusing on one high-profile variety of WE, Enokizono (2012) invites Japanese readers to the world of Indian English through a CD of dramatized skits recorded in Indian English, with explanations on the social and cultural background.

Recently, the Internet has made it easy to introduce learners to varieties of English. For example, D'Angelo (2012) reports on required oral communication classes at Chukyo University, an essential component of which is activities in listening to varieties of English via a website known as ELLLO. In my graduate applied linguistics class, when I assigned students to find examples of non-native varieties of English on the Internet, some of them referred to various YouTube videos making jokes about Singlish, although then I had to explain to them the difference between acrolectal, mesolectal, and basilectal varieties of Singaporean English.

94 Practices of EIL education

Role-plays as cross-cultural training

The next type of EIL pedagogy entails role-plays, arranged to prepare the students to cope with cultural differences that they are expected to encounter in EIL interactions.

Talk-and-Listen (Via & Smith, 1983) is a classic example of this approach. In this simplified role-play activity developed by former Broadway actor-turned educator Richard A. Via and pioneer EIL scholar Larry E. Smith, students are encouraged to be themselves even while acting, an idea that is at the heart of EIL philosophy.

Training for what Shiozawa (1999, 2016) calls "Affective Competence" could be also cited here as an example of cross-cultural role-play for EIL purposes. "Affective competence" is the ability to cope with cultural differences expected in EIL situations.

A role-play activity that I have developed for EIL is "Mt. Osorezan English Summit" (Hino, 2010). Mt. Osorezan is a mountain in the northern part of Japan where there are many spiritual mediums, mostly elderly women, who upon request call on the deceased and speak on behalf of the dead. In "Mt. Osorezan English Summit," each student chooses a historic figure and tries to speak like him or her. Those individuals, from various countries and different times of history, hold a conference on a given theme, at the end of which they are expected to issue a joint declaration. This is a cross-cultural simulation game in which the participants are required to overcome enormous differences in cultural values to reach a peaceful consensus.

In one Mt. Osorezan English Summit held in my graduate class, the students played the roles, which they freely chose, of Mother Teresa, John Lennon, Martin Luther (German religious reformer), Francisco Xavier, Pablo Casals (Spanish cellist), Sen no Rikyu (16th-century Japanese tea master), Sakamoto Ryoma (one of the key figures leading Japan to the Meiji Restoration), and even a war-time prime minister of Japan (whose name I would not mention here), with Prince Umayado (also known as Shotoku-taishi, a leader of Japan and a member of the royal family in the 7th century) for my own role as the chair. I wondered if I should turn down the student's wish to act as the war-time prime minister, but I decided to accept it, seeing that the student obviously had no intention of endorsing his war-time acts in any way.

In this summit meeting, the participants had a heated discussion on the theme "What should we do to achieve world peace?" Making compromises over various discrepancies such as religious differences among Catholics, Protestants, Shintoists, and Buddhists, together with enormous philosophical differences between warriors and pacifists, the delegates finally concluded a joint declaration for world peace, consisting of three clauses which were "1. Drink tea. 2. Love your neighbor, if you can. 3. Sing songs."

Mt. Osorezan English Summit would not be appropriate for use when any of the students feels it to be religiously offensive, while most Japanese take such a game simply as a harmless fiction (though the religious insensitivity of Japanese

Approaches and methods for teaching EIL   95

people can indeed be a problem in international settings). This activity is just an example of intercultural training in negotiations between different values, as a crucial skill for EIL users.

Content-based approach to EIL

A salient feature of EIL pedagogy is the popular use of the content-based approach, which is intended to help students learn EIL while learning content.

Two of my own methods referred to earlier in this chapter also belong to this category along with the other classifications, as they attempt to teach EIL by dealing with some actual content rather than the language per se. IPTEIL is based on real-time daily news, and the radio talk-shows with non-native speakers of English focused on the content, mainly global issues such as environment, international politics, international economy, and gender problems.

Takagaki and Tanabe (2007) reports on a home economics class taught in English by Filipino teachers at Onomichi Higashi High School, one of the "Super English Language High Schools" designated by the Ministry of Education. Although it is not necessarily clear if it is the intention of the school leadership to deliberately introduce the students to non-native English, this classroom practice may certainly be regarded as a form of content-based approach to EIL.

As for higher education, Galloway and Rose (2013) analyze a business course taught at a private Japanese university in English, where authentic ELF interactions take place as a result of the employment of seven international students, only one of whom comes from the Inner Circle, who assist Japanese students in the learning of business content. Along the similar line, Chapter 10 of the present volume will discuss the learning of EIL in EMI (English-Medium Instruction) classes in higher education as a form of CLIL (Content and Language Integrated Learning).

Some of the practices in "teaching about EIL" mentioned earlier in this section, such as the program discussed in Baker (2012), can be also regarded as a form of the content-based approach to EIL in a broad sense of the term, although the range of content may be relatively restricted in those cases.

Participation in a community of practice in EIL

Another major approach to the teaching of EIL is one that offers opportunities for participation in a community of EIL users, with or without reference to constructivist notions such as Legitimate Peripheral Participation (Lave & Wenger, 1991 cf. Wenger, 1998). This type of teaching is aimed at giving the students a certain authentic, real-life experience in EIL.

The IPTEIL method mentioned earlier in this chapter is one example along this line. IPTEIL leads the students to engage in the kind of activities shared by many of the real-life EIL users around the world – watch, read, and discuss

96 *Practices of EIL education*

real-time news that are broadcast and written in WE. These activities in the IPTEIL class are "legitimate" in the sense that watching, reading, and discussing real-time news are authentic uses of English rather than a mere simulation. This manner of participating in the community of EIL is also "peripheral," as the class is a somewhat sheltered environment, though still authentic, with no risk of bringing about any serious consequence even when the students make mistakes.

An educational project at Waseda University utilizing TV conference technology in collaboration with partner universities overseas, known as Cross-Cultural Distance Learning (CCDL), can also be considered to belong to this "learning-in-doing" approach. Ueda, Owada, Oya, and Tsutsui (2005) reports, for instance, that 20 students from Waseda University in Tokyo had discussions via TV conference with 20 counterparts from Korea University in Seoul. Waseda University has later added other measures such as voice chat to their CCDL activities (Nakano, Kondo, Owada, Ueda, & Yoshida, 2012), widening the modes of communication.

Chukyo University, with its college of World Englishes, has also held TV conferences with their partner institutions abroad, thereby teaching EIL through authentic interactions. In 2009, for example, undergraduates at Chukyo University had two talk sessions, one with diplomats from China and the other with military officers from Indonesia, both of whom were studying at the Regional Language Center (RELC) in Singapore at that time.

While TV conference is certainly a promising approach to EIL education, face-to-face interaction with EIL users has significant advantages as a more direct experience in EIL communication in person. For example, at an occasion that I was allowed to observe in February 2015, students from universities participating in CCDL, mainly from Asia, gathered at an off-line session at Waseda University, pursuing group projects across different nationalities, naturally using EIL as a means of communication.

When an EFL class is joined by international students, the class could be turned into a community of practice in EIL (Hino, 2003b). An interdepartmental class at Seikei University, reported by Kobayashi (2008), may be categorized as one effort in this direction. According to Kobayashi, foreign students are invited to the class as guest speakers, who engage in small group discussions with Japanese students. The guest speakers in 2006 were students who came from a wide range of countries – France, Germany, Italy, Sweden, Korea, Indonesia, Thailand, Myanmar, Tunisia, Australia, and the U.S.

Overseas study also constitutes EIL education if the learning environment is properly chosen in terms of EIL. For example, enrolling in English language schools on the island of Cebu, the Philippines, which is becoming popular among Japanese university students, provides opportunities for learning to interact with speakers of Filipino English, both inside and outside classrooms. Although the main motive for the students in choosing the Philippines for studying English is the lower cost compared with going to the U.S. or the

U.K., this still results in authentic experiences in communicating with users of a non-native variety of English (S. Oda, 2013).

Still another example of a program that leads learners to participate in a community of practice in EIL is one that was launched by the very pioneer of the concept of EIL, Larry E. Smith. This project, known as the Global Cultural Exchange Program (GCEP), makes extensive use of authentic EIL environments in Hawaii, assigning tasks such as interviewing tourists from across the world, as well as providing job-shadowing opportunities at places such as hotels and day-care centers.

Two principles for teaching EIL

In order to implement the teaching of EIL, in addition to the four methods discussed in the previous section, two overall principles should be also presented here. One is a need for locally-appropriate methodologies, and the other is the significance of presenting the local teacher's English as a model.

One of the principles for EIL pedagogy is an emphasis on locally-appropriate methodologies (Hino, 2003b). In other words, methods of teaching EIL should be compatible with the sociocultural values of the community that the learner belongs to (McKay, 2003). For the teaching of EIL in Japan, *yakudoku* (reading by translating) and *ondoku* (reading aloud), the latter being akin to traditional recitation practices in Hungary discussed in Duff (2007), may be viewed as two major candidates for such indigenous approaches (cf. Hino, 1988b, 1992a). Though age-old activities such as *yakudoku* and *ondoku* tend to be disregarded in Western schools of ELT, they are both embedded in the sociolinguistic structure of Japan including its *kanji* culture (Hino, 1991). It is more realistic and practical to build on these traditional methods, with which Japanese learners feel quite comfortable, than to make futile attempts to get rid of them.

The other principle is perhaps even more important. My classroom observations and interviews have revealed that the non-native English teacher's attitude to regard his or her own indigenous variety of English as legitimate could turn any EFL class into an EIL-oriented class to a considerable extent.

I interviewed a public senior high school teacher in Osaka Prefecture, right after observing her class with an Irish ALT in November 2008. She had a substantial background in the theories of EIL, as she had taken my graduate course in EIL education at Osaka University (Hino, 2017a) for three years while she was on a leave from the high school. In order to find out about the "before and after" of her EIL training, I asked her, "How does your graduate study in the concept of EIL influence your teaching in senior high school now?" Her answer may be summarized as follows:

> I think the biggest influence is that I stopped hesitating to present my own English in front of my students. I came to feel strongly that the students can learn from my conversations with the ALT.

98 *Practices of EIL education*

It should be noted here that in the Kachruvian WE paradigm, "Expanding Circle" varieties such as Japanese English for international communication, unlike postcolonial "Outer Circle" varieties such as Indian English with its intra-national functions, are not considered to be a valid educational model (B. Kachru, 1976, 1997). However, it is my standpoint, developed on the initial form of EIL by Smith (1976, 1978), to make no discrimination between Expanding and Outer Circle varieties when it comes to the issue of educational models of EIL (e.g., Hino, 2001, 2009). In my own framework of EIL, teachers' efforts to present their own English as one possible model are highly valued.

I also interviewed a national university professor in the Tokai region who teaches an EFL methodology course for prospective junior and senior high school teachers, immediately after my observation of the class in January 2009. Like the senior high school teacher, this college professor also used to be a student in my graduate course in EIL pedagogy. In the interview, I asked him, "What do you keep in mind when you teach this methodology course?" Below is a summary of his answer:

> I have been telling those future teachers that they should not depend on the CDs too much. I always make it clear that the primary model of English in class should be their own English.

My interviews with these two educators also identified the philosophy shared by them (and by myself) in demonstrating their own English as possible models in class. That is, if Japanese teachers do not exhibit confidence in their own Japanese English, we could not possibly expect the Japanese students to positively try to use their English. In other words, if the teachers treat their own Japanese English as inferior to native-speaker English, it would discourage their students from using English at the outset.

Conclusion

This chapter has looked into how classes are taught by teachers trying to incorporate the notion of EIL into their pedagogical practice.

A tendency observed in EIL-oriented classrooms is the popular use of content-based approach as well as active attempts at Legitimate Peripheral Participation in a Community of Practice. Both of these have the nature of holistic "learning-in-doing" approach rather than methods focusing on discrete points of grammar, pronunciation, vocabulary, etc.

It appears that there are two chief reasons for this tendency. One is the fact that training in EIL needs to be practical, due to the essentially pragmatic nature of EIL. The other reason is that specific linguistic details for teaching EIL have not been clearly identified thus far, making it more realistic to lead the students to "learn by doing."

Approaches and methods for teaching EIL   99

The present chapter is rather restricted in its size and scope, but it is hoped that it will encourage further research in discovering how EIL is being taught in actual classrooms.

Notes

1 Though I have some reservations about the idea that English is unique, I will not go into this issue here.
2 As far as the international functions of English are concerned, the question, "How many countries use English?" can actually be a bit confusing, though such an activity would still be useful in letting students think about the global spread of English.

8 A radio EIL education program

Introduction

This chapter will discuss an attempt to offer EIL perspectives on a radio English education program in Japan from 1989 to 1990, and then in 1992, for which the present writer was the host and also the text writer. This radio project was an attempt to render the EIL theory or "world Englishes paradigm" (K. Brown, 1993) into actual teaching practice by integrating EIL with the concept of Global Education. It was also an effort to bring about what Henrichsen (1989) called "diffusion of innovations in English language teaching" through a form of mass media that was aired all over Japan.

In the 1980s, Japan already had a considerable number of ELT teachers who were interested in the indigenous Japanese philosophy of international English (Kunihiro, 1970; T. Suzuki, 1975) or Larry E. Smith's concept of EIL (Smith, 1976, 1978, 1981b). However, they generally seemed to be at a loss when it came to actual teaching – "O.K., we understand EIL is important. But how can we teach it?" Being confused, most of those Japanese educators ended up with an attitude like, "Let's teach British and American English anyway. Let's teach how to interact with native speakers of English. And let's just hope that EIL will take care of itself." It may even be possible to say that EIL in Japan was interpreted simply as the "surrender value" (an ELT terminology originally used in life insurance) of failing to master American or British English. The radio EIL education programs discussed in this chapter were my attempts to bring about some changes to this sorry state of affairs.

Radio and television ELT programs in Japan

ELT programs on the radio and television have played significant roles in Japan in the post-war years. Due to the power of mass media, those programs still have major influence on learners of English in Japan even in the age of the Internet.

The dominant provider of those ELT programs is the public, national broadcasting corporation known as NHK. Despite the fact that most of those radio and television courses do not offer credits or certificates, they continue to be popular among Japanese learners of English. In 2017, there are as many as 11 ELT programs on NHK radio, seven of which are aired every weekday, and eight ELT programs on NHK television. The intended audience varies depending on each course, that is, children, junior high school students, senior high school students, and learners of English in general.

Most of those radio and television ELT programs have been, and still are, largely based on Anglo-American English, a stance partly reflected by the demographics of the regular hosts. In 2017, all the courses (whose main hosts are usually Japanese lecturers) come with international teaching assistants, or international lecturers in a few cases, all of whom are from Inner Circle countries such as the U.S. Although the demographics of the hosts may not necessarily mean that the courses are lacking in EIL perspectives (in fact, one of the current lecturers, Dr. Steve Soresi, is a recognized EIL expert), they can be too limiting from EIL perspectives in terms of the fact that international NNS/NNS interactions are not regular features of the programs.

The following sections discuss two radio ELT programs (not on NHK, though nationwide), one from 1989 to 1990 and the other in 1992, where I made efforts to teach EIL rather than the conventional American or British English.

Hino Nobuyuki's "Let's Read & Think" in *English for Millions*

Background

The radio program *English for Millions (Hyakuman-nin no Eigo)*, sponsored by the Japan English Educational Foundation of Japan, was aired daily for 34 years, from 1958 to 1992, on a commercial radio network that spanned the nation from Hokkaido to Okinawa. It basically consisted of seven independent weekly courses. The rare non-NHK radio ELT program had a wide range of listeners, from junior high school students to senior citizens.

English for Millions in its original form chiefly focused on American and British English just like NHK radio and television ELT programs. For example, one of the most popular series in this program started each broadcast with a chorus that said, "We love American English." The aim of that series was obviously to help Japanese listeners sound like Americans.

The present writer was the host, teacher, text writer, and editor for a series entitled "Let's Read & Think," which was broadcast once a week from July 1989 to March 1990, before assuming the same responsibility for another series in 1992, which will be discussed later. The series "Let's Read & Think" itself had been in existence for nine years when I took it over. My predecessor for this series was Masao Kunihiro, one of the first advocates of indigenous Japanese philosophy of EIL. Kunihiro (1970) proposed a concept that he called "de-Anglo-Americanized English," which is akin to the concepts of EIL, WE, and ELF today.

102   *Practices of EIL education*

What is interesting is that in this radio program Kunihiro did not necessarily practice what he preached. In spite of his ardent belief in the de-Anglo-Americanization of English, Kunihiro for nine years mainly used American and British materials. In fact, the course description for this program made no mention of de-Anglo-Americanization of English. Rather, the course description emphasized such factors as "Japan's relationship with America" or "familiarizing the listeners with native speakers' English." Here again, we see the gap between EIL theory and EIL practice. Kunihiro's dilemma is quite symbolic in this regard.

Format of the program

My program was composed of three parts. The first part was the explanation of reading materials written by native speakers of English (mostly Americans). The second part was discussions with an American journalist on topics related to the essays presented in the first part. The third part mainly consisted of my (i.e., the Japanese host's) interviews with a variety of non-native speakers of English.

Because I took over the program in the middle of the year, I followed the course description and the basic format set by my predecessor. Thus, the first and second parts continued to reflect the traditional EFL stance, or the American emphasis. The third part was where I was able to put my ideas on EIL and WE into practice. In fact, considering the ongoing importance for Japanese to communicate with native speakers of English, it was probably a good idea to retain some traditional EFL elements in this program rather than to discard them entirely.

Interviews such as the ones in the third part, known as "talk-shows," have been a popular genre in radio and television ELT programs in Japan. However, those talks have usually been either between a Japanese and a native speaker of English or between native speakers of English. In this sense, my talk-show series between non-native speakers of English was quite new to mass media ELT programs in Japan.

Objectives

As the host, text writer, and editor for this series, I had three objectives in having speakers of non-native varieties of English on the "talk-show." The first objective was to expose the listeners to WE, including both their linguistic and cultural features. The second was to present examples of interactions between non-native speakers of English. The third was to combine EIL with Global Education. Each of these objectives will be discussed in the following subsections.

Objective #1: exposing the learners to WE

As Smith and Bisazza (1982) indicated, exposure to varieties of English is effective training for successful communication in EIL situations. Therefore, for my talk-shows, I tried to invite guests from various countries in order to help my listeners get used to both linguistic and cultural features of WE.

As has been revealed by the great amount of research on WE, each variety of English has its own linguistic characteristics. It is certainly useful to have experience in listening to those different linguistic features to facilitate listening comprehension.

There are also some common traits shared by many non-native varieties of English. The most conspicuous of these is the frequent lack of phonological reduction, linking, elision, etc., that is, non-native speakers' tendency to pronounce every syllable distinctly, which presents a sharp contrast with native-speaker phonology such as American pronunciation. Some letters from the listeners of my program reported that non-native Englishes sounded clearer and therefore more intelligible than native-speaker English. Those observations lend support to the classic study by Smith and Rafiqzad (1979), which found that non-native varieties of English were no less intelligible than American English in EIL situations, as well as to recent studies such as Kirkpatrick (2010), which suggest that non-native speakers' syllable-timed rhythm, as opposed to native speakers' stress-timed rhythm, can actually enhance international intelligibility in EIL.

As has been shown by books such as Smith (1987), and more recently Y. Kachru and Smith (2008), along with numerous articles published in the journal *World Englishes*, sociocultural and sociolinguistic factors are often more important for international communication than phonological or syntactic factors. For example, the manner by which a speech act is performed in English often depends on the variety used by the speaker. The following dialogue between a Bangladeshi student and myself, which took place when I asked him to appear on the radio program as a guest, illustrates this point. Although this conversation itself was not taped, it was so interesting that it was presented in my talk in the program:

JAPANESE (HINO): Could you come to the studio next Wednesday?
BANGLADESHI: Well, maybe.
JAPANESE: I beg your pardon?
BANGLADESHI: I don't know, but I will try.

If interpreted within the framework of conventional Anglo-American English, this answer would sound rather negative, even to the extent that it can be taken as a polite refusal. At first, I also took it to mean that he was not very willing to come to the studio. However, in actuality, he was most willing to come. It was not a refusal, but an acceptance.

How could it be possible? The clue lies in the student's Islamic world views, which traditionally hold that only Allah knows the future. This Bangladeshi student later told me that he was a devout Muslim, and explained, citing the key Islamic concept of "Insha-Allah" (*God willing*), that making a promise with a human being would be blasphemy. He said that he was certainly eager to come, but that only Allah knew if he could actually make it to the studio on

104　*Practices of EIL education*

that day. In other words, he agreed to the request in a way that was very different from mainstream British or American English reared largely in the Judeo-Christian contexts. Most Americans would say "sure" or "certainly" when they perform the speech act of accepting a request.

It may be noted here, to evade oversimplification, that various positions actually exist within the Islamic world, and that this Bangladeshi student was perhaps relatively conservative, being strictly faithful to conventional Islamic principles. In fact, when I had a chance a few years later to ask another Bangladeshi Muslim student in Japan what he would have said if he had been in the same situation, his answer was, "Well, religiously speaking, I should also say 'I don't know, but I will try.' But I would probably just say 'Certainly' or 'Sure,' to avoid misunderstanding." Mahboob (2009) also points out, drawing on examples from Pakistani English, that "Insha-Allah" is indeed "sometimes used as a means of polite refusal or 'non-committing promise'" (p. 183). All in all, a correct interpretation has to be based, as always, on each particular situation.

This radio program gave the listeners chances to listen to non-native Englishes that represented various cultures different from that of Anglo-Americans. Judging from responses from the listeners, it seems that the program had some success in making them aware of the cultural diversity of WE, and in encouraging them to express their own cultural values through the medium of English (like the Bangladeshi guest) rather than someone else's values.

Objective #2: presenting NNS/NNS interactions

The interviewer Hino is a speaker of Japanese English. Traditionally, radio and television ELT programs in Japan have presented either NS/NS interactions or NS/NNS interactions. It was intended that this program would provide the missing element, that is, NNS/NNS interactions that characterize typical EIL situations.

Objective #3: combining EIL with Global Education

The teaching of EIL is given additional strength when combined with Global Education, even though introducing Global Education to ELT has been a controversial issue for many years.

It would be correct to say that the underlying philosophy, or perhaps even the ultimate goal, of Larry Smith's model of EIL is world peace, that is, to provide or ensure a means of cross-cultural communication in order to help peoples of the world live in harmony despite differences in their national or ethnic backgrounds (cf. Tanaka, 1978). This basic philosophy or the goal of EIL is in line with the concept of Global Education, which aims to help students become world citizens who can cope with global problems such as war and peace, environmental issues, hunger, or human rights. In my interviews with non-native speakers of English, I tried, as far as possible, to raise the kind of topics often dealt with in Global Education, as discussed later in this chapter.

I put a special emphasis on confronting Japanese prejudice towards their fellow Asians. While Japanese people often admire Europeans and Americans, they sometimes tend to look down upon non-Westerners, especially non-Caucasians such as those from Asia and Africa. This traditional Japanese attitude is a major hindrance to successful international communication, because it means that Japanese people are not even aware of the need to open communication channels with non-Westerners. I wanted to show that both the inferiority complex toward Westerners and the superiority complex toward Asians were totally unfounded and groundless.

Contents

Finding guests from various countries was by no means easy. It might have been easier if I had asked embassies or consulates to send their personnel to the program as guests, but I believed that it would be more useful to have sincere and honest opinions from ordinary people rather than official comments from government officials or diplomats.

Below are the contents of the talk-show series in my program, with the list of topics covered in each session:

July 1989 – Introduction

> 2nd week: Lecture on "Japanese English for international communication" I
> 3rd week: Lecture on "Japanese English for international communication" II

August 1989 – Talk with a university student from Malaysia

> 1st week: Ethnic groups in Malaysia, languages in Malaysia
> 2nd week: Geography of Malaysia, school education in Malaysia, language policy in school education
> 3rd week: Japanese society, housing in Japan, crime rates in Japan, Japanese people, Japanese university students, Japanese people in Malaysia, Japanese businesses in Malaysia
> 4th week: More on ethnicity in Malaysia, Chinese people/culture in Malaysia, Chinese Malaysians' feelings toward China, environmental issues, exploitation of tropical rain forests in Malaysia, Japanese involvement in environmental destruction in Malaysia

September 1989 – Talk with a university student from Hong Kong

> 1st week: School education in Hong Kong, languages in education
> 2nd week: Hong Kong's return to China in 1997, Hong Kong people's attitudes toward China, immigration issues
> 3rd week: Hong Kong people's attitudes toward Britain, Britain's attitudes toward Hong Kong, women's social status in Hong Kong

106 *Practices of EIL education*

4th week: Review of the above sessions – reflecting on Malaysian English and Hong Kong English, lecture on the significance of talking with non-native speakers of English, lecture on the need for familiarizing oneself with varieties of English

October 1989 – Talk with a graduate student from Sri Lanka

1st week: Brief history of Sri Lanka
2nd week: Basic facts about Sri Lanka, ethnic groups in Sri Lanka, ethnic conflicts in Sri Lanka, languages in Sri Lanka
3rd week: School education in Sri Lanka, languages in education, roles of English in Sri Lanka, women's status in Sri Lanka
4th week: Japanese society, Japanese people, Japan as a member of the world community, Japanese economy, trade friction

November 1989 – Talk with a university student from Bangladesh

1st week: Languages in Bangladesh, languages in education
2nd week: Religions in Bangladesh, Islamic values
3rd week: Ethnic groups in Bangladesh, foreign workers in Japan, "Opening Japan," labor markets in Japan, international relations of Bangladesh
4th week: Hunger in Bangladesh, illiteracy in Bangladesh, living in Japan, Japanese economy, Japanese technology

December 1989 – Talk with a university professor from the Philippines

1st week: Foreign students in Japan, foreign professors in Japanese universities, "internationalization" of Japanese universities
2nd week: Languages in the Philippines, languages in education, English in the Philippines, English in education, foreign students in Japan, Japanese students' attitudes toward foreign students
3rd week: Politics in the Philippines – revolution in February 1986, more on being a foreign professor at a Japanese university
4th week: "Opening Japan," need for international communication

January 1990 – Talk with a middle school English teacher from the Philippines

1st week: Linguistic background, English in education, on being a non-native speaking English teacher in Japan, evaluation of the JET program
2nd week: Immigration problems, Japanese prejudice, Japanese attitudes toward non-native speakers of English, shortcomings of school education in Japan, the teaching of English in Japan
3rd week: More on the teaching of English in Japan, school children and university students in Japan
4th week: "Opening Japan" – internationalization of Japan, Japanese admiration for Westerners and prejudice towards Asians, women's status in the Philippine society

A radio EIL education program   107

February 1990 – Lectures

> 1st week: Digests from the above talks, and lecture on their significance
> 2nd week: Lecture on an American author writing in Japanese, excerpts from Goodman (1987)

March 1990 – Talk with a university student from France

> 1st week: Japanese culture, Japanese people, Japanese university students
> 2nd week: Traditional values in Japanese life, unification of the EC in 1992, promoting friendship between French people and Japanese people

I started with guests from the Outer Circle, or ESL countries as they are traditionally called, who are defined in the WE paradigm as speakers of "institutionalized varieties." They were from Malaysia, Hong Kong, Sri Lanka, Bangladesh, and the Philippines. I would have liked to have additional guests from other Asian ESL countries such as India or Singapore, if it had been possible. Ideally, it would have been desirable if I had also been able to invite speakers of ESL varieties from African countries such as Kenya or Nigeria, or from the Pacific area such as Tonga or Papua New Guinea.

In the end, I had only one guest from the Expanding Circle, a speaker of a "performance variety" according to the WE theory, who was from France. However, I certainly had no intention of making light of Expanding Circle varieties. Rather, as one who insists on an indiscriminate treatment of speakers from the Outer and the Expanding Circle, it was important for me to include someone from the latter regions. In fact, if this series had been allowed to go on longer, I would have had chances to invite more guests from the Expanding Circle such as Korea, the Netherlands, or Brazil.

As can be seen in the summary of contents, I discussed a wide range of topics with the guests. Among those issues brought up in the talks, the following topics can be considered especially important in terms of Global Education:

- Exploitation of tropical rain forests in Malaysia
- Japanese involvement in environmental destruction
- A democracy movement in China (which occurred during this radio series)
- Hong Kong's return to China in the near future
- Ethnic problems in Sri Lanka (which Japanese are generally ignorant of)
- Japan's trade frictions with other countries
- Islamic values in Bangladesh (unfamiliar to most Japanese)
- Causes of hunger in Bangladesh
- The issue of opening the Japanese labor market to foreigners (heatedly debated at the time)
- The issue of internationalization or globalization of Japanese education (as viewed by a professor and a teacher from the Philippines)

108   *Practices of EIL education*

As 1989 was the year when women's social roles were hotly discussed in Japan, I asked several guests about women's social statuses in their home countries, again in an endeavor to combine EIL with Global Education.

For the February program, I brought up the concept of "Japanese for international communication," citing an article written in Japanese by American author David G. Goodman – "I have been using Japanese, not as a means of representing Japanese culture, but as a means of expressing my own philosophy and thought. . . . My act of writing in Japanese has nothing to do with Japan" (Goodman, 1987, p. 54. Translation mine). Essentially, Goodman is saying that what he express through the Japanese language is his own thoughts as a Jewish American, claiming that his use of the Japanese language is by no means based on Japanese culture.

On the radio, I tried to explain Goodman's standpoint by further referring to Smith (1981b. Reprinted in Smith, 1983, p. 10) which says "no one language is inextricably tied to any one culture." Thinking of the danger involved in treating English as "the" international language, that is, the risk of falling into the pitfall of linguistic imperialism, I wanted to illustrate that any language could potentially be used for international communication.

Reactions from the listeners

As a national broadcast, this radio program received numerous letters from the listeners.[1] Most of the reactions from the listeners were positive. Common reactions were, for example (Translation mine):

> "By listening to this program, I now have some confidence in my Japanese English."
>
> "This program is valuable, because an ELT program dealing with non-native Englishes is really rare."
>
> "Through this program, I have come to recognize the functions of English as an international language which go beyond the realms of Anglo-American culture."
>
> "I have realized that it doesn't matter if I cannot speak native-like English."
>
> "I have come to recognize the importance of understanding various cultures."
>
> "Now I look forward to communicating with people around the world, using my Japanese-style English as a tool."
>
> "I was surprised to find that non-native varieties of English are often easier to understand than native speaker English."
>
> "I am now well aware how ignorant I have been about my Asian neighbors, when I know quite a lot about Europe and America."

This program was certainly not free of criticisms from the listeners. However, as far as the efforts to introduce EIL were concerned, there was only one letter that was entirely negative, which said, "I don't want to listen to strange English like Filipino English." No other letters from the listeners expressed such prejudice against WE.

On the whole, reactions on this EIL talk-show project were overwhelmingly supportive. At a time when American English programs were abundant, those Japanese learners of English found it useful to listen to an EIL-oriented program partly because of its rarity.

Hino Nobuyuki's "Japan Today" in *English for Millions*

Background

After an interval of two years, I was given another chance to be a teacher for *English for Millions*, from April to September in 1992. This series, entitled *Japan Today*, had been on the air from half a year before, and I took on the responsibility, as in "Let's Read & Think," with the resignation of my predecessor. I decided to take this job because the prescribed goal of this *Japan Today* series was somehow in line with an important component of EIL philosophy, that is, expressing one's own cultural values in English. Once again, I served as the host, teacher, and the text writer for the program.

Format of the program

This program was basically composed of two parts. The first portion, which was the main part, presented sample dialogues on Japanese society and culture, followed by my discussions with a regular American guest. The second segment reported on current local news from all over Japan, again followed by some discussions.

There were several problems with the prearranged organization of the program, which I was not allowed to change. One of them was that I was restricted to have only one partner, who was American. Another problem was that all the sample dialogues were supposed to be interactions between a Japanese and an American. In terms of EIL, it would have been more desirable to have partners from several countries including non-native speakers of English. It would also have been more meaningful if the sample dialogues had taken place between a Japanese speaker of English and speakers of WE. However, in spite of these limitations, there were still chances to promote EIL through this program by highlighting the use of English in expressing the speaker's own values, that is, "non-Anglo-American" Japanese culture.

Goals of the program

The major goal of this series was to enable the listeners to talk about Japanese society and culture in English. This is one of the weak points in the teaching of English in Japan. For example, while it is not so difficult to find Japanese speakers of English who are able to discuss U.S. politics, very few of them could

110 *Practices of EIL education*

explain basic facts about the Meiji Restoration in English. In fact, this is a common problem not only in Japan but also in other Expanding Circle situations. For example, Wen (2016) observes that in mainland China "[q]uite a number of young Chinese scholars with high English proficiency often fail to explain what Confucianism is in English in international exchanges" (p. 157).

I also made one small attempt to help achieve this goal; that is, contrary to the longstanding custom in radio and television ELT programs in Japan, I started every program by saying "I'm your host Hino Nobuyuki" rather than "I'm your host Nobuyuki Hino." I wanted to show symbolically, by retaining the original order of names, that I was talking in EIL rather than EFL or ESL.

Contents

For each month, the first- and the third-week programs discussed traditional Japanese society/culture, and the second and the fourth programs dealt with modern Japanese society/culture. The themes of the sample dialogues were as follows:

April

> 1st week: Admission ceremony
> 2nd week: *Karoshi* (Death from overwork)
> 3rd week: Japanese names
> 4th week: Japanese word processor

May

> 1st week: Boys' Day
> 2nd week: The Constitution of Japan
> 3rd week: Name card
> 4th week: "English conversation" fads in Japan

June

> 1st week: Rice
> 2nd week: Enjoying a single life
> 3rd week: Japanese abacus
> 4th week: "Study abroad" boom

July

> 1st week: The Star Festival
> 2nd week: Job hunting in Japan
> 3rd week: Summer festivals
> 4th week: Foreign pop music

August

> 1st week: Education in Japan
> 2nd week: Cars in Japan

3rd week: The *Bon* Festival
4th week: Language learning in Japan

September

1st week: The Japanese language
Lecture on "Japanese English for international communication" I
2nd week: Japanese colleges
Lecture on "Japanese English for international communication" II
3rd week: Respect-for-the-Aged Day
Lecture on "Japanese English for international communication" III
4th week: Internationalization of Japan
Lecture on "Japanese English for international communication" IV

Reactions from the listeners

A large number of letters from the listeners acknowledged the importance of expressing Japanese society/culture through the medium of English.[2] However, it appears that this idea was not necessarily new to them.

One letter criticized the host's pronunciation for not sounding like that of a native speaker of English. On the other hand, several letters expressed their fondness for my kind of Japanese English pronunciation.

On the whole, in distinction to my previous series, not many letters commented on this program from the viewpoint of EIL. After all, under these circumstances, interactions presented in this program always took place between a Japanese and an American. It seems that the fact that no NNS/NNS interactions were shown blurred the EIL orientation of this program. It is certain that my first series had more impact than this second series as far as EIL philosophy is concerned. Still, some letters such as the following were received, which suggests that there were people who did gain a bit of insight into EIL by listening to this program (Translation mine):

> "Japanese people have a tendency to neglect the parts of the world other than Europe and America. I find this program really significant in that it proposes that we turn our eyes to the whole world including non-Western countries through our study of English."
>
> "Before I listened to this program, I took it for granted that I should put my given name first rather than my family name when I use English. However, now I am beginning to doubt that it is always a good idea to adapt ourselves to Western customs."

Conclusion

Although the two radio series discussed in this chapter, especially the first program, made a certain success in introducing Japanese learners of English to the concept of EIL, it seems that they did not exert a major influence on their later

112 *Practices of EIL education*

counterparts. That is, we see little evidence of EIL in today's radio and television ELT programs in Japan. Anyway, given the limited duration of my programs, it would have been too ambitious to expect any substantial change to the longstanding native-speakerism.

My radio series were just a small step. It is hoped that further endeavors will lead to a more thorough coverage of EIL in the teaching of English through mass media, toward the ultimate goal of constructing a peaceful society that is free from linguistic and cultural prejudice.

Notes

1 Unfortunately, most of these letters from the listeners were lost amid the turmoil of the Great Hanshin Earthquake on January 17, 1995. This is a loss of valuable primary sources. The comments from the listeners presented here are largely based on my memory at the time the original version of this chapter was written (in 1996).
2 Fortunately, these letters from the listeners, though they are not necessarily as significant as the letters to my first series, survived the Great Hanshin Earthquake.

9 Integrated Practice in Teaching English as an International Language (IPTEIL)

Introduction

Continuing with the discussion of EIL pedagogy, the present chapter reports on the author's classroom practice in undergraduate EFL classes at a university in Japan by extensively revising and updating Hino (2012a). The method of teaching allows the students to participate in the real world of EIL by watching, listening to, and discussing real-time news available on the Internet. In this course, TV news from non-native speaking English countries accessible on the Internet are utilized, as sources reflecting the wide linguistic and cultural variety of WE. In an effort to integrate the teaching of EIL with critical thinking and media literacy education, various electronic newspapers from around the world are also compared and contrasted, which exemplify a diversity of cultural values among worldwide users of EIL. This method, which grew out of my classroom teaching, is now known as IPTEIL (Integrated Practice in Teaching English as an International Language) (Hino, 2012a; Hino & S. Oda, 2015).

The undergraduate EFL classes, which I actually teach as EIL classes, discussed in this chapter are ones offered at Osaka University, a major national institution. The university covers most major disciplines with 11 undergraduate schools and 14 graduate schools, with approximately 16,000 undergraduate students and 6,500 graduate students. EFL classes at Osaka University are compulsory for all first-year and second-year students regardless of their major subjects of study.

The teaching with the IPTEIL method initially started as the author's individual project, but has gradually come to be recognized by the university administration on various subsequent occasions. They include "Osaka University Award for Outstanding Contributions to General Education" given to IPTEIL as many as 14 times, several FD (Faculty Development) seminars and official open classes in which I presented IPTEIL at the request of the university administration, along with the publication of a DVD by Osaka University Press that contains my classroom teaching with IPTEIL. In addition, the development of IPTEIL has recently been supported with a public research grant known as the Grants-in-Aid for Scientific Research provided by the Japan Society for the Promotion of Science. With some teachers beginning to apply this method to their classrooms (e.g., Orikasa, 2015), IPTEIL now seems to be going beyond a mere individual practice of my own.

114   *Practices of EIL education*

Background

As was mentioned in Chapter 4, the need for EIL has been recognized by Japanese ELT professionals, in some way or another, for nearly 90 years. However, the 20th century hardly saw the concept of EIL put into substantial teaching practice. Around the mid-1980s, there were some notable efforts by an EIL pioneer Larry E. Smith and his colleagues, evident in such works as Via and Smith (1983) and Weiner and Smith (1983), but those projects somehow did not provide further continuity. The question remained for a long time how we could not only raise the students' awareness in EIL, but also equip them with practical language skills and cross-cultural skills for EIL.

As for the present writer, though I had also attempted to incorporate the idea of EIL into my classrooms since the early 1980s, I was only able to achieve, till the end of the century, some sporadic success such as my radio program from 1989 to 1990 with non-native English-speaking guests, which was discussed in Chapter 8.

My chance for practicing EIL education in a more regular manner came with the installment of CALL (Computer-Assisted Language Learning) facilities with Internet access at my workplace, Osaka University, in the year 2000. I was assigned to a CALL classroom for one of my EFL classes, and saw it as an opportunity for practicing EIL. It may be noted here that in most EFL classes at Osaka University, just as at many other traditional universities in Japan, materials and methodologies are largely left to each teacher, which means I am relatively free to put into realization what I believe is best for my students.

In Japan, an EFL country where exposure to English in domestic life is rather limited, I regarded the Internet, on the rise at that time, as a major gateway to WE. I thought that I might be able to develop a concrete methodology for teaching EIL if I integrated multiple pedagogical concepts relevant to EIL in the Internet-connected CALL environment, which was an idea that gave birth to IPTEIL.

Description of the course

Curriculum

EFL classes at Osaka University, for first-year and second-year undergraduates, are basically arranged in accordance with each of the four linguistic skills.[1] Reading classes and listening classes consist of as many as 40 to 55 students, with speaking classes accommodating a little over 30, while writing classes only enroll 15 students. Each class meets once a week for 90 minutes, with the total of 15 sessions in a semester.[2] Most of the EFL classes are intended for EGP (English for General Purposes), though the concept of ESP (English for Specific Purposes) is also beginning to be incorporated into a part of the EFL curriculum. The majority of students are from Japan, with a limited number of international students chiefly from Asia. This university actually has a large number of students from abroad, but most of them are enrolled at the graduate level.

According to the results of TOEFL-ITP administered in 2013 for all first-year undergraduate students at this university, the average score was 490.36, with a wide range of 357 to 677 among 3,492 test-takers (Mori, 2015). Although TOEFL, dependent on the norms of American English, is not exactly a test of EIL, these scores provide some information on the proficiency level of the students.

I have mostly been assigned to reading classes, and they are largely where I have developed and employed the IPTEIL method, while also adding a bit of listening and speaking activities in an attempt to integrate multiple language skills. As to classroom equipment, IPTEIL takes place in CALL classrooms because of its extensive use of Internet news media from across the world.

Goals/objectives of IPTEIL

It is intended that by taking an IPTEIL class the students will:

- acquire identity as EIL users
- become familiar with the linguistic and cultural diversity of EIL
- gain cross-cultural awareness needed for communication in EIL
- nurture critical literacy to cope with the varieties of values in EIL
- acquire reading skills in EIL in combination with other skills

Teaching procedure

The basic classroom procedure for IPTEIL, though often with some modifications, is as follows:

1 The class (usually in a CALL classroom) watches a real-time English news video on a TV news station website, chosen by the teacher.
2 The teacher asks the students questions in English on the basic content of the news video, which are to be answered in English.
3 The class reads an article that corresponds to the news video, on the same TV news station website.
4 The teacher asks the students questions in English on the content of the article, requiring deeper understanding of the content than in number 2 earlier, which are to be answered in English.
5 The class reads another Internet news media chosen by the teacher, which represents social or cultural values different from the ones exhibited in the above media.
6 The teacher asks the students questions in English about the article in number 5, guiding their attention toward the diversity of values represented in the news media.
7 The teacher asks a few students to express their free opinions on the news topic. In case the student called upon is able to do so only in Japanese, the teacher orally translates the main points into English.
8 The class may repeat all or a part of the procedure above for another news topic, as far as time permits.

116 *Practices of EIL education*

All the questions and answers in this procedure consist of interactions between the teacher and the students. For reasons discussed later, I normally do not exercise peer interactions in this class.

Because of the use of real-time news as teaching materials, preparation for an IPTEIL class is often a race against time. As an IPTEIL teacher, I get up early and look at news media around the world on the Internet, whereby selecting appropriate news materials and thinking about questions to raise in class.

The English that I speak in class follows the production model of Japanese English (Hino, 2012a, 2012c) discussed in Chapter 4, which is a pedagogical policy explained to the students in the first session of the semester. For example, its phonology is characterized by relatively limited elision and linking, as a type of pronunciation that the students would find useful for enhancing intelligibility in interacting with NNS interlocutors in the future.

An important point to keep in mind for the teacher is to speak simple and comprehensible English, no matter what variety it may be. There is a gap between the difficult authentic news English and the students' current command of English. The teacher's English should function as a comprehensible input (Krashen, 1985) that bridges the gap between these two levels.

It may be noted that, while the language of instruction in this class is basically the target language (English), their native language (Japanese) is also used as an auxiliary aid, depending on the students' proficiency level. While the positive role of the first language in second/foreign language learning is not really unique to learners in Japan (cf. Widdowson, 1978; Cook, 2010), excluding the native language is especially counterproductive here with respect to the Japanese pedagogical beliefs in translation that have been formulated through their history of over a thousand years of practice in translating Chinese into Japanese (Hino, 1992a). Sociolinguistic aspects like this should not be neglected, since it is a central idea of EIL philosophy that teaching methodologies should be compatible with local values (McKay, 2002, 2003; McKay and J. Brown, 2016).

With a view to the emphasis on real-time experience in IPTEIL classes, no obligatory homework is given, though the students are encouraged to continue to watch and read daily news in English outside the classes.

Grades are based on class participation (50 percent) and the final examination (50 percent). The exam usually asks the students to write their comments in English on one of the recent newspaper articles provided by the teacher. Those articles are not the ones used in class, but are selected from the latest reports on the news topics discussed in previous sessions. Since IPTEIL focuses on real-life tasks as much as possible, the kind of exams that require inauthentic tasks, such as cloze tests, would lack "validity" for these classes, although cloze tests are certainly useful in some other educational contexts.

Teaching materials

Materials for IPTEIL are not textbooks but authentic materials, chiefly TV news videos and electronic newspapers available in real time on the Internet. The use of these resources, spoken or written in WE with their diversity of linguistic norms and cultural values, is one of the features of this teaching method. Examples of those news media are given in the following subsections, with some discussion of their significance from EIL perspectives.

TV news on the Internet from across the world

TV English news used in my classes, available on the Internet, include *CNN* (U.S.), *BBC* (U.K.), *Channel NewsAsia* (Singapore), *NDTV* (India), *ABS-CBN* (the Philippines), *KTN* (Kenya), and *NHK World* (Japan).

CNN and *BBC* news are news media with their dominant influence worldwide, the magnitude of which cannot be neglected irrespective of the relative de-emphasis on the U.S. and Britain in EIL education. *Channel NewsAsia* from Singapore, with reporters from various parts of Asia speaking their own varieties of English, extensively covers Asian news. Interactions between non-native speakers of English frequently occur in *Channel NewsAsia*, such as a dialogue between a Singaporean anchorperson and a Sri Lankan reporter, demonstrating authentic examples of typical EIL communication. *NDTV* and *ABS-CBN* are valuable sources of spoken Asian Englishes, representing Indian English and Philippine English, respectively. *KTN* demonstrates a variety of English in Africa, a region that Japanese are especially unfamiliar with, along with its social and cultural backgrounds. As shown in the classic study by Smith and Bisazza (1982), exposure to varieties of English is one of the important keys to successful comprehension in EIL.

NHK World presents news from Japanese viewpoints, with emphasis on domestic news, read by Japanese announcers. In terms of EIL, it is particularly useful for students to learn how to express their own culture in English. The English spoken by the Japanese anchors can generally serve as samples of good Japanese English, though with some disappointment at their occasional unnecessary imitation of American sociolinguistic norms, such as first-name calling between the anchors and some reporters.

In the 2000s, when news videos on the Internet were still limited, I usually videotaped news programs from satellite TV broadcasts for use in IPTEIL classes, in spite of time lags. I had to be also careful about copyright issues in using recorded TV programs in class. These problems have been solved thanks to the increase of news videos posted on TV station websites.

Electronic newspapers from around the world

In addition to reading the TV news station websites such as *CNN* and *Channel NewsAsia*, other electronic newspapers read in my IPTEIL classes include *Al Arabiya* (UAE), *The Jerusalem Post* (Israel), *Dawn* (Pakistan), *The Times of India* (India), *Bangkok Post* (Thailand), *Philippine Daily Inquirer* (the Philippines), *The Korea Herald* (Korea), *People's Daily* (China), *The Standard* (Hong Kong SRA, China), *Taipei Times* (Taiwan), *Hurriyet* (Turkey), *Ekathimerini* (Greece), *DW* (Germany),

118   *Practices of EIL education*

The Point (Gambia), *The Rio Times* (Brazil), *Pravda* (Russia), *The Globe and Mail* (Canada), and *Sydney Morning Herald* (Australia), among many others.

The use of these multiple news media provides a wide variety of viewpoints, which allows students to learn that the same phenomenon appears differently when looked at from divergent angles. Although there may not be significant grammatical or syntactical differences across these media worldwide, they nevertheless represent the cultural diversity of EIL.

As to such controversial problems as the Israeli-Palestinian conflict, it is particularly important to introduce the students to "the other side of the story." Comparing and contrasting the often-opposite opinions voiced in *The Jerusalem Post* and *Al Jazeera* on the Israeli-Palestinian conflict, for example, gives the students useful training in media literacy, global issues, and WE. This is a kind of experience that the students would not gain if the class only resorted to American media such as *CNN*. Reading Islamic media such as *Al Jazeera* is especially symbolic of EIL education, as the cultural basis of teaching English has long been associated with the Judeo-Christian tradition.

Comparing viewpoints in different media

Here is an example of comparing viewpoints in different media, from my recent IPTEIL class. In early June 2017, several Arab nations cut their diplomatic ties with Qatar. In my class on June 9, we read the coverage of this news in *Al Arabiya* (UAE), *Al Jazeera* (Qatar), and *Tehran Times* (Iran).

In the following articles, *Al Arabiya*, a UAE-based media often regarded as reflecting the positions of Saudi Arabia, focuses on the accusation on Qatar, while *Al Jazeera*, Qatar's flagship media, speaks for its country:

> Saudi Arabia, the United Arab Emirates, Egypt and Bahrain have collectively designated 59 individuals and 12 institutions that have financed terrorist organizations and received support from Qatar.
>
> (*Al Arabiya*, June 9, 2017)[3]

> Qatar will never surrender to the pressure being applied by its Arab neighbours and won't change its independent foreign policy to resolve disputes that have put the region on edge, Qatar's foreign minister has told Al Jazeera.
>
> (*Al Jazeera*, June 9, 2017)[4]

On the other hand, *Tehran Times*, a major English newspaper in Iran, sees the turmoil from its own perspective while basically siding with Qatar, calling it a business chance for Iranian companies:

> The condition in Qatar has created an opportunity for the Iranian food industry to embark on supplying products to the Persian Gulf nation. . . . food shipments sent from Iran can reach Qatar in 12 hours.
>
> (*Tehran Times*, June 9, 2017)[5]

By comparing articles such as the above, students learn that the same event looks very differently, with varied interpretations, depending on what angle is chosen. EIL represents a diversity of political, social, and cultural perspectives around the world, which often becomes evident by comparing their news media. In this particular example, the fact that Saudi Arabia, UAE, and Qatar are all Arab nations with Sunni Muslim majorities while Iran is a Shia-Muslim-dominated Persian nation also helps eradicate oversimplified stereotypes such as the conflicts between Arabs and Persians as well as between Sunnis and Shiites.

What is important in this classroom activity is to critically examine the messages from each source, always keeping in mind that any news media is inevitably biased in one way or another. Users of EIL, who have to wade through a vast diversity of values, may easily be lost unless they establish their own critical thinking while maintaining openness and flexibility for understanding different cultures. Nurturing critical literacy should be regarded as an indispensable part of EIL training.

It is also imperative for the teacher to exercise cultural sensitivity in the classroom. Political and religious issues are especially subtle by nature, and teachers always have to be careful not to inadvertently offend anyone in class, while exposing the students to a wide variety of views.

Relevant pedagogical concepts

As its name suggests, IPTEIL (Integrated Practice in Teaching English as an International Language) is an attempt to synthesize the teaching of EIL with other relevant pedagogical concepts. IPTEIL takes a form of Content-Based Instruction with the use of daily news for media literacy education in the promotion of critical thinking. Students are expected to nurture Learner Autonomy by experiencing in this class how to utilize authentic materials available in their daily life. They are also required to think globally (Global Education) and to use a combination of reading, listening, and speaking skills (Integrated Approach). This teaching method also shows one possible way of making effective use of the CALL (Computer-Assisted Language Learning) system. Above all, IPTEIL allows the students to learn by participating in the real world of EIL users, an approach that goes in line with the notion known as Legitimate Peripheral Participation in a Community of Practice.

In the following, some of these educational concepts and their relevance to EIL are discussed.

Legitimate Peripheral Participation in a Community of Practice

IPTEIL is a holistic approach to the teaching of EIL, aimed at involving the students in authentic EIL tasks. A central notion in IPTEIL, among others, is Legitimate Peripheral Participation in a Community of Practice (Lave & Wenger, 1991), a constructivist concept of learning chiefly associated with the neo-Vygotskian school of thought (e.g., Lantolf, 2000). An aspect of this theory

120 *Practices of EIL education*

particularly relevant to IPTEIL is its focus on "learning in doing," or "situated learning" in which the learner performs authentic tasks in a real-life environment.

In my IPTEIL classes, students watch and read real-time news given in WE, and then discuss those news in their own English, involving the teacher, Japanese students, and, as the case may be, international students. These activities have been chosen for this class, mainly because tasks that most EIL users perform daily are certain to include watching TV news, reading newspapers, and talking about them. They are common-core tasks for all EIL users regardless of their individual backgrounds. Also, the Internet is a major gateway to WE for students in Japan, where intra-national use of English is quite limited.

An IPTEIL class is intended to be a part of the real-life community of EIL, providing the students with opportunities for Legitimate Peripheral Participation in a Community of Practice in EIL (Hino, 2003b). The mode of participation is "legitimate" in the sense that it is authentic, as the primary reason for the use of real-time news in this class. It is also "peripheral" because no serious results will be brought about even when the students make mistakes, which is the kind of environment that the students need as novices. Through this participation process, the learners acquire new identity as members of the Community of Practice in EIL.

In the learning and teaching of EIL, as was discussed in Chapter 4, a minute description of target models is not available, at least thus far. Generally speaking, when it is difficult to specify a detailed educational model, a holistic approach is more realistic than a discrete-point approach. In other words, a practical method in such a situation is to "learn by doing." This partly explains why the notion of Legitimate Peripheral Participation is useful for EIL.

Another factor that makes the Legitimate Peripheral Participation relevant to EIL education is that communication in EIL is essentially an area where firsthand experience is of vital importance. Mere deductive teaching of EIL, or simple provision of knowledge of EIL, may inadvertently promote cultural stereotyping, which would prove counterproductive for EIL communication. It is highly desirable for learners to have actual experience in the use of EIL, or at least a direct exposure to it.

Content-Based Instruction

Content-Based Instruction (CBI) aims to teach a language through actual content rather than to teach the language per se. Besides the practicality of "two for one," CBI adds meaning and substance to the students' language learning. IPTEIL, whereby the students learn global issues via English, may be classified as a form of CBI.

As discussed in Chapter 7, teachers trying to practice EIL often employ CBI, intentionally or unintentionally. The reasons for this tendency are the same as the significance of Legitimate Peripheral Participation mentioned in the previous subsection. That is, one is the lack of comprehensive description of educational target models that makes such a holistic approach realistic, and the other is the importance of direct experience in communication in EIL.

Media literacy education/critical thinking/critical literacy

In advocating "literacy-based curriculum," Kern (2000) redefines the meaning of second/foreign language teaching by highlighting critical literacy as its integral part: "Instructional objectives shift. . . . to the development of learners' ability to interpret and critically evaluate language use in a variety of spoken and written contexts" (pp. 304–305). This view of language teaching is shared with IPTEIL.

In my IPTEIL class, as was shown earlier, students learn to process information from multiple perspectives by comparing and contrasting various news media. EIL users need to establish themselves by thinking on their own, so that they will not be overwhelmed by the diversity of cultural values that they encounter.

Global Education

Drawing upon the definition provided in every issue of the newsletter of the JALT "Global Issues in Language Education" SIG, Global Education may be defined, in the context of language teaching, as education that aims at "enabling students to effectively acquire and use a foreign language while at the same time empowering them with the knowledge, skills and commitment required by world citizens for the solution of global problems." Global awareness in this regard is an essential component of EIL. The IPTEIL class, which gives the students opportunities to analyze global problems through real-time world news, is one effort to incorporate Global Education into the teaching of EIL.

Responses to IPTEIL

This section discusses the results of EIL education with IPTEIL, based on the evaluation by the university administration, feedback from the students, and reactions from classroom observers.

University awards

A biannual award known as the Osaka University Award for Outstanding Contributions to General Education was given to the classroom teaching with IPTEIL 14 times since Fall 2002, including 12 consecutive semesters from Spring 2006 to the final semester with this award system, Fall 2011. The Osaka University Award for Outstanding Contributions to General Education was decided every semester on the basis of the results of faculty evaluation questionnaire for students administered by the university, coupled with reviews by a faculty committee in charge of general education. Reasons for the award, cited

122 *Practices of EIL education*

by the university, included the following, showing that EIL aspects of IPTEIL were highly evaluated:

> Overwhelmingly popular among the students, as the classes introduce them to varieties of English, whereby nurturing multiple perspectives in analyzing world news.
>
> (For Spring Semester, 2006. Translation mine)
> (Institute for Higher Education Research
> and Practice, 2010, p. 109)

> Gained recommendation from overwhelmingly many students, by introducing them to the diversity of English and leading them to analyze news from multiple perspectives, through activities such as comparing views of various news media real time.
>
> (For Fall Semester, 2006. Translation mine)[6]

"Varieties of English," "the diversity of English," and "multiple perspectives," found in the above evaluations, are key concepts of EIL and WE. Thus, a major national university in the Expanding Circle endorses the teaching of EIL, backed also by the students themselves. This fact should be encouraging for EIL educators.

Feedback from students

I regularly administer a survey on my own toward the end of each semester, independent of the official questionnaire run by the university, in all of my classes to obtain direct feedback from my students. Table 9.1 shows the results of a questionnaire administered most recently in five IPTEIL classes in July 2017. The original questionnaire, which is to be answered anonymously, is written in Japanese. Only the results of questions that are specifically relevant to EIL are listed in the table.

On the whole, the responses seem to indicate, along with the similar results of an earlier survey administered in 2010 and reported in Hino (2012a), that IPTEIL is largely producing its intended results in preparing the learners for EIL communication especially in cross-cultural aspects, at least as far as the students' perception goes.

As a main goal of IPTEIL, Questions 1 and 2 concern the learning of socio-cultural perspectives of EIL, "international understanding" and "the diversity of values" respectively, both of which received dominantly positive evaluations from the students.

Question 3 regards the improvement in linguistic skills, focusing here on reading skills as an official aim of the courses, though the responses are dependent on the subjective judgments by the students themselves. While this question garnered favorable answers from two-thirds of the respondents, it also met negative reactions from nearly 10 percent. These results suggest that IPTEIL

IPTEIL 123

Table 9.1 Results of a semester-end questionnaire on IPTEIL classes, July 2017

	Questions	Choices	Number of responses	Percentage (%)
1	This class has been useful for improving my international understanding.	Strongly agree	107	54.3
		Agree	75	38.1
		Neutral	11	5.6
		Disagree	3	1.5
		Strongly disagree	1	0.5
2	This class has been useful for learning the diversity of values.	Strongly agree	88	44.4
		Agree	82	41.4
		Neutral	19	9.6
		Disagree	8	4.4
		Strongly disagree	1	0.5
3	This class has been useful for improving my reading skills in English.	Strongly agree	39	19.8
		Agree	94	47.7
		Neutral	45	22.8
		Disagree	14	7.1
		Strongly disagree	5	2.5
4	Hino's effort in this class is useful, in which he attempts to demonstrate samples of "good Japanese English," which is intended to be expressive of Japanese values as well as internationally intelligible.	Strongly agree	98	50.0
		Agree	74	37.8
		Neutral	23	11.7
		Disagree	1	0.5
		Strongly disagree	0	0.0

(N=198 [Question 2], 197 [Questions 1 and 3], 196 [Question 4])

in its current form is more effective in the learning of social and cultural aspects than that of conventional linguistic domains.

The overwhelmingly positive responses to Question 4 are significant in pursuing the idea of Japanese English discussed in Chapter 4, showing that Japanese English as a target model has a promising potential for ELT in Japan. Some students reflect, in the open-ended section of the questionnaire, that they

124   *Practices of EIL education*

benefitted from the positive presentation of my Japanese English in class, which gave them the feeling that Japanese English could be one of the varieties of English as a means of international communication.

Among numerous comments written in the open-ended sections in my original surveys and in the university's official surveys, for example, one emblematic opinion in the latter reads (July 2017):

> I was really impressed with the goals and policies of this class. I believe that many other students would probably agree with me. The proposal for internationally intelligible "Japanese English," the use of real-time materials which leads us to recognize that we are a part of the global community, and the classroom procedure that promotes critical thinking through Q & As between the teacher and the students – All these were distinctly different from any other type of foreign language learning. However, I think there was one thing that should be improved, though this may actually be a problem for students. That is, some students appeared to be sleepy, by being inactive when they were not called on by the teacher. . . . I felt sorry about this, as the content of the class itself was extremely useful.
>
> (In Japanese. Translation mine)

As in the above comment, many students seem to accurately understand the aims of IPTEIL. This remark also appropriately points to a weakness of this class, which will be taken up again in the following sections.

Feedback from class observers

Over the years, my IPTEIL classes have had many observers including university professors, English teachers from the junior high to college level, graduate students of language education, and some journalists. Teaching assistants, who are graduate students, also provide their comments on my teaching practice. The feedback from these class observers may be summarized as follows, divided into comments on the strengths and weaknesses of IPTEIL.

IPTEIL classes seem to be successful in:

- letting the students experience the real world of English by using real-time materials
- letting the students acquire multiple perspectives about what is happening in the world
- getting the students to be interested in global issues
- introducing the students to the use of authentic materials to learn English on their own
- giving the students chances to learn English in meaningful contexts

IPTEIL classes seem to be weak in:

- offering varieties of activity
- giving the students enough chances for production
- giving the students opportunities for peer interaction

These comments by the classroom observers are largely in line with the impressions by the students themselves. In addition, the fourth item in the "strengths" column implies that IPTEIL has a potential for developing Learner Autonomy, which is part of my original intention for this method as well, in the hope of directing the students toward lifelong learning.

The "weaknesses," also mentioned earlier in the student's comment, are discussed in the next section.

Limitations

As evident or implied in the feedback from students and class observers, one of the major limitations with the current IPTEIL is that this method is teacher-centered in its form, where the participation by the students tends to be more passive than active. Though this shortcoming may be somewhat inevitable due to the fact that IPTEIL has been developed primarily for reading classes, it would be still possible to argue that some student-to-student interactions should be introduced instead of concentrating on teacher-to-student interactions.

However, this problem highlights the essential difficulty for the Expanding Circle in an effort to redefine an English class as an opportunity for real-life use of the language rather than a place for mere simulation. In Japan, it is simply unusual to communicate in English among the Japanese. When Japanese students are told to speak English with their fellow students in class, they cannot find any reason to do so other than the fact that it is the teacher's order. Many students feel strange or uncomfortable talking with their friends in English, because it is really unnatural. This has been a serious limitation when I intend my class to be a part of the real-life community of EIL users, where the use of English should come with authentic necessity.

One solution to this problem is to have international students in class. My IPTEIL classes, for first-year and second-year undergraduates, have occasionally had foreign students, mostly from Asian countries such as Thailand, Vietnam, China, and Korea, although very limited in number since the majority of international students study at the graduate level. It has been my experience that the presence of even one foreign student, who creates the real necessity to communicate in EIL, dramatically changes the nature of an EIL class from inauthentic to authentic. If it becomes possible to have a substantial number of international students in class, group work then will be really meaningful.

126 *Practices of EIL education*

Hino and S. Oda (2015) in fact examined a possibility of introducing peer interactions to IPTEIL classes. Still, after a few trials in consultation with teachers experienced in such activities, I have decided to continue with the current procedure, at least for the time being, since the concentration on teacher–student interactions seems to be an efficient use of class time in the present context after all, due to several factors including the large class size.

An English class that comprises Japanese students, non-native English-speaking students from overseas, native English-speaking students, and the teacher as the leader would constitute an ideal community of practice in EIL, in which everyone could learn from one another (Hino, 2003b). For this vision to come true, a major educational reform will be necessary so that the university may involve international students in the ELT curriculum.

Actually, while such curriculum reform would not be easy for ELT classes, it is quite feasible to make use of content EMI (English-Medium Instruction) courses, in which both international and local students enroll, for the interactive learning of EIL. This project will be discussed in the next chapter.

Conclusion

Before closing this chapter, it should be added, as a good example to illustrate the nature of EIL education, that I have had a few native speakers in my IPTEIL classes, including a first-year student from New Zealand. It might appear strange for native English-speaking students to enroll in an officially EFL (English as a *Foreign* Language) class, but it is actually fortunate from an EIL perspective that this university has no system of exempting native-speaker students from EFL classes. They took my IPTEIL classes, living up to the principle of EIL education that learners of EIL include native speakers of English (Smith, 1978; Kubota, 2001). In class, they were exposed to varieties of English via news media around the world, and also had a lot of contact with Japanese English. At the end of the semester, the New Zealander student, for example, told me that it had been a fruitful cross-cultural experience for him.

For the past 34 years, I have been attempting to put the concept of EIL (Hino, 2001; Smith, 1976, 1978) into actual teaching practice for my college EFL classes in Japan. Among the several methodologies that I have devised for this purpose, IPTEIL seems to be one of the most successful so far, though this method should certainly be subject to constant review for improvement through reflective teaching, or more generally, reflective practice (Richards & Lockhart, 1994; Richards & Farrell, 2005). It is hoped that IPTEIL will serve as a concrete sample to be referred to, beyond the author's individual practice, for pedagogical realization of the idea of EIL.

Notes

1 This curriculum could be subject to change in the future.
2 Technically speaking, Osaka University now has a quarter system, but EFL classes are operated practically with a semester system by bundling two terms together.

3 Arab powers list 59 individuals as Qatar-linked terrorism supporters. https://english.alarabiya.net/en/News/gulf/2017/06/09/Arab-countries-release-list-of-terrorist-financiers-supported-by-Qatar.html (Accessed on June 9, 2017).
4 Qatar 'not prepared to change its foreign policy'. www.aljazeera.com/news/2017/06/qatar-fm-ready-surrender-170608142453812.html (Accessed on June 9, 2017).
5 Abdi, M. Billion-dollar Qatari food market on tap. www.tehrantimes.com/news/414020/Billion-dollar-Qatari-food-market-on-tap (Accessed on June 9, 2017).
6 Institute for Higher Education Research and Practice, Osaka University. Osaka Daigaku Kyotsukyoikusho jushosha: Heisei 18-nendo koki [Recipients of the Osaka University Award for Outstanding Contributions to General Education: Fall semester, 2006]. www.cep.osaka-u.ac.jp/ourwork/prize (Accessed on September 24, 2010).

10 Content and English as a Lingua Franca Integrated Learning (CELFIL)

Introduction

The main aim of this chapter is to present the following thesis. In the recent quest for EIL pedagogy, utilization of university EMI (English-Medium Instruction) courses for the purpose of EIL education is worth considering, as those classes, especially ones with the participation of international students, provide valuable opportunities for students to acquire communication skills in authentic EIL situations.

Teaching content subjects in English, be it psychology, physics, or engineering, used to be more exceptional than normal in the Expanding Circle. This is rapidly changing now. EMI has recently been promoted across the world by education ministries (such as the "Super Global Universities" scheme in Japan) as well as by universities themselves (Doiz, Lasagabaster, & Sierra, 2013; Jenkins, 2014; K. Murata, 2016; Fenton-Smith, Humphreys, & Walkinshaw, 2017).

Two major motives are cited for the increase of EMI as a global trend. One is to attract more international students by alleviating the burden of learning local languages, and the other is to help local students gain higher proficiency in English. Regarding the latter aspect, the present chapter views EMI as an opportunity of EIL education not only for local but also for international students.

There is evidence that EMI in higher education in Japan has been a place for learning EIL since its inception. One of the first EMI programs in higher education in Japan was a graduate program in civil engineering at Tokyo University launched in 1982,[1] where classes were taught in English and dissertations were also written in English. After completing the Ph.D. program in its infancy, Benito M. Pacheco, from the Philippines, became an associate professor in the same department in 1989. I interviewed him in the same year on a radio English language education program *English for Millions*, discussed in Chapter 8, for which I served as a lecturer.

In his contribution to the textbook for this radio program, Professor Pacheco wrote about his experience as a teacher in the graduate EMI program – "they are also learning English from me, and from the many non-Japanese students here" (Pacheco, in Hino, 1989a, p. 133). "They" refers to Japanese students, and the majority of "non-Japanese students" in this situation are non-native speakers of English. In other words, local students learned EIL in this EMI class through their interactions with the professor from the Outer Circle as well as with non-native English-speaking international students. Thus, the potential of EMI for the learning of EIL was already suggested 28 years ago.

Lack of authentic EIL interaction in EFL classes

As mentioned in the previous chapter, a serious limitation is perceived in attempts to teach EIL in regular EFL classes in many Expanding Circle countries, where most students share the same first language. In this respect, it is difficult to fully construct a "community of practice in EIL" (Hino, 2003b, p. 75) in classes consisting chiefly of local students. In Japan, for instance, where the use of Japanese is almost exclusively dominant, talking in English among fellow nationals is felt to be too artificial.

In fact, for Japanese students, peer interaction in English between them is only bizarre. In my IPTEIL class, for example, after watching and reading about news reports on how Japan's national soccer team fought a game right before the class, I asked the students to talk about this topic in pairs. Despite the fact that the majority of students were excited about this news, what they did in this pair work were only chuckling and giggling about the unnaturalness of talking in English between them. This is quite understandable in view of the fact that they had no real reason to discuss it in English. In short, interaction in English between Japanese students is simply inauthentic.

Moreover, even if students stopped chuckling and started to engage in pair work in English, there is still one major problem. That is, there is no guarantee that the English that grows out of interactions between Japanese students will be internationally intelligible. Extremely heavily Japanized English can be highly communicative when the interaction takes place between compatriots, while such English would be internationally incomprehensible.

It is clear that authentic interaction in EIL/ELF is essential especially for the learning of communication strategies such as accommodation (Jenkins, 2000, 2007) and negotiation of meaning (Seidlhofer, 2009, 2011), which are of crucial importance for successful EIL/ELF communication. So then, what can we do for students in Japan, or other parts of the Expanding Circle? One solution nowadays is the use of communication technologies, as seen in CCDL (Cross-Cultural Distance Learning) at Waseda University, which connects Japanese students with their counterparts in several Asian countries through TV conferences and online chats.

Another approach is to send students to places outside their university campus where authentic interaction in EIL takes place. One such example is the GCEP (Global Cultural Exchange Program) (Smith, 2014), formerly known as the GCP (Global Challenge Program) in Hawaii, started by the late Larry E. Smith, an American pioneer in the field who is responsible for the very concept of EIL (Smith, 1983). Exploiting the multiethnic and multicultural environment of Hawaii,

130   *Practices of EIL education*

the GCEP offers a variety of activities outside of classrooms where the authentic use of EIL is required, ranging from tourist interviews to job shadowing.

In my observation in Hawaii in 2012, the job-shadowing tasks in the GCEP seemed particularly useful. Those work experiences included jobs such as a water park staff member, an assistant in a child day-care center, and a hotel clerk, all of which involved daily interactions with speakers of WE from various parts of the world (Hino, 2015a).

To provide students with opportunities to learn EIL in an authentic environment, is there any other available method, perhaps with an easy access for students? Actually, though often unnoticed, an ideal learning environment for EIL exists on many university campuses in Japan today, namely, EMI classes. The next section examines EMI classes as an opportunity for learning EIL.

CELFIL: CLIL for ELF in EMI classes

By definition, the primary aim of EMI classes is the teaching of content, such as economics, biology, and technology. However, they are also highly useful as a place for learning EIL. EMI classes are where international students often gather, the majority of whom are non-native speakers of English. Instructors may also be non-native or native speakers of English. Many of those courses are open to local students as well, giving them chances to mix with international students. Thus, interactions in EMI classes occur mostly between non-native speakers of English, which is a typical EIL situation. The authentic EIL environment in EMI courses makes it possible for students to learn communication skills such as accommodation and negotiation.

In terms of the learning of EIL, EMI in higher education naturally integrates three of the pedagogical approaches to EIL (Hino, 2013), that is, "exposure to the diversity of EIL," "content-based approach to EIL," and "participation in the community of EIL users." As for domains of language use, EMI classes at universities are also useful for learning academic ELF/EIL (Mauranen, 2012).

My intention, therefore, is to take advantage of EMI classes for helping students learn not only the content but also EIL skills by remodeling those courses with the addition of the concepts of CLIL (Content and Language Integrated Learning) (Coyle et al., 2010; Y. Watanabe, Ikeda, & Izumi, 2011) and EIL. As such, I call this approach CELFIL (Content and ELF Integrated Learning) (Hino, 2015b, 2017a, b). Here, I have employed the term "ELF" rather than "EIL," partly for the purpose of highlighting the interactive aspects of this pedagogy.

There have recently been a number of studies, chiefly by ELF scholars, on the linguistic and sociolinguistic aspects of EMI (e.g., Smit, 2010; Mauranen, 2012; Gotti, 2014; Kirkpatrick, 2014; Jenkins, 2014; Iino & K. Murata, 2016). However, methodology for utilizing EMI classes for the simultaneous teaching of content and ELF is still largely unheard of. A concept that Smit (2013) refers to as ICELF (Integrating Content and ELF) seems to share some philosophy with CELFIL, but thus far it appears that ICELF is intended more as implicit ideals than concrete pedagogy.

Principles of CELFIL

In order to gain clues for developing methodologies for CELFIL, I have observed numerous EMI classes, mainly in Japan, and interviewed some teachers and students, along with my practices in my own EMI classes. In the course of this research, a number of principles have surfaced for CELFIL, some of which are summarized in the following subsections under administrative and pedagogical categories.

Administrative principles

If the learning of English as well as the content is intended for EMI classes, policymakers and administrators should encourage or ensure the following:

1   *Collaboration between content teachers and EIL experts*

    This is highly important, just as with ESP (English for Specific Purposes) education (e.g., Fukui, Noguchi, & N. Watanabe, 2009), unless the EMI class is taught by an EIL education expert. However, with respect to the difficulty of interdepartmental cooperation at traditional universities in countries such as Japan, such interdisciplinary team work is easier said than done.

2   *Ready access to EMI classes both for local and international students*

    Local students are often found to shy away from EMI classes in Japan, missing a valuable learning opportunity. On the other hand, there are also EMI classes at Japanese universities taken solely by local students, due to reasons such as a separate curriculum and the lack of information for international students. Both local and international students should benefit from sharing their learning in the same EMI classroom, constituting a community of practice in EIL.

3   *No discrimination against NNS in the employment or assignment of EMI teachers*

    Some university administrators seem to assume that native speakers of English are preferable as EMI teachers. From EIL perspectives, such native-speakerism only exhibits misunderstanding of the nature of English for international communication.

Pedagogical principles

EMI teachers, if wishing to help their students not only with the content but also with English, should make efforts to pursue the following:

1   *Activities to utilize authentic EIL environments in EMI classes*

    As one example, a classroom activity that makes the best of a variety of student demographics for the learning of content and EIL is presented in the next section.

132   Practices of EIL education

2   *Refraining from identifying EMI pedagogy with Anglo-American pedagogy*

Just as the teaching of English has so often been confused with the spreading of Anglo-American culture, it seems to be unconsciously believed in Japan that EMI classes should employ methodologies used in American universities. When one attends a faculty development (FD) seminar on EMI in Japan, what he or she is often introduced to is how content subjects are taught at universities in the U.S. From the viewpoint of EIL, it needs to be reminded that "English" does not have to be accompanied by Anglo-American ways of life.

3   *Intercultural negotiation for appropriate pedagogy in EMI classes*

While the employment of "locally-appropriate pedagogy," in place of the imposition of Anglo-American methodology, has been a major tenet for EIL education, its premise is homogeneity among the students, or including the teacher. On the other hand, when participants in EMI represent a cultural diversity, the class should try to come up with a certain "intercultural pedagogy," acceptable to all students as well as to the teacher at the intersection of cultural differences. Recently in my own EMI class with Japanese and Chinese students along with an American TA, for example, there has been an interesting case of negotiations for intercultural pedagogy, seeking reconciliation between East Asian beliefs in harmony and American values in argumentation.

4   *Consideration of pedagogical tradition in each disciplinary field*

Each content subject has its own pedagogical tradition, which must be taken into account in order to produce successful educational results. For example, mathematics classes in Japan have traditionally been teacher-centered, with rare use of group work. In view of such a conventional practice, certain measures need to be skillfully worked out before introducing group work to those classes.

5   *Care for international students when the local language is additionally used in an EMI class*

As suggested by many studies, including ELF research on translanguaging such as Cogo (2012) and ELT theories on translation from Widdowson (1978) to Cook (2010), it is a useful strategy not to cling to the mono-lingual use of English. While for EFL classes this usually means the utilization of the local language, in EMI classes composed of both local and international students, care should be taken for the latter who may not be proficient in the local language. In such a case, measures such as adding translation into English save the international students from isolation.

6   *EMI teachers as role models of EIL users*

Though EMI classes are normally envisaged as having at least a sizable number of international students, those consisting only of local students are actually quite common. While international students' participation is desirable in order to create an authentic EIL environment in the classroom, even EMI classes with local students can be useful for CELFIL. That is, EMI teachers may serve as roles models of EIL users for their students. For instance, in my research (Hino, 2017b), a Japanese professor teaching an undergraduate course in education in English, taken only by Japanese students, was found to be regarded by enrollees as demonstrating how a Japanese person may speak English. A Singaporean professor for an undergraduate Asian studies class, also comprising Japanese students only, likewise proved to be respected as an encouraging example of a non-Anglophone speaker of English for international communication (cf. Ng, 2018).

OSGD (Observed Small Group Discussion): an activity for CELFIL

This section presents an activity that has grown out of my attempts at CELFIL in my graduate (master's level) EMI class in language education, which I have named OSGD (Observed Small Group Discussion) (Hino, 2017c, 2018). Though developed for CELFIL in EMI classes, OSGD as a "technique" could be combined also with some other approaches and methods of language teaching, as in the classic three-layer framework of "approach, method, and technique" (Anthony, 1963) where CELFIL is classified as an "approach."

Procedure for OSGD

The basic procedure for OSGD is as follows:

1   The teacher organizes one small group (preferably consisting of international diversity), and has other students surround the discussion group and observe their discussion. The ideal number of discussants is usually four, although it is not restricted to this number.
2   The teacher allows the discussion to continue for 10 to 15 minutes.
3   The teacher urges the observers to pay attention to a range of aspects, from the content of the discussion to the use of communication strategies.
4   After the discussion/observation session, the teacher leads a whole-class discussion, in which the discussants and the observers together reflect on the content of the discussion as well as the use of communication strategies. The teacher provides feedback in the whole-class discussion.

In the next OSGD session, the instructor sees to it that students take turns in the roles of discussants and observers. The discussants are encouraged to apply the skills and knowledge that they acquired as observers to their discussion. The observers are advised to further reflect on their experiences as previous discussants during their observation of the discussion.

134   *Practices of EIL education*

Practices of OSGD

In my graduate class in language education, thanks to the diversity of student demographics, it has been easy to set up an authentic EIL situation among the discussants, such as a group of two Chinese and two Japanese students, or one with an Iranian student, a Chinese student, and two Japanese students.

Through observations, reflections, and discussions, students learn communication skills in EIL as well as the content. In my class thus far, we picked up, from the small group discussions, examples of accommodation (Jenkins, 2000, 2007), negotiation of meaning (Seidlhofer, 2009, 2011), translanguaging (Cogo, 2012; Jenkins, 2015b), back-channels, turn-taking, and non-verbal cues, all of which are important conversational strategies in EIL. We have shared observations and reflections on those points with each other in the whole-class discussions, while I have attempted as a teacher to offer useful comments and to summarize key issues.

Rationale of OSGD

With respect to the notion of "intercultural pedagogy" as one of the pedagogical principles of CELFIL, OSGD is where the teacher-centered Confucian tradition of East Asia is typically required to make concessions to a more student-centered approach. Rationale of OSGD includes the following:

1   *Students learn to deal with the fluidity and dynamism of EIL by experiencing authentic international communication*

As mentioned in Chapter 1, ELF studies since the "ELF2" stage (Jenkins, 2015b) have emphasized the fluid nature of EIL. Hence, along with the teaching of content, CELFIL is required to train students to interact in dynamic EIL situations in a flexible manner through collaboration with their interlocutors. In this regard, OSGD is an activity in which students can learn strategies to communicate in fluid and dynamic EIL, such as accommodation and negotiation.

2   *Students learn autonomously how to communicate in EIL through observations and reflections*

OSGD makes use of observations and reflections by students themselves, enhancing the autonomous learning of EIL. OSGD in this respect is a type of reflective learning (Schön, 1983; Farrell, 2015), as an act of making sense of one's experience in search of future directions.

3   *The teacher is able to provide appropriate feedback at a proper time*

An inherent problem with conventional small-group discussions is the difficulty for the teacher to adequately monitor the students' interactions. In an ordinary small group discussion, the teacher goes around the classroom to watch discussion groups one after another, trying to give advice when necessary. Unfortunately, however, as he or she can only have a sporadic look at each group, the chance is rather slim for the teacher to be able to provide appropriate feedback at the right time. As a result, the teacher often ends up throwing the students into "sink-or-swim" situations. OSGD is a solution to such a problem. Instead of holding concurrent group discussion sessions, the teacher organizes just one small discussion group, allowing the rest of the class including the teacher himself/herself to observe its entire discussion. Thus, OSGD enables the teacher to provide appropriate and timely feedback to all students.

Conclusion

With the increase of EMI in higher education worldwide, CELFIL as an approach to modify EMI classes for the learning of EIL should be a promising endeavor for EIL education in the Expanding Circle. However, as CLIL for EIL, collaboration between content teachers and EIL experts is essential for CELFIL. For instance, it would be rather difficult for a law or a dentistry professor to use OSGD in their EMI classes without support from an EIL professional. In fact, I have been able to practice OSGD because I happen to be a content teacher and an EIL teacher at the same time.

Various difficulties in such interdisciplinary and interdepartmental cooperation have already been experienced by those involved in the teaching of ESP. There are both administrative and psychological problems that prevent such collaboration. However, it is certain that those are the barriers that need to be overcome for the cause of EIL education.

Note

1 Eigo niyoru kogakukei-daigakuin kyoiku [Graduate education in engineering in English]. *The Asahi Shimbun*, April 18, Evening edition (Tokyo), p. 5, 1987.

Conclusion

11 Toward the ownership of English for the Expanding Circle

Introduction

After all the theories and practices discussed in this book, how could the ownership of English, as an eventual goal of EIL education, become possible for the Expanding Circle beyond academic discourses and classroom efforts? The final chapter tackles this ultimate macro-sociolinguistic inquiry into the theme of the present volume.

The chance for learners of English to be true users of English will, in the end, amount to the question of feasibility for original varieties of English for the Expanding Circle. This notion is particularly salient in Japan, dating back to lexicographer H. Saito (1928), who called for the Japanization of English 90 years ago. The Japanese Association for Asian Englishes (JAFAE), established in 1997, lists the study of "Japanese English as a legitimate variety" in its official website as one of its seven main research objectives, thereby producing significant works on the topic such as Honna (2008) and Suenobu (2010). After all, owning an endonormative variety of English is the only way toward the full realization of what Nishiyama (1995) called "speaking English with a Japanese mind."

A website provided by Routledge as a supplement to Jenkins (2015a), a popular resource book on ELF, cites Hino (2012c) regarding my proposal for the models of Japanese English, and poses a discussion question, "Why do you think scholars have abandoned the description of new 'varieties' of English in European Expanding Circle contexts while the identification of 'varieties' seems to remain a research goal in Asia as Hino exemplified?"[1] Although the present volume will not attempt to directly answer this question, which involves a number of complex factors such as the concept of nation-state, traditional Asian values, and features of ELF as a school of thought, it is true that the idea of Expanding Circle varieties of English has been more ardently pursued in Asia than in Europe, as evident with China (Pan, 2015) and Japan, or broadly including Russia (Proshina & Eddy, 2016).

140   *Conclusion*

Inapplicability of conventional WE theories to the Expanding Circle

The path to the ownership of English for the Expanding Circle, severing the seemingly eternal cycle of mimicking native-speaker English, requires a considerably different approach from that of conventional WE theories tailored to the Outer Circle.

Unlike with the emergence of new Englishes in the postcolonial environment of the Outer Circle, indigenization of English in the Expanding Circle calls for active efforts by Expanding Circle users of English, just like the act of "customization" by computer users, to accommodate the language to their own cultural values. While the development of Outer Circle varieties has also been promoted partly as a result of conscious and painstaking endeavors such as the ones by creative authors of postcolonial literatures as well as by WE scholars themselves, it has essentially gone through a more or less inevitable process (cf. Mufwene, 2001; Schneider, 2007), which would not naturally happen in the Expanding Circle.

It should be noted that it is in some cases even counterproductive to directly apply WE theories, developed primarily for the intra-national use of English in the Outer Circle, to Expanding Circle situations. For example, if we mistakenly apply Schneider's Dynamic Model (2003, 2007), a theory for postcolonial Englishes, to non-postcolonial varieties such as China English and Japanese English, it would only appear that those varieties are presently much too primitive in their development to be used as models. Such inappropriate application would be misleading for the analysis of Expanding Circle Englishes used for international, rather than domestic, communication.

In the case of the Outer Circle, varieties of English have emerged, as a result of, and for the purpose of, the use of English in the intra-national discourse community. Those Outer Circle Englishes are also put to use in the international discourse community, though often with some modifications or accommodations. On the other hand, in the Expanding Circle, varieties of English develop as a result of, and for the purpose of, the use of English in the international discourse community, with the intra-national discourse community hardly playing any significant role. This sociolinguistic difference between the two circles in regard to discourse communities is crucial. That is, unlike in mainstream WE theories suited for the Outer Circle, intra-national use of English should not be regarded as a prerequisite for the development of Expanding Circle varieties.

A roadmap to original Englishes for the Expanding Circle

How might pedagogical efforts presented in this book help achieve the ultimate goal of equipping Expanding Circle users of English with the kind of English capable of expressing their own values as well as being internationally communicative?

Toward the ownership of English 141

In discussing the developmental process of Japanese English as an example from the Expanding Circle, let us once again refer to an influential theory on the evolution of postcolonial Englishes, the Dynamic Model by Schneider (2003, 2007). This theory illustrates the developmental stages of postcolonial Englishes in accordance with the following five phases:

Phase 1: Foundation
Phase 2: Exonormative stabilization
Phase 3: Nativization
Phase 4: Endonormative stabilization
Phase 5: Differentiation

Though this process has often been cited in analyzing the development of Englishes in the Expanding Circle, Schneider himself has made it clear that he has no intention of applying this theory to Expanding Circle Englishes (Schneider, 2014). In fact, while a highly useful theory for postcolonial Englishes in the Outer Circle, and the Inner Circle in some cases, the Dynamic Model should not be expected to account for the future of Englishes in the Expanding Circle. The Dynamic Model is based on various sociolinguistic factors that are nearly non-existent in the Expanding Circle, such as interactions between colonizers and the colonized, along with intra-national communication in English.

As to the lack of intra-national use of English in the Expanding Circle, it may be counter-argued that English is increasingly present even in countries such as Japan. However, it is not an issue in our present discussion, because "intra-national" here does not refer to geographical location, but is synonymous with "between compatriots." Even today, Japanese people normally do not speak or write English among themselves, but use it only when the communicative event involves some international participants.

Below, I illustrate a roadmap for the creation and diffusion of endonormative Englishes in the Expanding Circle, which was initially presented in Hino (2012d) with Japanese English as an example. Though this roadmap is partly hypothetical, the Expanding Circle would have to go through such a process, rather than the one described in the Dynamic Model, if it desires to have original Englishes capable of representing its own cultures while being internationally communicative. The roadmap, or a socio-educational vision for Englishes in the Expanding Circle, consists of the following seven phases:

Phase 1: Advocacy of EIL philosophy
Phase 2: Efforts to put EIL philosophy into practice
Phase 3: Design of partial models of original English
Phase 4: Design of relatively detailed models of original English
Phase 5: Incorporation of the models of original English into the national curriculum
Phase 6: Birth of users of original English
Phase 7: Continuous development of the models of original English

142 Conclusion

Since sociolinguistic environments in the Expanding Circle are by no means monolithic, there are limitations in applying this roadmap, primarily based on situations surrounding Japanese English, to the whole Expanding Circle. Especially, as it assumes a centralized education system, this vision would be more relevant, for example, to China English, Taiwanese English, Korean English, Indonesian English, and Thai English than to German English, Belgian English, and Finnish English. Most typically, with the major influence of education on the users of English in Japan, the development of Japanese English will have to be socio-educational in nature.

A socio-educational vision for Englishes in the Expanding Circle

Unlike the Dynamic Model, which is already verifiable to a considerable extent in reference to existing varieties, this roadmap is basically a "vision" or a "prospect" at the moment. On the other hand, it is not entirely hypothetical, as the first three phases have already occurred in Japan. The seven phases are described in the following subsections, with Japanese English as an example, which are hoped to serve as guideposts on the rocky road to the true ownership of English.

Phase 1: advocacy of EIL philosophy

At this first stage, the philosophy of de-Anglo-Americanized EIL is advocated through books, papers, lectures, the Internet, and other media, with a claim for the significance of original English for the Expanding Circle.

Phase 2: efforts to put EIL philosophy into practice

In this phase, teachers and researchers of ELT as well as some Japanese learners and users of English explore how the philosophy of EIL might be practiced in a concrete manner. Research on the international intelligibility, comprehensibility, and interpretability of varieties of English (Smith & C. Nelson, 1985) is conducted. Those users of English who are conscious of EIL philosophy produce some original innovations irrespective of native-speaker models. There are also accidental innovations, though limited, even by native speaker-oriented users of English. Teachers influenced by EIL philosophy also reflect on their own experiences in international communication about what kind of English has been actually effective in communicating their thoughts.

Phase 3: design of partial models of original English

By synthesizing relevant research results, innovations by users of English, and reflections on one's own experiences in international communication, some teachers who are action researchers at the same time come up with partial and tentative models of original English for their classes. Proposals are made on those models by way of a limited number of conference presentations and publications.

Phase 4: design of relatively detailed models of original English

Collaborations among teachers/researchers, as well as their individual efforts, more widely take place, which lead to the devising of relatively detailed models of original English. Conference presentations, lectures, papers, and books on the models are frequently produced in this phase.

Phase 5: incorporation of the models of original English into the national curriculum

At this stage, models of original English are gradually incorporated by the education ministry into the Courses of Study, or the national curriculum that defines the content of ELT. Textbooks for the public school system are required to reflect those models. As a result, school teachers at large refer to the models of original English in their classes. Many instructors at the university level and teachers at private sectors also employ those models. The models of original English are adopted for entrance exam questions for high schools and universities, giving a major impact on ELT from elementary to senior high schools as a backwash effect.

Phase 6: birth of users of original English

With the adoption of the models of original English in most schools and many university classes, full users of original English gradually emerge.

Phase 7: continuous development of the models of original English

As the users of original English engage in international communication, their experiences reveal the need for further development and continuous revision of the models, which will work as feedback to teachers and researchers, subsequently to the education ministry. Models of original English will see constant and continuous development.

The processes explored in this section will not automatically happen, but will be dependent on deliberate endeavors. What is envisaged here is a bottom-up reform movement in education, which is expected to ultimately bring about major changes in governmental policies.

As for Japan as an example, Japanese English is currently at Phase 3, with a limited number of teachers of English presently making attempts to design partial models of Japanese English (e.g., Hino, 2012a; Suenobu, 2010; Tachibana,

144   *Conclusion*

2012). Transition from Phase 3 to Phase 5 is expected to be especially crucial, requiring a great deal of efforts and cooperation by many.

It may be noted that the plural form "models" is used where possible throughout the present chapter in support of diversity, since an imposition of one single model as "the" norm is against the basic philosophy of EIL.

It should be recognized as one of the missions of academic and professional organizations in EIL such as IAWE (the International Association of World Englishes) and JAFAE (the Japanese Association for Asian Englishes) to promote such reform efforts toward the equality of all users of English. Unless we act, the Expanding Circle will not be able to get out of the dark ages, in a foreseeable future, of merely imitating native speakers like parrots. Indeed, this issue concerns fundamental human rights. That is, being entitled to your own variety of English to express yourself is to gain freedom for your soul in international communication.

Conclusion

For the purpose of liberating the Expanding Circle from conventional native-speakerism, this book has proposed a theoretical foundation for the concept of EIL, or de-Anglo-Americanized varieties of English for international communication, followed by discussions of its pedagogical application to the teaching of English, and finally closing with socio-educational prospects for the future. Japan was taken up as a primary example, though often with wider implications for the Expanding Circle, especially for that of Asia.

The introductory chapter (Chapter 1) provided an overview of the whole theme, in which the need for EIL education was discussed with reference to the sociolinguistic environment of the Expanding Circle.

In Part I (Chapters 2 and 3), the construction of an analytical framework for EIL education was attempted with the goals of systematically organizing key issues of EIL, and of identifying major principles for EIL education.

Part II (Chapters 4, 5, and 6) was intended to serve as a bridge between theories and practices in EIL education, concerning materials, methodologies, and models for teaching EIL in the Expanding Circle. Chapter 4 investigated the controversial issue of models of English for the Expanding Circle including Japan, in search of pedagogical models of EIL capable of expressing indigenous values while at the same time being internationally communicative. Chapter 5 analyzed the content of English textbooks as an expression of cultural values beyond the traditional Anglo-American framework, while Chapter 6 explored from sociohistorical perspectives the notion that methodologies for teaching EIL need to be appropriate for local contexts.

Part III (Chapters 7, 8, 9, and 10) examined actual practices in teaching EIL, which long used to be one of the neglected areas in EIL studies. First, an attempt was made in Chapter 7 to classify existing pedagogical approaches for EIL into five categories, with two additional guiding principles. Chapter 8 went on to analyze the author's radio ELT program 28 years ago as a pioneering effort in

Toward the ownership of English 145

EIL education through mass media, while Chapter 9 reported on the author's present practice in teaching EIL in undergraduate classes at Osaka University, which integrates multiple pedagogical concepts. As the author's latest project, Chapter 10 discussed an approach to take advantage of content EMI classes in higher education for the purpose of helping students acquire EIL skills.

The present and final chapter (Chapter 11) ventured to conclude with an illustration of a roadmap to the development of original Englishes for the Expanding Circle, as an ultimate measure to the ownership of English.

There are, however, various limitations to this volume. For example, the analytical framework for EIL education proposed in Part II remains tentative, and will need to go through constant modifications, especially with a view to the rapid development of ELF studies as a new school of thought. It also needs to be further investigated, with more objective data, to what degree the students' EIL skills actually improve through the pedagogical practices presented in Part III. Moreover, while largely drawing on cases from Japan as a typical Asian Expanding Circle situation, the extent to which the theses presented in this book are actually applicable to other parts of the Expanding Circle has not been made clear.

Though with such limitations, the intended aim of the present volume is to pave the way for innovative approaches to the teaching of English that will free Expanding Circle users of English from conventional native-speaker norms in coping with the need for expressing themselves in the age of globalization. It is hoped that such endeavors will help the world become more tolerant of cultural diversity. For the author, the eventual goal of EIL education is to contribute to the construction of a symbiotic society, where people with varieties of values are allowed to live in peaceful harmony with each other. EIL education for the Expanding Circle is one effort in that direction.

Note

1 http://www.routledgetextbooks.com/textbooks/9780415638449/strand.php (Accessed on January 11, 2018)

References

(School textbooks approved by the Japanese Ministry of Education are separately listed at the end.)

Alatis, J., & Straehle, C. A. (1997). The universe of English: Imperialism, chauvinism, and paranoia. In L. E. Smith & M. L. Forman (Eds.), *World Englishes 2000* (pp. 1–20). Honolulu: University of Hawaii Press.

Alsagoff, L. (2007). Singlish: Negotiating culture, capital and identity. In V. Vaish, S. Gopinathan, & L. Yongbing (Eds.), *Language, capital, culture: Critical studies of language and education in Singapore* (pp. 25–46). Rotterdam: Sense Publishers.

Alsagoff, L., McKay, S. L., Hu, G., & Renandya, W. A. (Eds.). (2012). *Principles and practices for teaching English as an international language*. New York: Routledge.

Anderson, F. E. (1996). Intelligibility, identity, and models for English as an international language: A Japan perspective. *Bulletin of Fukuoka University of Education*, 45(1), 15–25.

Ando, S., Kuroda, K., Narita, Y., & Osawa, S. (1978). *Gendai no eigoka-kyoikuho* [*More successful teaching of English*]. Tokyo: Nan'undo.

Andreasson, A. (1994). Norm as a pedagogical paradigm. *World Englishes*, 13(3), 395–409.

Anthony, E. M. (1963). Approach, method, and technique. *English Language Teaching* (presently titled *ELT Journal*), 17(2), 63–67.

Bailey, R. W., & Görlach, M. (Eds.). (1982). *English as a world language*. Ann Arbor: University of Michigan Press.

Baker, W. (2012). *Using e-learning to develop intercultural awareness in ELT: A critical evaluation in a Thai higher educational setting*. ELT Research Papers 12–03. London: British Council.

Baker, W. (2015). *Culture and identity through English as a lingua franca: Rethinking concepts and goals in intercultural communication*. Berlin: De Gruyter Mouton.

Bamgbose, A. (1998). Torn between the norms: Innovations in world Englishes. *World Englishes*, 17(1), 1–14.

Barron, A. (2017). The speech act of 'offers' in Irish English. *World Englishes*, 36(2), 224–238.

Baxter, J. (1980). Interactive listening. *TESL Reporter*, Fall, 3–9. Reprinted in L. E. Smith (Ed.). (1983) *Readings in English as an international language* (pp. 103–110). Oxford: Pergamon Press.

References 147

Bayyurt, Y., & Akcan, S. (Eds.). (2015). *Current perspectives on pedagogy for English as a lingua franca*. Berlin: De Gruyter Mouton.

Bayyurt, Y., & Altinmakas, D. (2012). A WE-based English communication skills course at a Turkish university. In A. Matsuda (Ed.), *Principles and practices of teaching English as an international language* (pp. 169–182). Bristol: Multilingual Matters.

Bayyurt, Y., & Sifakis, N. (2017). Foundations of an EIL-aware teacher education. In A. Matsuda (Ed.), *Preparing teachers to teach English as an international language* (pp. 3–18). Bristol: Multilingual Matters.

Berns, M. (2008). World Englishes, English as a lingua franca, and intelligibility. *World Englishes, 27*(3&4), 327–334.

Bhabha, H. K. (1994). *The location of culture*. London: Routledge.

Bhatia, V. K. (1997). Introduction: Genre analysis and world Englishes. *World Englishes, 16*(3), 313–319.

Bolton, K. (2003). *Chinese Englishes: A sociolinguistic history*. Cambridge: Cambridge University Press.

Bolton, K., Graddol, D., & Meierkord, C. (2011). Towards developmental world Englishes. *World Englishes, 30*(4), 459–480.

Brown, K. (1993). World Englishes in TESOL programs: An infusion model of curricular innovation. *World Englishes, 12*(2), 59–73.

Brumfit, C. (Ed.). (1982). *English for international communication*. Oxford: Pergamon Press.

Butler, S. (1997). World English in the Asian context: Why a dictionary is important. In L. E. Smith & M. L. Forman (Eds.), *World Englishes 2000* (pp. 90–125). Honolulu: University of Hawaii Press.

Butler, S. (2012). [Review of the book *A dictionary of Hong Kong English: Words from the fragrant harbor*, by P. J. Cummings & H.-G. Wolf]. *World Englishes, 31*(4), 549–551.

Byram, M. (1997). *Teaching and assessing intercultural communicative competence*. Clevedon: Multilingual Matters.

Canagarajah, S. (2007). Lingua franca English, multilingual communities, and language acquisition. *The Modern Language Journal, 91*, 923–939.

Cates, K. A. (2002). Teaching for a better world: Global issues and language education. *Human Rights Education in Asian Schools, 5*, 41–52.

Chiba, R., Matsuura, H., & Yamamoto, A. (1995). Japanese attitudes toward English accents. *World Englishes, 14*(1), 77–86.

Cogo, A. (2012). ELF and super-diversity: A case study of ELF multilingual practices from a business context. *Journal of English as a Lingua Franca, 1*(2), 287–313.

Connor, U. (2004). Intercultural rhetoric research: Beyond texts. *Journal of English for Academic Purposes, 3*, 291–304.

Cook, G. (2010). *Translation in language teaching: An argument for reassessment*. Oxford: Oxford University Press.

Coyle, D., Hood, P., & Marsh, D. (2010). *CLIL: Content and language integrated learning*. Cambridge: Cambridge University Press.

Crystal, D. (1997). *English as a global language*. Cambridge: Cambridge University Press.

Crystal, D. (2003). *English as a global language* (2nd ed.). Cambridge: Cambridge University Press.

Cummings, P. J., & Wolf, H.-G. (2011). *A dictionary of Hong Kong English: Words from the fragrant harbor*. Hong Kong: Hong Kong University Press.

148 References

D'Angelo, J. (2005). Educated Japanese English: Expanding oral/aural core vocabulary. *World Englishes, 24*(3), 329–349.

D'Angelo, J. (2012). WE-informed EIL curriculum at Chukyo: Towards a functional, educated, multilingual outcome. In A. Matsuda (Ed.), *Principles and practices of teaching English as an international language* (pp. 121–139). Bristol: Multilingual Matters.

Davies, A. (2003). *The native speaker: Myth and reality.* Clevedon: Multilingual Matters.

Davydova, J. (2012). Englishes in the Outer and Expanding Circles: A comparative study. *World Englishes, 31*(3), 366–385.

Delbridge, A. et al. (Eds.). (1997). *The Macquarie dictionary.* North Ryde, NSW: Macquarie Library.

Deterding, D., & Kirkpatrick, A. (2006). Emerging South-East Asian Englishes and intelligibility. *World Englishes, 25*(3–4), 391–409.

Dewey, M. (2009). English as a lingua franca: Heightened variability and theoretical implications. In A. Mauranen & E. Ranta (Eds.), *English as a lingua franca: Studies and findings* (pp. 60–83). Newcastle upon Tyne: Cambridge Scholars Publishing.

Doiz, A., Lasagabaster, D., & Sierra, J. M. (Eds.). (2013). *English-medium instruction at universities: Global challenges.* Bristol: Multilingual Matters.

Dörnyei, Z. (2009). The L2 motivational self system. In Z. Dörnyei & E. Ushioda (Eds.), *Motivation, language identity and the L2 self* (pp. 9–42). Bristol: Multilingual Matters.

Duff, P. (2007). Second language socialization as sociocultural theory: Insights and issues. *Language Teaching, 40*(4), 309–319.

Dunworth, K., & Zhang, G. (Eds.). (2014). *Critical perspectives on language education.* Cham, Switzerland: Springer.

Enokizono, T. (2012). *Indo-eigo no risuningu* [*Indian English: Listening practice*]. Tokyo: Kenkyusha.

Erikawa, H. (2008). *Nihonjin wa eigo o dou manandekitaka: Eigokyoiku no shakaibunka-shi* [*How the Japanese have been learning English: A socio-cultural history of English language education*]. Tokyo: Kenkyusha.

Farrell, T. S. C. (2015). *Promoting teacher reflection in second language education: A framework for TESOL professionals.* New York: Routledge.

Fenton-Smith, B., Humphreys, P., & Walkinshaw, I. (Eds.). (2017). *English as a medium of instruction in higher education in Asia-Pacific: From policy to pedagogy.* Cham, Switzerland: Springer.

Fujita, K. (1987). Eigokyoiku to kokusairikai [The teaching of English and international understanding]. *Modern English Teaching, 24*(6), 10–11.

Fujiwara, Y. (2014). *Kokusaieigo toshiteno "Nihon-eigo" no kopasukenkyu* [*A corpus study on "Japanese English" as English as an international language*]. Tokyo: Hituzi Shobo.

Fukui, K., Noguchi, J., & Watanabe, N. (Eds.). (2009). *ESP-teki bairinguaru o mezashite: Daigaku-eigokyoiku no saiteigi* [*Towards ESP bilingualism: Redefining university English education in Japan*]. Osaka: Osaka University Press.

Galloway, N., & Rose, H. (2013). 'They envision going to New York, not Jakarta': The differing attitudes toward ELF of students, teaching assistants, and instructors in an English-medium business program in Japan. *Journal of English as a Lingua Franca, 2*(2), 229–253.

References 149

Gerritsen, M., Van Meurs, F., Planken, B., & Korzilius, H. (2016). A reconsideration of the status of English in the Netherlands within the Kachruvian Three Circles model. *World Englishes, 35*(3), 457–474.

Goodman, D. G. (1987). Anata ga anata de aru yue ni watashi ga watashi de aru [You are you. Therefore, I am me]. *The World of Translation, 12*(9), 52–55.

Görlach, M. (1991). *Englishes: Studies in varieties of English 1984–1988.* Amsterdam: John Benjamins.

Görlach, M. (1995). *More Englishes: New studies in varieties of English 1988–1994.* Amsterdam: John Benjamins.

Gotti, M. (2014). Explanatory strategies in university courses taught in ELF. *Journal of English as a Lingua Franca, 3*(2), 337–361.

Graddol, D. (1997). *The future of English?* London: The British Council.

Graddol, D. (2006). *English next.* London: The British Council.

Granger, S. (1996). Learner English around the world. In S. Greenbaum (Ed.), *Comparing English worldwide: The international corpus of English* (pp. 13–24). Oxford: Clarendon Press.

Greenbaum, S. (1988). A proposal for an international computerized corpus of English. *World Englishes, 7*(3), 315.

Greenbaum, S. (Ed.). (1996). *Comparing English worldwide: The international corpus of English.* Oxford: Clarendon Press.

Greenbaum, S., & Nelson, G. (1996). The international corpus of English (ICE) project. *World Englishes, 15*(1), 3–15.

Halliday, M. A. K., McIntosh, A., & Strevens, P. (1964). *The linguistic sciences and language teaching.* Bloomington: Indiana University Press.

Hashiuchi, T. (1989). Eibeigo, shin-eigo, kokusaieigo [Anglo-American English, new Englishes, and international English]. *Modern English Teaching, 26*(9), 10–12.

Henrichsen, L. (1989). *Diffusion of innovations in English language teaching: The ELEC effort in Japan, 1956–1968.* Westport, CT: Greenwood Press.

Hilgendorf, S. K. (2007). English in Germany: Contact, spread and attitudes. *World Englishes, 26*(2), 131–148.

Hilgendorf, S. K. (2015). Plurality and world Englishes: The social realities of language use. *World Englishes, 34*(1), 55–67.

Hinds, J. (1990). Inductive, deductive, quasi-inductive: Expository writing in Japanese, Korean, Chinese, and Thai. In U. Connor and A. M. Johns (Eds.), *Coherence in writing: Research and pedagogical perspectives* (pp. 89–109). Alexandria, VA: Teachers of English to Speakers of Other Languages.

Hino, N. (1987a). The concept of international English in the history of English textbooks in Japan. *The Journal of Tokyo International University: The Department of Commerce, 35,* 69–83.

Hino, N. (1987b). *TOEFL de 650-ten: Watashi no eigoshugyo* [*650 on the TOEFL: My experiences in learning English*]. Tokyo: Nan'undo.

Hino, N. (1988a). Nationalism and English as an international language: The history of English textbooks in Japan. *World Englishes, 7*(3), 309–314.

Hino, N. (1988b). Yakudoku: Japan's dominant tradition in foreign language learning. *JALT Journal, 10*(1&2), 45–55.

Hino, N. (1989a). Let's read & think. *English for Millions,* December, 132–139.

Hino, N. (1989b). *Take a chance: 650 on the TOEFL.* Tokyo: Nan'undo.

Hino, N. (1989c). Nihonshiki-eigo no kanosei [The possibility of Japanese English]. *Modern English Teaching, 26*(9), 8–9.

150 References

Hino, N. (1989–1990). Let's read & think. *English for Millions* (monthly textbook), July 1989–March 1990.

Hino, N. (1991). The impact of the kanji culture on the teaching of English in Japan. In K. Ito (Ed.), *Gendai no eigokyoikugaku-kenkyu* [*Recent studies on English language teaching*] (pp. 265–280). Tokyo: Yumi Press.

Hino, N. (1992a). The yakudoku tradition of foreign language literacy in Japan. In F. Dubin & N. A. Kuhlman (Eds.), *Cross-cultural literacy: Global perspectives on reading and writing* (pp. 99–111). Englewood Cliffs, NJ: Regents/Prentice Hall.

Hino, N. (1992b). Japan today. *English for Millions* (monthly textbook), April–September.

Hino, N. (1997). EIL in a radio English program in Japan. *Studies in Language and Culture*, *23*, 95–113.

Hino, N. (2001). Organizing EIL studies: Toward a paradigm. *Asian Englishes*, *4*(1), 34–65.

Hino, N. (2003a). Kokusaieigo-kenkyu no taikeika ni mukete: Nihon no eigokyoiku no shiten kara [Toward a systematization of EIL studies for ELT in Japan]. *Asian English Studies*, *5*, 5–43.

Hino, N. (2003b). Teaching EIL in Japan. In G. French & J. D'Angelo (Eds.), *Proceedings: First conference on World Englishes in the classroom* (pp. 67–78). Nagoya: Chukyo University.

Hino, N. (2009). The teaching of English as an international language in Japan: An answer to the dilemma of indigenous values and global needs in the Expanding Circle. *AILA Review*, *22*, 103–119.

Hino, N. (2010). EIL in teaching practice: A pedagogical analysis of EIL classrooms in action. In N. Hino (Ed.), *Gengobunka-kyoiku no aratanaru riron to jissen* [*New theories and practice in education in language and culture*] (pp. 1–10). Osaka: Osaka University.

Hino, N. (2011). WE in the Expanding Circle need our own models too!: Quest for equality in World Englishes. *The Humanities and Social Studies in the Far East*, *32*(4), 256–260.

Hino, N. (2012a). Endonormative models of EIL for the Expanding Circle. In A. Matsuda (Ed.), *Principles and practices of teaching English as an international language* (pp. 28–43). Bristol: Multilingual Matters.

Hino, N. (2012b). Participating in the community of EIL users through real-time news: Integrated practice in teaching English as an international language (IPTEIL). In A. Matsuda (Ed.), *Principles and practices of teaching English as an international language* (pp. 183–200). Bristol: Multilingual Matters.

Hino, N. (2012c). Negotiating indigenous values with Anglo-American cultures in ELT in Japan: A case of EIL philosophy in the Expanding Circle. In A. Kirkpatrick & R. Sussex (Eds.), *English as an international language in Asia: Implications for language education* (pp. 157–173). Dordrecht: Springer.

Hino, N. (2012d). *A socio-educational vision for the creation and diffusion of Japanese English: A prospect for the Expanding Circle.* Paper presented at the 18th Annual Conference of International Association for World Englishes. City University of Hong Kong & Sun Yat-Sen University, Hong Kong & Guangzhou, China, December 6–9. Also in N. Hino (Ed.) (2016). *Saishin no eigokyoiku-kenkyu* [The latest research in English language teaching] (pp. 1–13). Osaka: Graduate School of Language and Culture, Osaka University.

References 151

Hino, N. (2013). Kokusaieigo ni okeru komyunikeshon-noryoku no yosei [Teaching communicative competence in English as an international language]. In K. Kataoka & K. Ikeda (Eds.), *Komyunikeshon-noryoku no shoso* [*Aspects of communicative competence*] (pp. 429–455). Tokyo: Hituzi Syobo.

Hino, N. (2015a). Learning EIL through participation in the community of EIL users in Hawaii. In M. Imura & K. Haida (Eds.), *Nihon no gengokyoiku o toinaosu* [*Reconsidering language education in Japan*] (pp. 375–384). Tokyo: Sanseido.

Hino, N. (2015b) Toward the development of CELFIL (Content and ELF integrated learning) for EMI classes in higher education in Japan. *Waseda Working Papers in ELF, 4*, 187–198.

Hino, N. (2016a). English for Japan: In the cultural context of the East-Asian Expanding Circle. In G. Leitner, A. Hashim, & H.-G. Wolf (Eds.), *Communicating with Asia: The future of English as a global language* (pp. 28–42). Cambridge: Cambridge University Press.

Hino, N. (2016b). Negotiation between East Asian values and Anglophone culture in the teaching of English in Japan. In H.-H. Liao (Ed.), *Critical reflections on foreign language education: Globalization and local interventions* (pp. 29–45). Taipei: The Language Training & Testing Center.

Hino, N. (2017a). Training graduate students in Japan to be EIL teachers. In A. Matsuda (Ed.), *Preparing teachers to teach English as an international language* (pp. 87–99). Bristol: Multilingual Matters.

Hino, N. (2017b). The significance of EMI for the learning of EIL in higher education: Four cases from Japan. In B. Fenton-Smith, P. Humphreys, & I. Walkinshaw (Eds.), *English as a medium of instruction in higher education in Asia-Pacific: From policy to pedagogy* (pp. 115–131). Cham, Switzerland: Springer.

Hino, N. (2017c) Tabunkakyosei no tame no kokusaieigo-kyoiku [EIL education for multicultural symbiosis]. In Y. Imao, Y. Okada, I. Koguchi, & N. Hayase (Eds.), *Eigokyoiku tettei rifuresshu: Gurobaruka to 21-seikigata no kyoiku* [*Completely refreshing the teaching of English: Globalization and education for the 21st century*] (pp. 2–13). Tokyo: Kaitakusha.

Hino, N. (2018). Pedagogy for the post-native-speakerist teacher of English. In S. A. Houghton & K. Hashimoto (Eds.), *Towards post-native-speakerism: Dynamics and shifts* (pp. 217–233). Singapore: Springer Nature.

Hino, N., & Oda, S. (2015). Integrated practice in teaching English as an international language (IPTEIL): A classroom ELF pedagogy in Japan. In Y. Bayyurt and S. Akcan (Eds.), *Current perspectives on pedagogy for English as a lingua franca* (pp. 35–50). Berlin: De Gruyter Mouton.

Holliday, A. (1994). *Appropriate methodology and social context.* Cambridge: Cambridge University Press.

Holliday, A. (2006). Native-speakerism. *ELT Journal, 60*(4), 385–387.

Honna, N. (1999). *Ajia o tsunagu eigo* [*English connects Asia*]. Tokyo: ALC Press.

Honna, N. (2008). *English as a multicultural language in Asian contexts: Issues and ideas.* Tokyo: Kurosio Publishers.

Honna, N. (2013). *Kokusai-gengo to shiteno eigo: Bunka o koeta tsutaeai* [*English as an international language: Communication across cultures*]. Tokyo: Fuzambo International.

Honna, N., Kirkpatrick, A., & Gilbert, S. (2001). *English across cultures.* Tokyo: Sanshusha.

152 References

Honna, N., Tajima, T. H., Enokizono, T., & Kawahara, T. (2002). *Ajia-eigo jiten* [*Sanseido dictionary of Asian Englishes*]. Tokyo: Sanseido.

Honna, N., & Takeshita, Y. (1998). On Japan's propensity for native speaker English: A change in sight. *Asian Englishes*, *1*(1), 117–134.

Hoshiyama, S. (1980). Senjika no eigokyoikukai [The English teaching circle during the war]. In S. Wakabayashi (Ed.), *Showa 50-nen no eigokyoiku* [*50 years of English language teaching in the Showa Period*] (pp. 46–62). Tokyo: Taishukan Shoten.

Houghton, S. A., & Hashimoto, K. (Eds.). (2018). *Towards post-native-speakerism: Dynamics and shifts*. Singapore: Springer Nature.

Houghton, S. A., & Rivers, D. J. (Eds.). (2013). *Native-speakerism in Japan: Intergroup dynamics in foreign language education*. Bristol: Multilingual Matters.

Howatt, A. P. R. with Widdowson, H. G. (2004). *A history of English language teaching* (2nd ed.). Oxford: Oxford University Press.

Hu, G. (2012). Assessing English as an international language. In L. Alsagoff, S. L. McKay, G. Hu, & W. A. Renandya (Eds.), *Principles and practices for teaching English as an international language* (pp. 123–143). New York: Routledge.

Iino, M., & Murata, K. (2016). Dynamics of ELF communication in an English-medium academic context in Japan: From EFL learners to ELF users. In K. Murata (Ed.), *Exploring ELF in Japanese academic and business contexts: Conceptualization, research and pedagogic implications* (pp. 111–131). London: Routledge.

Ikeda, T. (1968). Eigokyokasho (English textbooks). In K. Takanashi et al. (Eds.), *Nihon no eigaku 100-nen: Meiji-hen* [*100 years of the English studies in Japan: The Meiji Period*] (pp. 358–378). Tokyo: Kenkyusha.

Ikenaga, K. (1969). Eigokyokasho (English textbooks). In K. Takanashi et al. (Eds.), *Nihon no eigaku 100-nen: Showa-hen* [*100 years of the English studies in Japan: The Showa Period*](pp. 346–363). Tokyo: Kenkyusha.

Imura, M. (1997). *Palmer to nihon no eigokyoiku* [*Harold E. Palmer & Teaching English in Japan*]. Tokyo: Taishukan Shoten.

Institute for Higher Education Research and Practice. (2010). Kyotsukyoiku-sho [*Osaka University Award for Outstanding Contributions to General Education*]. In Institute for Higher Education Research and Practice (Ed.), *Miryoku aru jugyo no tameni 2* [*For attractive classroom teaching 2*] (pp. 126–142). Osaka: Osaka University Press.

Inui, T. (2010). *John Manjiro no eikaiwa* [*The first manual of English conversation in Japan by John Mung*]. Tokyo: J-Research-shuppan.

Ito, K. (1978). Traditional methods and new methods: A study on the methods suited for the Japanese. In I. Koike, M. Matsuyama, Y. Igarashi, & K. Suzuki (Eds.), *The teaching of English in Japan* (pp. 204–219). Tokyo: Eichosha.

Iwasaki, Y. (1994). Englishization of Japanese and acculturation of English to Japanese culture. *World Englishes*, *13*(2), 261–272.

Jenkins, J. (2000). *The phonology of English as an international language*. Oxford: Oxford University Press.

Jenkins, J. (2002). A sociolinguistically based, empirically researched pronunciation syllabus for English as an international language. *Applied Linguistics*, *23*(1), 83–103.

Jenkins, J. (2006). Global intelligibility and local diversity: Possibility or paradox? In R. Rubdy & M. Saraceni (Eds.), *English in the world: Global rules, global roles* (pp. 32–39). London: Continuum.

References   153

Jenkins, J. (2007). *English as a lingua franca: Attitude and identity.* Oxford: Oxford University Press.

Jenkins, J. (2009). English as a lingua franca: Interpretations and attitudes. *World Englishes, 28*(2), 200–207.

Jenkins, J. (2014). *English as a lingua franca in the international university: The politics of academic English language policy.* London: Routledge.

Jenkins, J. (2015a). *Global Englishes: A resource book for students* (3rd ed.). London: Routledge.

Jenkins, J. (2015b). Repositioning English and multilingualism in English as a lingua franca. *Englishes in Practice, 2*(3), 49–85.

Jenkins, J. (2016). International tests of English: Are they fit for purpose? In H.-H. Liao (Ed.), *Critical reflections on foreign language education: Globalization and local interventions* (pp. 3–28). Taipei: The Language Training & Testing Center.

Jespersen, O. (1904). *How to teach a foreign language.* London: George Allen & Unwin Ltd.

Kachru, B. B. (1965). The Indianness in Indian English. *Word, 21*(3), 391–410.

Kachru, B. B. (1976). Models of English for the Third World: White man's linguistic burden or language pragmatics. *TESOL Quarterly, 10*(2), 221–239.

Kachru, B. B. (1980). Models for new Englishes. *TESL Studies, 3,* 117–150.

Kachru, B. B. (1985). Standards, codification and sociolinguistic realism: The English language in the Outer Circle. In R. Quirk & H. G. Widdowson (Eds.), *English in the world: Teaching and learning the language and literatures* (pp. 11–30). Cambridge: Cambridge University Press.

Kachru, B. B. (1986). *The alchemy of English: The spread, functions and models of non-native Englishes.* Oxford: Pergamon Press.

Kachru, B. B. (1987). The bilingual's creativity: Discoursal and stylistic strategies in contact literatures. In L. E. Smith (Ed.), *Discourse across cultures: Strategies in world Englishes* (pp. 125–140). Hertfordshire: Prentice Hall.

Kachru, B. B. (1988). The spread of English and sacred linguistic cows. In P. H. Lowenberg (Ed.), *Georgetown University Round Table on Languages and Linguistics 1987* (pp. 207–228). Washington, DC: Georgetown University Press.

Kachru, B. B. (1997). World Englishes 2000: Resources for research and teaching. In L. E. Smith & M. L. Forman (Eds.), *World Englishes 2000* (pp. 209–251). Honolulu: University of Hawaii Press.

Kachru, B. B. (2017). *World Englishes and culture wars.* Cambridge: Cambridge University Press.

Kachru, B. B., & Smith, L. E. (1985). Editorial. *World Englishes, 4*(2), 209–212.

Kachru, Y. (1992). Speech acts in world Englishes. *World Englishes, 10*(3), 299–306.

Kachru, Y. (1997). Culture and argumentative writing in world Englishes. In L. E. Smith and M. L. Forman (Eds.), *World Englishes 2000* (pp. 48–67). Honolulu: University of Hawaii Press.

Kachru, Y., & Smith, L. E. (2008). *Cultures, contexts, and world Englishes.* New York: Routledge.

Kaplan, R. B. (1966). Cultural thought patterns in inter-cultural education. *Language Learning, 16*(1–2), 1–20.

Kawasumi, T. (1976). Yakudoku no rekishi [The history of yakudoku]. *The English Teachers' Magazine,* July Special Issue, 14–19.

154 References

Kawasumi, T. (Ed.). (1978). *Shiryo nihon-eigakushi 2: Eigokyoiku-ronsoshi* [*Collection of primary sources on the history of English studies 2: Controversies on English language teaching*]. Tokyo: Taishukan Shoten.

Kelly, L. G. (1969). *25 Centuries of language teaching.* Rowley, MA: Newbury House.

Kern, R. (2000). *Literacy and language teaching.* Oxford: Oxford University Press.

Kimura, S. (Ed.). (2004). *Posutokoroniaru-bungaku no genzai* [*Contemporary postcolonial literatures*]. Kyoto: Koyo Shobo.

Kirkpatrick, A. (2007). *World Englishes: Implications for international communication and English language teaching.* Cambridge: Cambridge University Press.

Kirkpatrick, A. (2010). *English as a lingua franca in ASEAN: A multilingual model.* Hong Kong: Hong Kong University Press.

Kirkpatrick, A. (2012). English as an international language in Asia: Implications for language education (pp. 29–44). In A. Kirkpatrick & R. Sussex (Eds.), *English as an international language in Asia: Implications for language education.* Dordrecht: Springer.

Kirkpatrick, A. (2013). The Asian Corpus of English: Motivation and aims. In S. Ishikawa (Ed.), *Learner corpus studies in Asia and the world 1: Papers from ICSAW2013* (pp. 17–30). Kobe: School of Language and Communication, Kobe University.

Kirkpatrick, A. (2014). The language(s) of HE: EMI and/or ELF and/or multilingualism? *The Asian Journal of Applied Linguistics, 1*(1), 4–15.

Kobayashi, M. (2008). *Ryugakusei tono koryu kara manabu: World Englishes jissenhokoku* [*Introducing world Englishes through exchange with international students*]. Paper presented at the 47th national convention of the Japan Association of College English Teachers. Waseda University, Tokyo, Japan, September 12.

Koike, I., et al. (1983). *General survey of English language teaching at colleges and universities in Japan: Teachers' view.* Tokyo: Research Group for College English Teaching in Japan.

Koike, I., et al. (1985). *General survey* of *English language teaching at colleges* and *universities in Japan: Students' view.* Tokyo: Research Group for College English Teaching in Japan.

Komiya, T. (2007). Nihonjin-eigo ni okeru teikanshi no tokucho to anteika ni tsuite [On possible stabilization of the definite article in Japanese English]. *Asian English Studies, 9,* 7–24.

Komiya, T. (2016). Nihonjin-eigo no bunpo [Grammar of Japanese English]. In T. Shiozawa et al. *"Kokusaieigo-ron" de kawaru nihon no eigokyoiku* [*Changing the teaching of English in Japan with the concept of "English as an international language"*] (pp. 119–152). Tokyo: Kurosio Publishers.

Krashen, S. D. (1985). *The input hypothesis: Issues and implications.* London: Longman.

Kubota, R. (1999). Japanese culture constructed by discourses: Implications for applied linguistics research and ELT. *TESOL Quarterly, 33*(1), 9–35.

Kubota, R. (2001). Teaching world Englishes to native speakers of English in the USA. *World Englishes, 20*(1), 47–64.

Kubota, R. (2012). The politics of EIL: Toward border-crossing communication in and beyond English. In A. Matsuda (Ed.), *Principles and practices of teaching English as an international language* (pp. 55–69). Bristol: Multilingual Matters.

References 155

Kubota, R. (2015). Inequalities of Englishes, English speakers, and languages: A critical perspective on pluralist approaches to English. In R. Tupas (Ed.), *Unequal Englishes: The politics of Englishes today* (pp. 21–41). Basingstoke, UK: Palgrave Macmillan.

Kubota, R., & Lehner, A. (2004). Toward critical contrastive rhetoric. *Journal of Second Language Writing, 13*, 7–27.

Kunihiro, M. (1970). *Eigo no hanashikata* [*English works for you*]. Tokyo: Simul Press.

Kuteeva, M. (2015). Academic English as 'nobody's land': The research and publication practices of Swedish academics. In R. Plo Alastrué & C. Pérez-Llantada (Eds.), *English as a scientific and research language: Debates and discourses* (pp. 261–280). Berlin: De Gruyter Mouton.

Lantolf, J. P. (Ed.). (2000). *Sociocultural theory and second language learning*. Oxford: Oxford University Press.

Lave, J., & Wenger, E. (1991). *Situated learning: Legitimate peripheral participation*. Oxford: Oxford University Press.

Lim, L. (Ed.). (2004). *Singapore English: A grammatical description*. Amsterdam: John Benjamins.

Llurda, E. (Ed.). (2005). *Non-native language teachers: Perceptions, challenges and contributions to the profession*. New York: Springer.

Low, E. L. (2010). The acoustic reality of the Kachruvian circles: A rhythmic perspective. *World Englishes, 29*(3), 394–405.

Low, E. L. (2015). *Pronunciation for English as an international language: From research to practice*. London: Routledge.

Lowenberg, P. H. (Ed.). (1988). *Georgetown University Round Table on Languages and Linguistics 1987*. Washington, DC: Georgetown University Press.

Lowenberg, P. H. (1993). Issues of validity in tests of English as a world language: Whose standards? *World Englishes, 12*(1), 95–106.

Lummis, D. (1976). *Ideorogi to shite no eikaiwa* [*English conversation as an ideology*]. Tokyo: Shobunsha.

Lummis, D. (1982). Nihonjin no ningenkankei o eigo de hyogen dekiruka. *Honyaku no sekai, 7*(5), 26–27.

Mahboob, A. (2009). English as an Islamic language: A case study of Pakistani English. *World Englishes, 28*(2), 175–189.

Marlina, R., & Giri, R. A. (Eds.). (2014). *The pedagogy of English as an international language: Perspectives from scholars, teachers, and students*. Cham, Switzerland: Springer.

Martin, I. P. (2014). Philippine English revisited. *World Englishes, 33*(1), 50–59.

Matsuda, A. (2002). Representation of users and uses of English in beginning Japanese EFL textbooks. *JALT Journal, 24*(2), 182–200.

Matsuda, A. (2003). The ownership of English in Japanese secondary schools. *World Englishes, 22*(4), 483–496.

Matsuda, A. (Ed.). (2012a). *Principles and practices of teaching English as an international language*. Bristol: Multilingual Matters.

Matsuda, A. (2012b). Teaching materials in EIL. In L. Alsagoff, S. L. McKay, G. Hu, & W. A. Renandya (Eds.), *Principles and practices for teaching English as an international language* (pp. 168–185). New York: Routledge.

Matsuda, A. (Ed.). (2017a). *Preparing teachers to teach English as an international language*. Bristol: Multilingual Matters.

156 References

Matsuda, A. (2017b). Introduction. In A. Matsuda (Ed.), *Preparing teachers to teach English as an international language* (pp. xiii–xxi). Bristol: Multilingual Matters.

Matsuda, A., & Duran, C. S. (2012). EIL activities and tasks for traditional English classrooms. In A. Matsuda (Ed.), *Principles and practices of teaching English as an international language* (pp. 201–237). Bristol: Multilingual Matters.

Matsuda, A., & Friedrich, P. (2011). English as an international language: A curriculum blueprint. *World Englishes, 30*(3), 332–344.

Matsuda, A., & Matsuda, P. K. (2010). World Englishes and the teaching of writing. *TESOL Quarterly, 44*(2), 369–374.

Matsui, M. (1984). *Nihonshiki-eigo de kamawanai [Japanese English is all right]*. Tokyo: Daisan-shokan.

Matsuura, H., Chiba, R., & Yamamoto, A. (1994). Japanese college students' attitudes towards non-native varieties of English. In D. Graddol & J. Swann (Eds.), *Evaluating language: Papers from the annual meeting of the British Association of Applied Linguistics held at the University of Essex, September 1992* (pp. 52–61). Clevedon: Multilingual Matters.

Mauranen, A. (2012). *Exploring ELF: Academic English shaped by non-native speakers*. Cambridge: Cambridge University Press.

McKay, S. L. (1992). *Teaching English overseas: An introduction*. Oxford: Oxford University Press.

McKay, S. L. (2002). *Teaching English as an international language*. Oxford: Oxford University Press.

McKay, S. L. (2003). Teaching English as an international language: The Chilean context. *ELT Journal, 57*(2), 139–148.

McKay, S. L., & Bokhorst-Heng, W. D. (2008). *International English in its sociolinguistic contexts: Towards a socially sensitive EIL pedagogy*. New York: Routledge.

McKay, S. L., & Brown, J. D. (2016). *Teaching and assessing EIL in local contexts around the world*. New York: Routledge.

Mead, M. (1965, first published in 1942). *And keep your powder dry: An anthropologist looks at America*. New York: William Morrow and Co.

Ministry of Education, Culture, Sports, Science, and Technology. (2001). *Eigoshidohoho to kaizen no suishin ni kansuru kondankai hokoku [Committee report on the improvement of English language teaching]*. Retrieved from www.mext.go.jp/b_menu/houdou/13/01/010110a.htm. (Accessed on June 12, 2001).

Modiano, M. (1996). The Americanization of Euro-English. *World Englishes, 15*(2), 207–215.

Mohan, B. A. (1986). *Language and content*. Reading, MA: Addison-Wesley.

Mori, Y. (Ed.). (2015). *Heisei 25-nendo TOEFL-ITP jisshi ni kansuru hokokusho [A report on the results of TOEFL-ITP administered in 2013]*. Osaka: Center for Education in Liberal Arts and Sciences & Graduate School of Language and Culture, Osaka University.

Mufwene, S. S. (2001). *The ecology of language evolution*. Cambridge: Cambridge University Press.

Mufwene, S. S. (2008). *Language evolution: Contact, competition, and change*. London: Continuum.

Mufwene, S. S. (2015). Colonization, indigenization, and the differential evolution of English: Some ecological perspectives. *World Englishes, 34*(1), 6–21.

References 157

Munro, M. J., & Derwing, M. J. (1995). Foreign accent, comprehensibility, and intelligibility in the speech of second language learners. *Language Learning, 45*(1), 73–97.

Murata, K. (Ed.). (2016). *Exploring ELF in Japanese academic and business contexts: Conceptualization, research and pedagogic implications.* London: Routledge.

Murata, N., & Sugimoto, K. (2009). *World Englishes education in high school.* Paper presented at the 35th annual JALT International Conference on Language Teaching and Learning. Granship, Shizuoka, Japan, November 22.

Nakagawa, Y. (2011). Koko-eigokyokasho ni mirareru nihonjin no eigokan no ichikosatsu [Study of the Japanese views of English reflected in English textbooks for senior high schools]. *Asian English Studies, 13*, 39–62.

Nakano, M., Kondo, Y., Owada, K, Ueda, N., & Yoshida, S. (2012). English language education as a lingua franca in Asia. *Proceedings: The Asian Conference on Education 2012*, pp. 1368–1389.

Nakayama, Y. (1980). Kokusaieigo: Saiko (International English reconsidered). *English Language Education Forum, 9*, 20–26.

Nakayama, Y. (1990). Non-neitibu supika ingurisshu: Nippon-jin to Amerika-jin no kangaekata [Non-native speaker English: Japanese views and American views]. In N. Honna (Ed.), *Ajia no eigo [Englishes in Asia]* (pp. 287–307). Tokyo: Kurosio Publishers.

Narasimhan, R. (1997). Steven Pinker on 'Mentalese'. *World Englishes, 16*(1), 147–152.

Nelson, C. L. (1991). New Englishes, new discourses: New speech acts. *World Englishes, 10*(3), 317–323.

Nelson, C. L. (2011). *Intelligibility in world Englishes: Theory and application.* New York: Routledge.

Newbold, D. (2015). Engaging with ELF in an entrance test for European university students. In Y. Bayyurt and S. Akcan (Eds.), *Current perspectives on pedagogy for English as a lingua franca* (pp. 205–222). Berlin: De Gruyter Mouton.

Ng, C. L. P. (2018). Overcoming institutional native-speakerism: The experience of one teacher. In S. A. Houghton & K. Hashimoto (Eds.), *Towards post-native-speakerism: Dynamics and shifts* (pp. 3–15). Singapore: Springer Nature.

Nihalani, P. (2010). Globalization and international intelligibility. In M. Saxena & T. Omoniyi (Eds.), *Contending with globalization in world Englishes* (pp. 23–44). Bristol: Multilingual Matters.

Nijuisseiki Nihon no Koso Kondankai [The Prime Minister's Commission on Japan's Goals in the 21st Century]. (2000). *Nihon no furontia wa nihon no naka ni aru [The frontier within]*. Tokyo: Kodansha.

Nishinoh, H., Yamamoto, T., & Taguchi, T. (Eds.). (1994). *From English to Englishes: Drills for listening comprehension.* Tokyo: Eihosha.

Nishiyama, S. (1995). Speaking English with a Japanese mind. *World Englishes, 14*(1), 27–36.

Norton, B. (1997). Language, identity, and the ownership of English. *TESOL Quarterly, 31*(3), 409–429.

Obari, H. (1995). Global education in teaching English. *Gaikokugo-kyoiku Ronshu, 17*, 99–115. Univeristy of Tsukuba Foreign Language Center.

Obunsha. (Ed.). (2016). *Eiken 1-kyu sogotaisaku kyohon [A comprehensive preparation book for the STEP 1st grade test]* (Revised ed.). Tokyo: Obunsha.

158   References

Oda, Makoto. (1970). English to Englanto [English and Englanto]. In T. Umesao & N. Nagai (Eds.), *Watashi no gaikokugo [My foreign languages]* (pp. 59–65). Tokyo: Chuokoronsha.

Oda, Masaki. (2017). CELF reflection: A journey to the establishment of a university ELF program. *JACET ELF SIG Journal, 1*(1), 3–17.

Oda, S. (2013). Kokusaieigo-kyoiku to shite no firipin deno eigokenshu [Learning English in the Philippines as EIL education]. In N. Hino (Ed.), *Eigokyoiku no atarashii choryu [New currents in English language teaching]* (pp. 21–28). Osaka: Graduate School of Language and Culture, Osaka University.

O'Dwyer, F. (2012). Mini world Englishes research. In A. Matsuda (Ed.), *Principles and practices of teaching English as an international language* (pp. 206–210). Bristol: Multilingual Matters.

Ogden, C. K. (1930). *Basic English*. London: Routledge and Kegan Paul.

Oishi, S. (1993). Eigo-shihai shuen ni mukete no kojinteki-sonen [Personal thought toward the end of the hegemony of English]. In Y. Tsuda (Ed.), *Eigo-shihai eno iron [The objections to the hegemony of English]* (pp. 69–118). Tokyo: Daisan Shokan.

Orikasa, M. (2015). English learners' perception of world English. *Proceedings of the 41st convention of the Japan Society of English Language Education*, pp. 138–139.

Otani, Y. (1985). *Gendai no gakusei to korekarano eigokyoiku [Today's students and future English education]*. Paper presented at the 24th national convention of the Japan Association of College English Teachers. Sugiyama Jogakuen University, Nagoya, Japan, October 27.

Otani, Y. (2007). *Nihonjin ni totte eigo towa nanika [What does the English language mean to the Japanese?]*. Tokyo: Taishukan Shoten.

Otsubo, Y. (1999a). Maegaki [Preface]. In Y. Otsubo (Ed.), *Shogakko de eigo o oshieyo [Let's teach English in elementary school]* (pp. 4–6). Tokyo: Soeisha/ Sanseido.

Otsubo, Y. (1999b). 'World Englishes' to eigoka-kyoin no yosei ['World Englishes' and training of English teachers]. In Y. Otsubo (Ed.), *Shogakko de eigo o oshieyo [Let's teach English in elementary school]* (pp. 19–32). Tokyo: Soeisha/Sanseido.

Otsubo, Y. (2017). *Kyoin no tameno 'kokusaigo toshiteno eigo' gakushuho no susume [Invitation for teachers to an approach to the learning of 'English as an international language']*. Tokyo: Kaitakusha.

Ozasa, T. (1995). *Harold E. Palmer no eigokyojuho ni kansuru kenkyu: Nihon ni okeru tenkai o chushin to shite [A study of Harold E. Palmer's methodology for teaching English: With an emphasis on its development in Japan]*. Tokyo: Daiichigakushusha.

Pakir, A. (2000). The development of English as a 'glocal' language: New concerns in the old saga of language teaching. In W. K. Ho & C. Ward (Eds.), *Language in the global context: Implications for the language classroom* (pp. 14–31). Singapore: SEAMEO Regional Language Centre.

Palmer, H. E. (1921). *The oral method of teaching languages*. Cambridge: W. Heffer & Sons Ltd.

Pan, L. (2015). *English as a global language in China: Deconstructing the ideological discourses of English in language education*. Cham, Switzerland: Springer.

Pennycook, A. (1994). *The cultural politics of English as an international language*. London: Longman.

References   159

Pennycook, A. (2009). Plurilithic Englishes: Towards a 3D model. In K. Murata & J. Jenkins (Eds.), *Global Englishes in Asian contexts: Current and future debates* (pp. 194–207). New York: Palgrave Macmillan.

Phillipson, R. (1992). *Linguistic imperialism.* Oxford: Oxford University Press.

Pitzl, M.-L. (2009). 'We should not wake up any dogs': Idiom and metaphor in ELF. In A. Mauranen & E. Ranta (Eds.), *English as a lingua franca: Studies and findings* (pp. 298–322). Newcastle upon Tyne: Cambridge Scholars Publishing.

Pitzl, M.-L. (2016). World Englishes and creative idioms in English as a lingua franca. *World Englishes, 35*(2), 293–309.

Platt, J., Weber, H., & Ho, M. L. (1984). *The new Englishes.* London: Routledge & Kegan Paul.

Prator, C. H. (1968). The British heresy in TESL. In J. Fishman et al. (Eds.), *Language problems of developing nations* (pp. 459–476). Oxford: Random House.

Pride, J. B. (Ed.). (1982). *New Englishes.* Rowley, MA: Newbury House.

Proshina, Z. G., & Eddy, A. A. (Eds.). (2016). *Russian English: History, functions, and features.* Cambridge: Cambridge University Press.

Quirk, R. (1981). International communication and the concept of Nuclear English. In L. E. Smith (Ed.), *English for cross-cultural communication* (pp. 151–165). London: Macmillan.

Richards, J. C. (1977). Variation in Singapore English. In W. Crewe (Ed.), *The English language in Singapore* (pp. 68–82). Singapore: Eastern Universities Press.

Richards, J. C. (2015). *Key issues in language teaching.* Cambridge: Cambridge University Press.

Richards, J. C., & Farrell, T. S. C. (2005). *Professional development for language teachers: Strategies for teacher learning.* New York: Cambridge University Press.

Richards, J. C., & Hino, N. (1983). Training ESOL teachers: The need for needs assessment. In J. Alatis, H. H. Stern, & P. Strevens (Eds.), *Georgetown University Round Table on Languages and Linguistics 1983* (pp. 312–326). Washington, DC: Georgetown University Press.

Richards, J. C., & Lockhart, C. (1994). *Reflective teaching in second language classrooms.* Cambridge: Cambridge University Press.

Richards, J. C., & Rodgers, T. S. (2014). *Approaches and methods in language teaching* (3rd ed.). Cambridge: Cambridge University Press.

Rivers, D. J. (2013). Institutionalized native-speakerism: Voices of dissent and acts of resistance. In S. A. Houghton & D. J. Rivers (Eds.), *Native-speakerism in Japan: Intergroup dynamics in foreign language education* (pp. 75–91). Bristol: Multilingual Matters.

Rubdy, R., & Saraceni, M. (2006). Introduction. In R. Rubdy & M. Saraceni (Eds.), *English in the world: Global rules, global roles* (pp. 5–16). London: Continuum.

Saito, H. (1928). *Saito's Japanese-English dictionary.* Tokyo: Nichieisha. (Reprinted in 2002. Tokyo: Nichigai Associates).

Saraceni, M. (2015). *World Englishes: A critical analysis.* London: Bloomsbury.

Schell, M. (2009). Colinguals among bilinguals. *World Englishes, 27*(1), 117–130.

Schneider, E. W. (2003). The dynamics of new Englishes: From identity construction to dialect birth. *Language, 79*(2), 233–281.

Schneider, E. W. (2007). *Postcolonial English: Varieties around the world.* Cambridge: Cambridge University Press.

Schneider, E. W. (2014). New reflections on the evolutionary dynamics of world Englishes. *World Englishes, 33*(1), 9–32.

160 *References*

Schön, D. A. (1983). *The reflective practitioner: How professionals think in action.* New York: Basic Books.

Seidlhofer, B. (2006). English as a lingua franca in the Expanding Circle: What it isn't. In R. Rubdy & M. Saraceni (Eds.), *English in the world: Global rules, global roles* (pp. 40–50). London: Continuum.

Seidlhofer, B. (2009). Common ground and different realities: World Englishes and English as a lingua franca. *World Englishes, 28*(2), 236–245.

Seidlhofer, B. (2011). *Understanding English as a lingua franca.* Oxford: Oxford University Press.

Seidlhofer, B. (2012). Anglophone-centric attitudes and the globalization of English. *Journal of English as a Lingua Franca, 1*(2), 393–407.

Sewell, A. (2016). Beyond 'variety' and 'community': A conceptual challenge for the study of English in Asia. In M. O'Sullivan, D. Huddart & C. Lee (Eds.), *The future of Engish in Asia: Perspectives on language and literature* (pp. 57–74). London: Routledge.

Sharifian, F. (2009). English as an international language: An overview. In F. Sharifian (Ed.), *English as an international language: Perspectives and pedagogical issues* (pp. 1–18). Bristol: Multilingual Matters.

Shim, R. J. (1999). Codified Korean English: Process, characteristics and consequence. *World Englishes, 18*(2), 247–258.

Shimaoka, T. (1968). Eigokyokasho [English textbooks]. In K. Takanashi et al. (Eds.), *Nihon no eigaku 100-nen: Taisho-hen [100 years of the English studies in Japan: The Taisho Period]* (pp. 305–317). Tokyo: Kenkyusha.

Shiozawa, T. (1999). 'Affective competence': Sono riron to jissen ['Affective competence': Its theory and practice]. *Chubu Daigaku Jinbungakubu Kenkyu Ronshu, 2*, 1–33.

Shiozawa, T. (2016). Ima naze kokusaieigo-ron no shiten ga hitsuyo ka [Why we need EIL perspectives now]. In T. Shiozawa et al. (Eds.), *'Kokusaieigo-ron' de kawaru nihon no eigokyoiku [Changing the teaching of English in Japan with the concept of 'English as an international language']* (pp. 27–51). Tokyo: Kurosio Publishers.

Siegel, J. (1997). Pidgin and English in Melanesia: Is there a continuum? *World Englishes, 16*(2), 185–204.

Silva, M. (1991). Bilingualism and the character of Palestinian Greek. In S. E. Porter (Ed.), *The language of the New Testament: Classic essays* (pp. 205–226). Sheffield: Sheffield University Press.

Silva, P. (Ed.). (1996). *A dictionary of South African English on historical principles.* Oxford: Oxford University Press.

Smit, U. (2010). *English as a lingua franca in higher education: A longitudinal study of classroom discourse.* Berlin: De Gruyter Mouton.

Smit, U. (2013). Learning affordances in integrating content and English as a lingua franca ('ICELF'): On an implicit approach to English medium teaching. *Journal of Academic Writing, 3*(1), 15–29.

Smith, L. E. (1976). English as an international auxiliary language. *RELC Journal 7*(2), 38–42. Also in L. E. Smith (Ed.). (1983). *Readings in English as an international language* (pp. 1–5). Oxford: Pergamon Press.

Smith, L. E. (1978). Some distinctive features of EIIL vs. ESOL in English language education. *The Culture Learning Institute Report,* June, 5–7 & 10–11. Also in L. E. Smith (Ed.). (1983). *Readings in English as an international language* (pp. 13–20). Oxford: Pergamon Press.

References 161

Smith, L. E. (Ed.). (1981a). *English for cross-cultural communication*. London: Macmillan.

Smith, L. E. (1981b). English as an international language: No room for linguistic chauvinism. *Nagoya Gakuin Daigaku Gaikokugo Kyoiku Kiyo* 3, 27–32. Also in L. E. Smith (Ed.). (1983). *Readings in English as an international language* (pp. 7–11). Oxford: Pergamon Press.

Smith, L. E. (Ed.). (1983). *Readings in English as an international language*. Oxford: Pergamon Press.

Smith, L. E. (1984). A communicative approach to teaching English as an international language. *Cross Currents, 11*(1), 37–48.

Smith, L. E. (Ed.). (1987). *Discourse across cultures: Strategies in world Englishes*. Hertfordshire: Prentice Hall.

Smith, L. E. (1988). Language spread and issues of intelligibility. In P. H. Lowenberg (Ed.), *Georgetown University Round Table on Languages and Linguistics 1987* (pp. 265–282). Washington, DC: Georgetown University Press.

Smith, L. E. (1992). Spread of English and issues of intelligibility. In B. B. Kachru (Ed.), *The other tongue: English across cultures* (2nd ed., pp. 75–90). Urbana: University of Illinois Press.

Smith, L. E. (2001). International communication in world Englishes. In T. C. Kiong, A. Pakir, B. K. Choon, & R. B. H. Goh (Eds.), *Ariels: Departures & returns, Essays for Edwin Thumboo*. Singapore: Oxford University Press.

Smith, L. E. (2004). From English as an international auxiliary language to world Englishes. In Y. Otsubo & G. Parker (Eds.), *Development of a teacher training program* (pp. 72–80). Tokyo: Soueisha/Sanseido.

Smith, L. E. (2014). Teaching English as an international language (EIL) in Hawaii: The case of the Global Cultural Exchange Program (GCEP). In T. Shiozawa, T. Enozokizono, Y. Kurahashi, T. Komiya, & M. Shimouchi (Eds.), *Gendaishakai to eigo: Eigo no tayosei o mitsumete [World Englishes in changing society]* (pp. 133–139). Tokyo: Kinseido.

Smith, L. E., & Bisazza, J. A. (1982). The comprehensibility of three varieties of English for college students in seven countries. *Language Learning, 32*(2), 259–269. Also in L. E. Smith (Ed.). (1983). *Readings in English as an international language* (pp. 59–67). Oxford: Pergamon Press.

Smith, L. E., & Nelson, C. L. (1985). International intelligibility of English: Directions and resources. *World Englishes, 4*(3), 333–342.

Smith, L. E., & Rafiqzad, K. (1979). English for cross-cultural communication: The question of intelligibility. *TESOL Quarterly, 13*(3), 371–380. Also in L. E. Smith (Ed.). (1983). *Readings in English as an international language* (pp. 49–58). Oxford: Pergamon Press.

Smith, L. E., & Via, R. A. (1983). English as an international language via drama techniques. In L. E. Smith (Ed.), *Readings in English as an international language* (pp. 111–116). Oxford: Pergamon Press.

Sridhar, K. K. (1991). Speech acts in an indigenized variety: Sociocultural values and language variation. In J. Chershire (Ed.), *English around the world: Sociolinguistic perspectives* (pp. 308–318). Cambridge: Cambridge University Press.

Sridhar, K. K., & Sridhar, S. N. (1986). Bridging the paradigm gap: Second language acquistion theory and indigenized varieties of English. *World Englishes, 5*(1), 3–14.

Stanlaw, J. (2004). *Japanese English: Language and culture contact*. Hong Kong: Hong Kong University Press.

162 References

Suenobu, M. (1990). Nihon-eigo [Japanese English]. In N. Honna (Ed.), *Ajia no eigo* [*Englishes in Asia*] (pp. 257–286). Tokyo Kurosio Publishers.

Suenobu, M. (2010). *Nihon-eigo wa sekai de tsujiru* [*Japanese English communicates to the world*]. Tokyo: Heibonsha.

Suzuki, T. (1971). English kara Englic e [From English to Englic]. *The English Teachers' Magazine*, January, 64–67.

Suzuki, T. (1975). *Tozasareta gengo, nihongo no sekai* [*A closed language: The world of Japanese*]. Tokyo: Shinchosha.

Sweet, H. (1964, originally published in 1899). *The practical study of languages*. London: Oxford University Press.

Tachibana, H. (2012). Koksaihojogo toshiteno eigo ni okeru 'Nihoneigo' no kochiku [Constructing 'Japanese English' as EIAL]. *Nichiei gengobunka kenkyu*, 3, 111–122.

Takagaki, T., & Tanabe, N. (2007). High school freshmen's responses to home economics conducted in a non-native variety of English: A three-year survey on content-based instruction in Japan. *The Asian EFL Journal*, 9(2), 7–18.

Takanashi, K. (1975). Eigakushi kara mita Nihon no eigokyoiku [The teaching of English in Japan from the viewpoint of the history of English studies]. In K. Takanashi & K. Omura (Eds.), *Nihon no eigokyoikushi* [*The history of English teaching in Japan*] (pp. 1–55). Tokyo: Taishukan.

Takashi, K. (1990). A sociolinguistic analysis of English borrowings in Japanese advertising texts. *World Englishes*, 9(3), 327–341.

Tanaka, H. (1978). Eibeijin dake no mono dewa nai kokusaihojogo to shite no eigo [English as an international auxiliary language not owned solely by Anglo-Americans]. *The English Teachers' Magazine*, January, 64–67.

Tanner, P. D. (2012). Developing an awareness of English in the world. In A. Matsuda (Ed.), *Principles and practices of teaching English as an international language* (pp. 201–204). Bristol: Multilingual Matters.

Toh, G. (2015). English in Japan: Indecisions, inequalities, and practices of relocalization. In R. Tupas (Ed.), *Unequal Englishes: The politics of Englishes today* (pp. 111–129). Basingstoke, UK: Palgrave Macmillan.

Trudgill, P. (2014). Before ELF: GLF from Samarkand to Sfakia. *Journal of English as a Lingua Franca*, 3(2), 387–393.

Trudgill, P., & Hannah, J. (1982). *International English: A guide to varieties of standard English*. London: Edward Arnold.

Tsuda, Y. (1990). *Eigo-shihai no kozo* [*The structure of the hegemony of English*]. Tokyo: Daisan Shokan.

Tsuda, Y. (2003). *Eigoshihai towa nanika* [*What is the hegemony of English?*]. Tokyo: Akashi Shoten.

Tsuruta, C., & Shibata, S. (2008). *Dabosu-kaigi de kiku sekai no eigo* [*Listening to world Englishes at the Davos conference*]. Tokyo: Cosmopier.

Tupas, T. R. F. (2006). Standard Englishes, pedagogical paradigms, and their conditions of (im)possibility. In R. Rubdy & M. Saraceni (Eds.), *English in the world: Global rules, global roles* (pp. 169–185). London: Continuum.

Turner, N. (1991). The language of Jesus and his disciples. In S. E. Porter (Ed.), *The language of the New Testament: Classic essays* (pp. 174–190). Sheffield: Sheffield University Press.

Ueda, N., Owada, K., Oya, M., & Tsutsui, E. (2005). Shakai e tsunageru daigaku-eigokyoiku [University English language education in social contexts]. In M. Nakano (Ed.), *Eigokyoiku gurobaru dezain* [*Global design for Engilsh language teaching*] (pp. 135–173). Tokyo: Gakubunsha.

References 163

Via, R. A. (1981). Via-Drama: An answer to the EIIL problem. In L. E. Smith (Ed.), *English for cross-cultural communication* (pp. 200–210). London: Macmillan.

Via, R. A., & Smith, L. E. (1983). *Talk and listen: English as an international language via drama techniques.* Oxford: Pergamon Press.

Walker, R. (2010). *Teaching the pronunciation of English as a lingua franca.* Oxford: Oxford University Press.

Watanabe, M. (2007). Nichi-futsu-bei no kokugokyoiku o yomitoku: 'Yomikaki' no rekishishakaigakuteki kosatsu [A comparison of language arts education in the three countries, Japan, the United States and France: Sociohistorical analyses of 'reading and writing']. *Nihon Kenkyu, 35,* 573–619.

Watanabe, T. (1983). *Japalish no susume [An invitation to Japalish].* Tokyo: Asahi Shimbunsha.

Watanabe, Y., Ikeda, M., & Izumi, S. (2011). *CLIL: Jochi Daigaku gaikokugo-kyoiku no aratanaru chosen [New challenges in foreign language education at Sophia University] Volume 1. Genri to hoho [Principles and methodologies].* Tokyo: Sophia University Press.

Weiner, E. S., & Smith, L. E. (1983). *English as an international language: A writing approach.* Oxford: Pergamon Press.

Wen, Q. (2016). Teaching culture(s) in English as a lingua franca in Asia: Dilemma and solution. *Journal of English as a Lingua Franca, 5*(1), 155–177.

Wenger, E. (1998). *Communities of practice: Learning, meaning, and identity.* Cambridge: Cambridge University Press.

Widdowson, H. G. (1978). *Teaching language as communication.* Oxford: Oxford University Press.

Widdowson, H. G. (1994). The ownership of English. *TESOL Quarterly, 28*(2), 377–389.

Widdowson, H. G. (1997). EIL, ESL, EFL: Global issues and local interests. *World Englishes, 16*(1), 135–146.

Widdowson, H. G. (2015). ELF and the pragmatics of language variation. *Journal of English as a Lingua Franca, 4*(2), 359–372.

Wilkins, D. A. (1976). *Notional syllabuses.* London: Oxford University Press.

Yamagishi, K. (Ed.). (1991). *The new anchor Japanese-English dictionary.* Tokyo: Gakken.

Yano, Y. (2001). World Englishes in 2000 and beyond. *World Englishes, 20*(2), 119–132.

School textbooks approved by the Japanese Ministry of Education
(In the alphabetical order of the titles)

Shibata, T. et al. (2010). *Kotogakko koten kanbun-hen [Classical Chinese for senior high schools].* Tokyo: Sanseido.

Kuroda, T. et al. (1960). *New approach to English 2.* Tokyo: Taishukan Shoten.

Ota, A. et al. (1986). *New horizon English course 3* (Revised ed.). Tokyo: Tokyo Shoseki.

Inamura, M. et al. (1968). *New prince readers 2.* Tokyo: Kairyudo.

Nakamura, K. et al. (1984). *The new crown English series 2* (Revised ed.). Tokyo: Sanseido.

Nakamura, K. et al. (1984). *The new crown English series 3* (Revised ed.). Tokyo: Sanseido.

Nakajima, F. et al. (1984). *Total English 3* (New ed.). Tokyo: Shubun Shuppan.

Yada, H. et al. (2016). *Total English 3.* Tokyo: Gakko Tosho.

Index

Note: Page numbers in *italics* denote references to Figures and page numbers in **bold** denote references to Tables.

ABS-CBN 117
accommodation 27–28, 37, 134
Affective Competence 94
African-American vernacular English 30
Alsagoff, L. 32
ALTs (Assistant Language Teachers) 39, 47–48, 52
argumentative writing 43–44, 67–68
artificial English 21
Asian Corpus of English (ACE) 33
Asian Expanding Circle 92
audio WE materials 42
authentic interactions in EIL/ELF 129–130

back-channeling 67, 134
Baker, W. 92
Basic English 21
Baxter, J. 42
Bayyurt, Y. 53, 92, 93
BBC news 117
Bhatia, V. K. 45
Bisazza, J. A. 93, 102–103
Bolton, K. 23, 35
Brown, K. 47

CALL (Computer-Assisted Language Learning) 114, 119
Cates, Kip 24
CCDL (Cross-Cultural Distance Learning) 96, 129
CELFIL (Content and ELF Integrated Learning) 130–135
Channel NewsAsia 117
chauvinism 26, 73–74, 81
Chiba, R. 38

Chinese language 83–86
Chukyo University 96
classroom practices: communication skills course 92; content-based approach to EIL 95; exposure to varieties of English 92–93; oral communication classes 93; participating in community of practice 95–97; role-plays as cross-cultural training 94–95; teaching about EIL 91–92
CLIL (Content and Language Integrated Learning) 95
CNN 117
Cogo, A. 132
communicability 62
communication skills course 92
communicative aspects of EIL 36–38
communicative language teaching (CLT) 43
comprehensibility, communication 37
contact linguistics 35–36
Content-Based Instruction 25, 40, 44, 63, 119–121
continuous development of models 143–144
contrastive rhetoric 69
Cook, G. 87, 132
corpus linguistics 33
cross-cultural understanding in EIL 44
Crystal, D. 21, 27, 31

D'Angelo, J. 93
Davies, A. 47
Davydova, J. 35

Index 165

de-Anglo-Americanized English
101–102
definite article usage 64
Delbridge, A. 34
developmental World Englishes 23
Dewey, M. 64
*dictionary of South African English on
historical principles, A* 34
discourse models in MJE 67–69
discursive rules in EIL 32
diverse EIL 19–20, *19*
Dörnyei, Z. 71
Duff, P. 97
Dunworth, K. 24
Dynamic Model 27, 30, 61, 141

Edo period 74
EFL (English as a foreign language) 13,
129–130
EGP (English for General Purposes)
114
EIL (English as an international
language): anthropological aspects
of 28–30; concept of 17–18; as
de-Anglo-Americanized English 18;
definition of 7, 16–17; ELF vs. 13;
ESP vs. 45; forms of 18–21; historical
aspects of 25–28; ideology and
development of 26–28; social factor
prompting 12; taxonomy of views
on forms of *19*; terms to express 17;
users' identities and 23–24; WE vs.
12–13, 59
EIL education: analytical framework
for 11–12; face-to- face interactions
96; general principles for **53–54**;
learners in 53, **54**; materials for
49–50, **53**; methodologies 50–51,
53; models in **54**; overseas studies
96–97; production models 51;
public school textbooks 50; repeated
reading aloud practice 51; teachers
52–53; testing interactive skills 52,
54; testing productive skills 51–52,
54; testing receptive skills 51, **54**;
word-by-word translation 50–51;
see also IPTEIL (Integrated Practice in
Teaching English as an International
Language) method, TEIL (Teaching
English as an International
Language)
EIL methodology: content-based
approach to EIL 95; exposure
to varieties of English 92–93;

participating in community of practice
95–97; principles for 97–98; role-
plays as cross-cultural training 94–95
EIL research 13–16
EIL studies *14*, 15–16
ELF (English as a Lingua Franca) 5, 7,
20, 59
ELF2 stage 20
ELF3 phase 20
EMI (English-Medium Instruction)
courses 128
endonormative Englishes in Expanding
Circle 141
English: dictionaries 33–34; as a
global language 32; intra-national
use of 59, 141; language attitudes
toward varieties of 38; linguistic
characteristics in 103; monolingual
use of 132; non-native varieties of
103; in postcolonial environment 61;
in postcolonial literatures 36; as a
public language 31; spread of 31
English as a Lingua Franca in Academic
Settings (ELFA) 33
English for Millions (radio program):
description of 93; Japan Today
109–111; Let's Read & Think
101–109
English textbooks in Japan: emphasizing
native English-speaking cultures 77;
fifth period 77–80; first period 74–75;
focusing on indigenous Japanese
values 75–76; fourth period 76–77;
highlighting Japanese contribution
to international community 79–80;
imitating Anglo-American cultures
74–75; nationalism influencing 75;
presence of Japanese characters 79;
second period 75; shifting to foreign
cultures 77–78; third period 75–76
Enokizono, T. 42, 93
Erikawa, H. 79
ESP (English for Specific Purposes) 45,
114
European Expanding Circle 92
examination English 35
Expanding Circle: definition of 7;
Dynamic Model applied to 30;
EIL more relevant than WE in 13;
endonormative Englishes in 141;
indigenization in 29; intra-national
use of English in 59; limitations
of 5; Model of Japanese English
in 57–59; original Englishes for

166 *Index*

140–142; socio-educational vision for Englishes in 142–144; sociolinguistic environments in 141–142

face-to-face interactions 96

Galloway, N. 95
GCEP (Global Cultural Exchange Program) 43, 129–130
GIL (Greek as an International Language) 25–26
global awareness 24–25
Global Cultural Exchange Program (GCEP) 97
Global Education 24, 104–105, 107–108, 121
Global Education in ELT 24–25
global Englishes 7, 25, 27
Goodman, David G. 108
Görlach, M. 27
Graddol, D. 23, 31
Graded Direct Method (GDM) 21
Grammar-Translation Method 87
grammatical models of MJE 64–65
Greenbaum, Sydney 33

Halliday, M. A. K. 26, 27
Hashimoto, K. 38
Henrichsen, L. 82, 100
Hinds, J. 69
Holliday, A. 47
Honna, N. 92, 139
Houghton, S. A. 38
Hu, G. 46
Humboldt, K. W. 28

Ideal L2 Self 71
identity and communication 36–37
identity markers 23
idiomatic expressions 66–67
Indian English 23, 26, 93
indigenization of English 3–4, 29–30, 58
Inner Circle, definition of 7
Insha-Allah 103–104
institutionalized varieties 34–35, 40–41
intelligibility, communication 37
interactive listening 42
intercultural pedagogy 132, 134
intercultural understanding in EIL 44
interlanguage corpus 33
International Association for World Englishes (IAWE) 26
international communication: accommodation in 27–28; exposure

to varieties of English 92–93; Japanese attitude as hindrance to 105; Japanese for 108; MJE criteria for 62; nationalism and 81; need for 12; significance of English for 92; sociocultural factors for 103–104
International Corpus of English (ICE) 33
International Corpus of Learner English (ICLE) 33
international English, new form of 21
international languages 18, 25–26
International Singapore English (ISE) 32
interpretability, communication 37, 42
intra-national use of English 59, 141
IPTEIL (Integrated Practice in Teaching English as an International Language) method: background of 114; class observers 124–125; classroom practices 93; classroom procedure for 115–116; curriculum for 114–115; definition of 111; with electronic newspapers 117–118; as form of Content-Based Instruction 119; goals/objectives of 115; grades 116; legitimate peripheral participation in community of practice 119–120; limitations of 125–126; literacy-based curriculum and 121; participating in community of practice 95–96; peer interactions to 125–126; responses to 121–125; semester-end questionnaire 123; student feedback 122–124; teaching materials 116–117; university awards 121–122; *see also* TEIL (Teaching English as an International Language)

Japan: designating English as an official second language 31; examination English in 35; teaching Chinese in 83–85; written language as primary aspect of language 85–86
Japanese Association for Asian Englishes (JAFAE) 139
Japanese English 23, 57, 60; *see also* Model of Japanese English (MJE)
Jenkins, Jennifer13, 27, 37, 59, 63
JET (Japan Exchange and Teaching) program 47–48
Jewish Greek 26
Journal of English as a Lingua Franca 13

Kachru, B. 26, 59
Kachru, Y. 32, 103

Index 167

Kaplan, R. B. 44, 69
Kern, R. 86, 121
Kirkpatrick, Andy 33, 39, 42, 92, 93, 103
Koike, I. 87
Komiya, T. 64
Korean English 35
KTN 117
Kubota, R. 23
kundoku method 83–85, 86
Kunihiro, Masao 17–18, 21, 101–102
kunten 83
Kuteeva, M. 45

language policies, EIL 31
Learner Autonomy 119
learner corpus 33
Legitimate Peripheral Participation in a Community of Practice 119–120
Let's learn English (textbook) 76–77
Let's Read & Think (radio program): combining EIL with Global Education 104–105; concept of 101–102; contents 105–108; Expanding Circle guests 107; exposing learner's to WE 102–104; listener reactions 108–109; objectives 102–105; Outer Circle guests 105–107; presenting NNS/NNS interactions 104; program format 102
lexical models in MJE 66–67
LFC (Lingua Franca Core) 5, 20
Lim, L. 30
linguistic chauvinism 26
linguistic equality 22–23
linguistic imperialism 18, 22, 108
literacy-based curriculum 121
locally-appropriate pedagogy 132
Low, E. L. 32, 35
Lowenberg, P. H. 46
Lummis, D. 70

Macquarie dictionary, The 34
macro-sociolinguistic aspects of EIL 30–31
Malaysia 31
Matsuda, A. 47, 86
Matsuura, H. 38
Mauranen, Anna 33, 35
McIntosh, A. 26
McKay, S. L. 82
Mead, Margaret 65
media 42, 118–119

Meierkord, C. 23
metaphors 66–67
micro-sociolinguistic aspects of EIL 32–36
Mid-Atlantic English 21
model, definition of 5–6
Model of Japanese English (MJE): class demonstrations 70–71; criteria for 62; definite article usage 64; definition of 5; description of 62–63; developing 59; discourse models 67–69; in the Expanding Circle 57–59; expressing Japanese values 58; features of 58; foundations of 60–62; grammatical models 64–65; implementing 70–71; learners' reactions to 71; lexical models 66–67; as pedagogical creation 61; phonological models 63–64; radio series 70–71; rationale for 60; sociolinguistic models 69–70; "will" vs. "be going to" 64–65; word-initial voiceless plosives 63–64; "You had better~" 65; *see also* Japanese English
models of original English 143
Modiano, M. 21
monolingual use of English 132
monolithic EIL 19–20, *19*, 21
Mt. Osorezan English Summit 94–95
Murata, K. 128

Nakano, M. 96
Nakayama, Y. 23
national identity/nationalism 23, 60, 73–74, 75–76, 80–81
native-speakerism 5, 48, 52, 112
NDTV 117
negotiation of meaning 36–37, 134
Nelson, Cecil L. 37
neutral English 21
new anchor Japanese-English dictionary, The 34
Newbold, D. 46
New prince readers 78–79
NHK radio 101
NHK World 117
Nihalani, Paroo 63
Nishiyama, S. 139
non-verbal cues 134
Nuclear English 21

Oda, Makoto 17
Oda, Masaki 52
Ogden, C. K. 21

168   *Index*

ondoku (reading aloud) 97
Oral Method 87
oral communication classes 93
Osaka University 111
Osaka University Award for
    Outstanding Contributions to
    General Education 121
OSGD (Observed Small Group
    Discussion) 133–135
Otani, Y. 80
Otsubo, Y. 39
Outer Circle 7, 29
overseas studies 96–97
Oxford EnglishDictionary (OED)
    33–34

Pacheco, Benito M. 128
Pakir, A. 32
Pakistani English 104
Palestinian Greek 26
Palmer, H. E. 87
Pennycook, A. 18, 20
performance varieties 34–35, 40–41
Phillipson, R. 18
phonological intelligibility 37
phonological models of MJE 63–64
pidgins/creoles 35–36
Pitzl, M.-L. 67
plosives, word-initial 63–64
postcolonial Englishes 61
postcolonial English literatures 36
postcolonialism 74
Prator, C. H. 26
pronunciation 27, 37, 39, 42–43, 111

Quirk, R. 21

radical nationalism 81; *see also* national
    identity/nationalism
radio ELT programs 93, 100–101
radio series 70–71
Rafiqzad, K. 37, 103
Rao, Raja 36
reordering symbols 83–85
repeated reading aloud practice 51
Richards, J. C. 21, 47, 87
Rivers, D. J. 48
Rodgers, T. S. 87
Rose, H. 95
Rubdy, R. 20

Saito, Hidezaburo 3–4, 5, 58, 139
Sapir, Edward 28
Sapir-Whorf hypothesis 28–29
Saraceni, M. 7, 20

Schell, M. 29–30
Schneider, Edgar W. 27, 30, 61, 141
second language acquisition (SLA) 39
Seidlhofer, Barbara 33, 59
Sharifian, F. 12
Shikiba, Ryuzaburo 76
Shim, R. J. 35
Shiozawa, T. 94
Sifakis, N. 53
Silva, Penny 34
similect 35, 41, 61
Singapore 31
Singaporean English 93
Smit, U. 130
Smith, Larry E. 59, 93–94, 102–103,
    108, 114, 129–130
sociocultural factors for international
    communications 103–104
sociolinguistic models in MJE 69–70
sociolinguistic rules in EIL 32
Soyinka, Wole 36
speaking English with a Japanese mind
    139
Spivak, Gayatri 23
Stanlaw, J. 60
strategic essentialism 23
Strevens, P. 26
student-to-student interactions 125
Suenobu, M. 139
Suzuki, T. 17

Takanashi, K. 77
Talk-and-Listen role-play 43, 94
Tamagawa University 52
Tanaka, H. 104.
teachers 47–48, 52, **54**; *see also* EIL
    education, TEIL (Teaching English as
    an International Language)
teacher-to-student interactions 125
teaching EIL *see* EIL education, TEIL
    (Teaching English as an International
    Language)
teaching materials 73, 116–117; *see also*
    English textbooks in Japan
TEIL (Teaching English as an
    International Language):
    administrative matters 38–39;
    analyzing course of study 44–45;
    background of 14–15, 25–38;
    curriculum for 38–45; developing
    teaching materials 45; EIL as
    basis for 12; evaluation/testing
    of 46–47; examination questions
    cultural content 46; foundations
    of 15–16; global education and

24–25; listening in EIL 41–42; methodologies 45–46; models in 40–41; practice of 16, 38; pronunciation in EIL 42–43; rationale for 22–25; reading in EIL 43; speaking in EIL 42–43; syllabus 39–40; teacher training 47–48; writing in EIL 43–44; *see also* EIL education, IPTEIL (Integrated Practice in Teaching English as an International Language) method
television ELT programs 100–101
third space, the 24
TOEFL (Test of English as a Foreign Language) 47, 114–115
TOEIC (Test of English for International Communication) 47
translanguaging 5, 20, 134
Tsuda, Y. 18
Tupas, T. R. F. 22–23
turn-taking 134

unification of English 21

Via, R. A. 40, 94, 114
Vienna-Oxford International Corpus of English (VOICE) 33

voiceless word-initial plosives 63–64

Waseda University 96, 129
Watanabe, T. 23
Weiner, E. S. 40, 44, 114
Wen, Q. 110
Whorf, Benjamin 28
Widdowson, H. G. 45, 132
Wilkins, D. A. 40
"will" vs. "be going to" 64–65
word-by-word translation 50–51, 85
word-initial voiceless plosives 63–64
World Englishes (WE): definition of 7; EIL vs. 12–13, 59; Expanding Circle in 4–6; inapplicability of theories 140; pidgins/creoles 35–36
World Standard Spoken English (WSSE) 21

yakudoku tradition 86, 87, 97
Yamagishi, Katsuei 34
Yamamoto, A. 38
Yano, Y. 21
"You had better~" 65

Zhang, G. 24